POVERTY AND OPPORTUNITY: 100 YEARS OF THE BIRMINGHAM SETTLEMENT

POVERTY AND OPPORTUNITY: 100 YEARS OF THE BIRMINGHAM SETTLEMENT

Jon Glasby

With a foreword by Dr. Carl Chinn

First published by Brewin Books Ltd.
Studley, Warwickshire B80 7LG in 1999.

British Library Cataloguing in Publication Data
A catalogue record for this book is available from
The British Library

ISBN: 1 85858 150 8 (Hardback)
ISBN: 1 85858 151 6 (Paperback)

Typeset in Plantin
and made and printed in Great Britain
by Warwick Printing Company Limited,
Theatre Street, Warwick, Warwickshire CV34 4DR.

Acknowledgements

No book can be written in isolation, and this is no exception. So many people have contributed to this book that it is impossible to thank them all by name. They know who they are, and I greatly appreciate their support. This being said, there are a number of individuals and groups whose input has been such that they deserve a specific mention.

First and foremost, I wish to thank the staff, service users and supporters of the Birmingham Settlement (past and present) for their ongoing assistance with and interest in this project. In particular, I appreciate the time, support and knowledge of people such as Carl Bayliss, Dawn Clifford, Pat Conaty, Sue Freedman, Sara Griffin, Pat Hetherington, Peter Houghton, Christian Johnson (previously Kunz), Angus McCabe, Gemma Ogbeide, Janine Phillips, Susan Spencer and Maisie Smith. Secondly, I am grateful to Pete Alcock and Ann Davis at the University of Birmingham's Department of Social Policy and Social Work for their supervision, comments and ideas. Thirdly, I am indebted to Carl Chinn for his advice, for his enthusiasm, for reading drafts of this text and for supplying a foreword to the final version. I was also touched by the generous response of listeners to Carl's Radio WM show and readers of the Birmingham Voice, who supplied me with letters and memories about the work of the Birmingham Settlement and the history of Newtown and Kingstanding. Fourthly, I greatly appreciate the support of Joyce Rimmer, whose history of the first eighty years of the Birmingham Settlement gave me such an insight into the topic and made my job so much easier. I am also very grateful for the commitment and input of everybody at Brewin Books, whose speedy and efficient contribution meant that this book could be published in time for the Settlement's centenary.

In addition, I also wish to thank individuals and organisations such as the Aston Reinvestment Trust, the Aston Ward Team, Paul Beecham, Birmingham Chamber of Commerce, Birmingham Citizens' Advice Bureaux, Birmingham City Council, Birmingham Enterprise Limited, Birmingham Health Authority, Birmingham Law Society, Birmingham Voluntary Services Council, the British Association of Settlements and Social Action Centres, Broadening Choices for Older People, the City Central, University of Birmingham and Selly Oak Colleges libraries, Community Transport, the City Challenge Company, Focus, the International Federation of Settlements, iSSUE, Sydney Jacobs, Jennifer Jones, Lee Longland and Co., Newtown/South Aston Credit Union, Ring and Ride, Cecile Simon, the South and East Birmingham Family Service Units, Toynbee Hall, the University of Birmingham, the West Midlands Employment Information Unit and West Midlands Special Needs Ltd.

Last but not least, I am grateful to Anne-Marie and to my family, without whom this book could not have been written.

Contents

Chapter headings for chapters 3 to 7 are based on categories defined by William Beveridge, a key figure in the Settlement movement and in the foundation of the Welfare State. Deriving from his 1942 report (see introduction), they are based on language which would no longer be used to describe the problems of poverty and which does not reflect the Birmingham Settlement's attitude to these issues.

Foreword

by Dr. Carl Chinn

Why were so many poor in the midst of plenty? This was the question that raced through the minds of so many social commentators in the Late Victorian and Edwardian periods. Was it because the poor were feckless and workshy or was it because of adverse economic conditions over which the poor themselves had no control? The work of Charles Booth, Seebohm Rowntree, Bowley and Burnett-Hurst and other social scientific investigators made it clear that overall the poor were not to blame for their poverty. Of course, there were those folk who mis-spent their money and wasted their incomes, but the overwhelming majority of poor people were poor through no fault of their own. They were in poverty because of low wages, irregular earnings, illness, disability and widowhood and they battled daily to overcome the harsh circumstances in which they found themselves.

Alongside the debate on the causes of poverty there arose a concern that rich and poor were sundered. Such a preoccupation had been obvious in the mid-1800s when Disraeli had written *Sybil or the Two Nations* and Elizabeth Gaskell had brought out *North and South,* but it took on greater meaning as the century waned. By then, the greatest portion of Britons were living in towns and cities in which residential segregation between the classes was marked. It was feared that the urban working class was lacking the positive influence of upper and middle-class people and that to solve this problem it was necessary to re-establish contact between the rich and the poor. This imperative led to the settlement movement. The first settlers were students from Oxford University who had been fired by the vision of Canon Samuel Barnett, vicar of St. Jude's, Whitechapel in the East End of London. In 1884 he had been able to set up Toynbee Hall, a place where young men from the university could stop for a while and through their example raise up the local people socially and intellectually. Importantly, Barnett also believed that the settlers could find out at first hand about the difficulties faced by the working class.

By 1914, there were 25 settlements in London with another twelve elsewhere in England. They became important centres of social work, helping to improve the health and welfare of those in poverty. Many settlers themselves went on to make major contributions to thinking about social welfare. Amongst the most notable were E.G. Howarth, co-author of an important study of West Ham, and William Beveridge, a sub-warden at Toynbee Hall and the man who is credited as the architect of the Welfare State. Yet for all its good work and its significance, the settlement movement was based on social superiority. The word settlement itself stresses this, indicating the belief that the settlers knew best. This characteristic was satirised powerfully by Arthur Morrison in his novel *A Child of the Jago* (1896) and it was a characteristic which worried those settlers who realised that they had something to learn from the poor.

Increasingly, those who worked in settlements came to appreciate both the vitality and independence of working-class life and the close-knit nature of working-class neighbourhoods. Summer Lane was one such neighbourhood. Viewed by outsiders as one of the toughest parts of Birmingham, it was actually the scene of strong neighbourly and kinship ties. A long road running north-eastwards from the edge of the city centre to the border with Aston, Summer Lane had a host of courtyards lying off it and was criss-crossed by streets whose people were drawn to 'The Lane' by its shops and pubs. So strong were the neighbourhood bonds that Summer Lane is the only part of Birmingham about which an anthem has been written. 'See the Palm Trees Swaying Way Down Summer Lane' indicates not only local pride but also the manner in which 'The Lane' came to be regarded by Brummies as the archetypal working-class neighbourhood.

The Summer Lane of today is still often shunned by outsiders who know little of the qualities of the people who live in an area which the council has re-named Newtown. Yet as in the past, the people of 'The Lane' are battling with dignity and determination against the hardships with which they are faced. As they have been since 1899, they are joined in that battle by the Settlement on Summer Lane. Crucially, although the name settlement survives there remains no trace of the class superiority which imbued the settlement movement in the early twentieth century. Today the folk of Summer Lane and Newtown are in partnership with the workers at the Settlement. It is a successful partnership which is based on trust, respect and learning from each other. As we approach the year 2000, the Settlement's importance needs to be recognised more widely so that it can continue with its much-valued work into the new millennium.

'Overviews and Underpasses': an introduction

Heading out of Birmingham on the Aston Expressway, most drivers could be forgiven for overlooking Newtown altogether. Birmingham is fortunate enough to have a series of under- and over-passes which conveys traffic across the central business district on a single road – the A38 – without encountering the hustle and bustle of city centre driving. While this reduces congestion at peak times, it also renders almost invisible the inner city areas which lie on either side of the A38. As a result, drivers can pass through them oblivious to their existence, not so much ignoring them as not even realising that they are there. Should the occasional driver venture off the main thoroughfare, however, he would find himself in a district which is nothing if not controversial. At first glance, he might only see the empty, dreary streets, concrete tower blocks and industrial units. This is a place that most outsiders only drive through when they have to, making sure that their windows are wound up and their car doors locked when they stop even at traffic lights. At the same time, however, local people know that this fleeting glimpse through the window of a passing car - sometimes the only image non-residents have of the inner city - is hopelessly superficial, conveying nothing of the heritage of the area, the community spirit or the daily struggle against poverty. Over the years, Birmingham's inner city has provoked many reactions, some positive and some negative - few have been neutral, for these are places that it is difficult to be neutral about:

> *"What d'you wanna write about Newtown for? If you wanna tell the truth just write 'crap' at the top of the sheet. It should all be pulled down. It probably will be. It's all gonna be office blocks soon. There's nothing to do and nowhere to go except the pub... It's all right if you're a thug. You could do well as a thug. But there's nothing here. I'll probably move."*

> *"People who don't live here say it's a deprived area – that annoys me. Newtown has got hell of a lot going for it, swimming baths, community centre and a far better nursery provision than, shall we say, the upper class areas."*

> *"They don't even riot in Newtown – it's not worth it. You can look around all day and not see people. You're not aware of the population; there's an intangible awfulness, almost an atmosphere. There's no street life, all there is are tall tower blocks which make wind tunnels."*

> *"If people slag off Newtown I always defend it... When I got to know that I had got a flat back in this area, I was pleased... I like Newtown because it's where I grew up and where I know people."*

> (Local people, quoted Edwards and Lewis, 1992, pp. 6 and 35-36)

This is Newtown and this, for one hundred years, has been the home of the Birmingham Settlement.

The Birmingham Settlement is an independent voluntary agency serving Birmingham from its base in Newtown, but with a national and international influence and reputation in several areas of its work. It first opened its doors on 29th September 1899 and from 1931 to 1974 also operated from a base in Kingstanding on the edge of the city. One hundred years later, this publication is intended to celebrate the Birmingham Settlement's centenary. With over 120 members of staff and more than 250 volunteers, the Settlement today is responsible for 24 different projects ranging from a nursery scheme to a day centre, from money advice to business training and from home-based care to energy conservation (Birmingham Settlement, 1999). Dedicated to developing and implementing effective ways of overcoming social disadvantage, the Birmingham Settlement seeks to achieve this aim by helping people to help themselves, by building awareness and access to opportunities and by working with all concerned to develop and deliver new services to meet people's needs (Birmingham Settlement, 1998b). These themes and ways of working, although only recently expressed in this exact formulation of words, have characterised the Settlement's work throughout its hundred-year history and will emerge time and time again in the following pages.

The Birmingham Settlement at its opening, 29th September 1899.

The Birmingham Settlement is based at 318 Summer Lane, a street which runs from the foot of Snow Hill and Constitution Hill northwards towards Aston High Street. Mentioned in documents as far back as 1260, Summer Lane is neglected in official city histories but has a long heritage and for a time gave its name to the area around it (Chinn, 1997b). It is also one of the few areas of the city to have inspired its own song. Although the verses describe the city centre as a whole, the chorus is dedicated to Summer Lane and to the good times had by all in local pubs such as 'The Salutation':

> *"You can see the palm trees swaying down Summer Lane.*
> *Every night there's a jubilation, See the folks a singing at the 'Salutation.'*
> *No snow in Snow Hill, there's no need to catch a train*
> *To your southern home where the weather is warm*
> *It's always summer in Summer Lane."*

(Berry and Gines, quoted Chinn, 1997b, p.65)

Above all, however, Summer Lane is a place of contrasts. On the one hand, it is an area of grinding poverty, infamous for its pubs, its drinking and its street-fights at closing time. Authors who have written about the area describe policemen walking in three's in case of attack and keeping to the middle of the street for fear that the local people would drop chamber pots on their heads (Douglas, 1979). At the same time, 'The Lane' is remembered by the people who lived there as a poor but happy place, renowned for its community spirit and the hard-working dignity of its inhabitants (Chinn, 1997b; Dayus, 1994). In many ways, these contrasts still exist today, with some locals hating where they live and desperate to leave, but others proud of Newtown's heritage and fighting hard to defend themselves and their home against the criticisms of outsiders who know nothing about the people living there or the daily struggle against poverty. This tension is even mirrored in accounts of the area, with local residents Pauline and Bernard Mannion (1985) publishing their memories of Summer Lane in direct response to unduly negative descriptions of the area by a non-resident (Douglas, 1979, 1983).

Newtown – a place of contrasts

"Newtown South Aston is surrounded by success and regeneration, yet the same success has to date eluded it. Its physical environment remains poor and people have lost confidence in it. Lack of skills, low incomes and unemployment are long term problems with which poverty, deprivation, ill-health, crime and the fear of crime go hand in hand. Residents only have a limited choice of housing with little private rented accommodation or property to buy. Many of the local authority owned flats, houses and maisonettes are in urgent need of repair and renovation. In addition, the range of community, childcare and shopping facilities are poor. Overall, the area has some of the worst socio-economic and environmental problems in the city."

(Birmingham City Council, 1992d, p.1)

"Hockley [near Newtown] is an area of warehouses and factories today and I shouldn't think anybody lives there except the landlords of the pubs that are dotted about here and there on corners. It was a different story seventy years ago, though. Then this whole district was so crammed with humanity it was more like a rabbits' warren. There were still factories and lots of small workshops and foundries and the same pubs were crowded all day long... Then, this was what people today would call a 'slum' I suppose, and the people who lived here would be pitied as the 'have-nots'. But then there was no pity and we were left to sink or swim, rise or fall, as best we could. Yes, this was where I was born in 1903 and the poor people who struggled to live until that struggle killed them were my people."

(Dayus, 1994, p.5)

"Summer Laners were typical of Brummies as a whole. Whether they were English, Irish, Welsh or Italian, they were hard-working, gritty and determined. They were forthright and plain-speaking. They had a dry sense of humour and knew how to have a knees up and a good shindig. They were loyal and true. Many of them were poor, but they were proud and dignified. It was the people of 'The Lane' and neighbourhoods like it who were the real builders of Brum. It was they who forged Birmingham's reputation as the city of a thousand trades. And it was they who made Brummagem a place renowned throughout the world for its manufacturing and goods. Yes, Summer Lane was a tough quarter. Yes, there were many fights. Yes, it did have a boozer on every corner. But babbies could play safely in the streets of Summer Lane. Women could walk out late at night and have no fear of being attacked. And old people could go for a mooch and have no worries about muggers. 'The Lane' may have been hard but it was also caring. It was a place where thousands of people worked together to create strong communities. There was plenty of poverty in Summer Lane, but families bonded with one another and helped each other unselfishly... The people of 'The Lane' knew how to be real neighbours. Brummies through and through."

(Chinn, 1997b, p.66)

Despite these contrasts, the fact remains that Summer Lane and the neighbourhood around it has been one of the most impoverished areas in the city throughout the hundred years of the Birmingham Settlement's existence. There have been many changes – political, social, economic and cultural – but the poverty of Summer Lane's inhabitants not only continues, but shows no signs of abatement. Throughout all these changes, the only constant has been the Settlement and its commitment to working with people in need to alleviate their material circumstances and support them to regain their independence.

Outline

In honour of the Birmingham Settlement's centenary, this publication aims to examine the work of the Settlement over the last hundred years. It is not a chronological history – a very detailed and comprehensive account of the first 80 years of the Birmingham Settlement has already been produced (Rimmer, 1980) and numerous texts are available for Settlements elsewhere (Barnett, 1918a, 1918b; Briggs and Macartney, 1984; Carson, 1990; Davis, 1984; Gorst, 1895; Meacham, 1987; Pimlott, 1935; Stocks, 1956; Trolander, 1987; Woods and Kennedy, 1922). Nor is it a person-centred history, for although the Settlement's work has relied on the commitment of its staff and supporters, a detailed account of all the individuals involved would be beyond the scope of this book and inaccessible to the more general reader. Instead, this book adopts a thematic approach, exploring the issues with which the Birmingham Settlement has grappled over the last hundred years.

Newtown, 1975.

After a brief description of the origins and development of the Settlement movement in general and of the Birmingham Settlement in particular, this book sets the work of the Birmingham Settlement in its historical context, charting Birmingham's emergence as a major industrial centre and its subsequent social, economic, demographic and cultural development over time. The remainder of the book then focuses on 5 distinct aspects of the Settlement's work:

- financial and material deprivation
- health
- education and training
- housing and community
- employment and recreation

These themes, which are by no means exclusive and frequently overlap, are based on Beveridge's 'Five Giants' identified in his report on *Social Insurance* (Beveridge, 1942, p.6): want, disease, ignorance, squalor and idleness. The choice of Beveridge's categories as a structure for a history of the Birmingham Settlement is by no means co-incidental:

- To begin with, Beveridge was sub-warden at the first settlement, Toynbee Hall in Whitechapel, from 1903 to 1905 and completed the research for his treatise on unemployment there (Pimlott, 1935). Later in life, Beveridge recalled his time at Toynbee Hall with fondness, describing his decision to go there as "the best choice of occupation that I could have made" and stating that he owed his future jobs to the "special knowledge" he had acquired there (Beveridge, 1953, pp. 19-20).

- It was Beveridge's 1942 report and the subsequent introduction of the Welfare State that revolutionised British social policy and forced a change in the way that the Settlement movement conducted its work (Matthews and Kimmis, n.d.). In a new age and with a new government, many Settlements found their very existence threatened. Funds were short and traditional aspects of the Settlements' work had been overtaken by policy developments. It was only those Settlements able to adapt to the rapid and fundamental changes of the post-war world that have survived. This sense of crisis was also experienced in Birmingham, but the Settlement proved flexible and resilient enough to reappraise its work and carve out a new role for itself in the second half of the twentieth century. This process is described in more detail in chapter 7 of this book.

Writing a history of the Birmingham Settlement is difficult for a variety of reasons:

- The last hundred years have seen such profound social, economic, political and cultural changes that it is impossible to encapsulate them all in this work.

In a centenary publication such as this, all that can be attempted is an overview of the Settlement's work, with occasional reference wherever applicable to national or city-wide developments to place the Settlement's contributions in context.

- The administrative boundaries within Birmingham have changed during the present century, and this has influenced the nature and quality of statistical information available. When the Settlement was founded in 1899, it was situated in an area between Aston and Hockley in the ward of St. Mary's (although its work also extended into the nearby ward of St. George's). This later became known as Newtown following the redevelopment which took place after the Second World War, but is now technically part of the ward of Aston. Interestingly, none of these names seem to have endeared themselves to local people, and for many years the area around the Birmingham Settlement took its name from its main road and focal point: Summer Lane (Chinn, 1997b). As a result, the names St. Mary's, Newtown and Summer Lane are used interchangeably throughout the rest of this publication.

- The people who chose to involve themselves with the Settlement have tended to be very active and committed, working also for a number of other voluntary organisations. It is therefore extremely difficult to establish whether a particular initiative was the result of action by the Settlement or the product of a different agency altogether. This confusion is exacerbated by the Settlement's close relationships with other organisations working in the same area and by its role as an originator of innovative projects. On a number of occasions an initiative developed by the Settlement has branched out on its own after an initial period of growth and consolidation, making it hard to know whether its success should be credited to the Settlement or not.

- Frequent changes in the format of the Settlement's annual reports and periods of relatively poor documentation sometimes obscure the true extent of the Settlement's work. It is not uncommon, for example, for an annual report to refer to a particular project in a single sentence without explaining what the project entails. Although it is often possible to rectify this situation from other sources, there are occasions when no other written record of the project's existence remains and its exact nature is hidden forever.

To rectify these problems, the information in this book has been triangulated at every feasible opportunity and supplemented by oral histories from Settlement workers and local people in order to obtain as accurate a picture of the Settlement's work as possible. Any errors that remain are the responsibility of the author, not of the many individuals involved in producing this publication. Unless otherwise stated, all references are to the Birmingham Settlement's annual reports.

Chapter 1:

Origins, influences and development

This chapter charts the origins and subsequent development of the Settlement movement in general and of the Birmingham Settlement in particular. In the process, it:

- Identifies the factors and leading figures responsible for the first Settlement, Toynbee Hall.
- Outlines the growth of the Settlement movement from its origins in 1884 to the present day.
- Describes the foundation of the Birmingham Settlement and its subsequent development.
- Provides an overview of the changing structure of the Birmingham Settlement.

A. The Settlement Movement

There was no one founder of the Settlement movement: instead it was the product of a groundswell of public opinion outraged by the plight of the poor and of the endeavours of leading social reformers. The first Settlement, Toynbee Hall, was founded in 1884 in the East End of London at a time when the educated classes were becoming increasingly aware of the stark contrast between their own wealth and the poverty of the working classes (Young and Ashton, 1956). Shocked by the revelations of pamphlets such as Andrew Mearns' *The Bitter Outcry of Outcast London,* university men turned their attention to the inner city with a genuine desire to serve the poor. Through their efforts was created what was to become one of the most enduring and influential social movements of the last hundred years. International in its appeal, the Settlement movement has influenced some of the most important figures of the twentieth century. Examples in the United Kingdom include politicians such as William Beveridge and Clement Attlee, academics such as R.H. Tawney and clergymen such as Cosmo Gordon Lang, all of whom have had close links with the Settlement movement at one stage or another in their careers (Briggs and Macartney, 1984). At the time of its inception, however, none of these future developments could be foreseen. On the contrary,

Toynbee Hall and other early Settlements began their existence in relatively obscure and humble circumstances, with no sign of the success to come:

> *"On Christmas eve 1884, two Oxford University students slept in a half-completed building in the slums of East London. They did not come for a brief visit to an exciting underworld, nor did they intend to dole out charity to the needy. They expected to become residents of the neighbourhood, and to learn as well as to teach. They were the first settlement workers, and the half-completed Toynbee Hall, the first settlement."*

> (Davis, 1984, p.3)

Although much has been written about the Settlement movement, much of the available literature shies away from defining what a Settlement actually is, assuming that readers will already have a basic knowledge of the topic in question. In the late 1990s, this can perhaps no longer be taken for granted, and a working definition is a useful place to begin an overview of the origins and development of the Settlement movement. Writing of Toynbee Hall, Werner Picht sought to define what a Settlement was and what being a settler entailed:

> *"A settlement is a colony of members of the upper classes, formed in a poor neighbourhood with the double purpose of getting to know the local conditions of life from personal observation, and of helping where help is needed. The settler gives up the comfort of a West End home, and becomes a friend of the poor. He sacrifices to them his hours of leisure, and fills his imagination with pictures of misery and crime, instead of impressions of beauty and happiness. For a shorter or longer period, the slum becomes his home. Only seldom does he show himself at his Club, at the Theatre, in Society. This means the loosening of social and personal ties, in many cases the foregoing of the prospect of an early marriage, and the neglect of favourite pursuits. It means a sacrifice of life."*

> (Picht, 1914, p.1)

Although this description focuses on aspects of the settler's sacrifice which might not seem particularly relevant today, Picht's definition nevertheless touches upon several of the key features of the Settlement movement:

1. First and foremost, Picht reveals the class background of early settlers. Settlements initially consisted of educated people who had come to live among the poorer classes in order to raise their expectations and teach them by example what could be achieved. As time has passed, Settlements have inevitably become less paternalistic in their nature, yet early links with the universities often remain (see chapter 5).

2. In addition, Picht highlights the residential nature of Settlements. Traditionally, settlers have not only worked but also resided in Settlement houses. This was true of the Birmingham Settlement from its foundation in 1899 up until 1982 (see chapter 5).

3. Next, Picht emphasises the reciprocal nature of Settlement work. Settlers came not just to teach, but also to learn, living side by side with people in the direst poverty and sharing their experiences. This knowledge was then employed to influence policy debates and highlight areas of unmet need.

4. Finally, Picht describes the hardships faced by those who chose to involve themselves in the Settlement movement and, by implication, points towards the dedication and commitment which settlers throughout the years have undoubtedly displayed.

In some ways, the idea of settling in a poor area, even at the time of the creation of Toynbee Hall, was nothing new. There had been settlers long before there were Settlements, many of whom were enlightened and committed members of the clergy who lived and worked among their impoverished parishioners. Examples include J.R. Green of St. Philip's, Stepney and the Rev. E.C. Hawkins of Hackney (Pimlott, 1935). These men, however, were not strict settlers in the sense in which the word later came to be used since they lived in poor areas not as the colonists described by Picht above, but in the exercise of their professional duties. Perhaps the first true settler and the man later credited for inspiring Canon Barnett to found Toynbee Hall was Edward Denison.

Edward Denison (1849-1870)

The son of a Bishop and the nephew of the speaker of the House of Commons, Denison himself seemed destined for a career in Parliament before deciding to prepare for politics by acquiring personal experience of poverty issues (Briggs and Macartney, 1984; Woods and Kennedy, 1922). During the economic hardships of the 1860s, he came from Oxford to live in the impoverished Mile End Road district of London. Working initially for the London Society for the Relief of Distress, Denison quickly came to realise that material aid alone was insufficient: indiscriminate almsgiving served only to demoralise the working classes and did nothing to tackle the root of the problem. "The evil condition of the poor," he believed, "is largely due to the total absence of residents of a better class – to the dead level of labour which prevails over that wide region" (quoted in Pimlott, 1935, p.13). The solution, he thought, lay in education, self-help and increased contact between the rich and the poor. Himself the founder of an adult education class and a night school, it was Denison who first proposed the idea of a Settlement at a meeting with other reformers in 1868 (Pimlott, 1935). Weakened by the poverty he had voluntarily experienced, he died of tuberculosis at the age of 30 before his ideas could come to fruition.

Arnold Toynbee (1852-1883)

A second key figure in the development of the Settlement movement was Arnold Toynbee. An undergraduate and later a tutor at Balliol College, Oxford, Toynbee was one of the most brilliant scholars of his age. Renowned for popularising the term 'The Industrial Revolution' and for focusing British historiography away from political issues towards the social conditions of the masses, Toynbee was also a committed social reformer determined to improve the lot of the ordinary man (Pimlott, 1935). During his short career, Toynbee served as a poor-law guardian in Oxford, lived for a time in voluntary poverty in East London, lectured to working class audiences and campaigned for adult education (Meacham, 1987). His burning desire was to share the benefits of his own culture and education with the labouring classes (Davis, 1984) and his friends referred to him only half in jest as 'Apostle Arnold' (Pimlott, 1935). Like Denison before him, Toynbee sought to live among and learn from those living in poverty and to bridge the gulf between the educated elite and the working man. Like Denison too, his constitution was not strong and he died in 1883 at the age of 31.

Samuel Barnett (1844-1913)

If men such as Denison and Toynbee laid the foundation of the Settlement movement, the man to bring their ideas to fruition was Samuel Augustus Barnett. The Bristol-born son of an iron founder, Barnett was a spoilt, sickly, nervous child who disliked going to school (Barnett, 1918a). In spite of this, he was able to achieve a second-class degree in history and law at Wadham College, Oxford and, in 1868, entered the Church. In 1870 he was introduced to Henrietta Rowland (his future wife) at the birthday of the renowned housing reformer, Ocatvia Hill. The couple married in 1873 and in the same year made the decision to accept the living of St. Judes in Whitechapel. Described by the Bishop as "the worst parish in my diocese" (quoted Barnett, 1918a, p.68), St. Judes was one of the most notorious slums in London. Within a decade, however, the Barnetts had begun to transform the parish, establishing an adult education class, a night school for girls, a literacy society, an annual art exhibition, mothers' meetings, a penny bank and a pension scheme (Meacham, 1987). During the course of their work, the Barnetts, like Denison and Toynbee before them, came to realise that the solution to the problem of poverty lay not in indiscriminate almsgiving, but in making education available to the working classes and in bringing rich and poor people together to learn from each other. It was this realisation, coupled with ready support from the universities in the wake of Toynbee's untimely death, that led to the creation of Toynbee Hall, the first Settlement.

The Foundation of the Settlement Movement

In 1883, Samuel Barnett was asked to give two lectures, one at Oxford and the other at Cambridge. In the second of these lectures, at St. John's College, Oxford, he proposed the idea of a University Settlement in a paper entitled *Settlements of University Men in Great Towns* (quoted in full in Pimlott, 1935). In this paper, Barnett contrasted the traditional concept of a religiously motivated college mission with a new and more effective way of working with the poor. To bridge the growing divide between the rich and the poor, Barnett proposed a colony of educated men in a poor area of a large city. These people would live among the poor, educating them, learning from them, socialising with them and promoting social reform. Barnett's idea was greeted with enthusiasm, and by early 1884 a committee had been formed to found and maintain a Settlement in East London under the wardenship of Barnett himself. Support was soon received from Cambridge and a Universities Settlement Association was registered as a joint stock undertaking in July 1884. It had four main objectives (quoted Briggs and Macartney, 1984, p.9):

● to provide education and the means of recreation and enjoyment for the people in the poorer districts of London and other great cities; to inquire into the condition of the poor and to consider and advance plans calculated to promote their welfare;

● to acquire by purchase or otherwise and to maintain a house or houses for the residence of persons engaged in or connected with philanthropic or educational work;

● to provide in whole or for part of the salary of maintenance of any person or persons engaged in promoting the aforesaid objectives; and

● to receive and apply donations and subscriptions from persons desiring to promote the objectives aforesaid or any of them and to hold funds in trust for the same.

Partially financed by a memorial fund set up in response to the death of Arnold Toynbee, the Settlement was established on Commercial Street, Whitechapel under the name of Toynbee Hall (Young and Ashton, 1956).

Spread of the Settlement Idea

Often referred to as the mother of all Settlements, Toynbee Hall set an example which was to be repeated throughout the world. Nine more Settlements were founded in the UK in the 1880s and another 22 in the 1890s (Rimmer, 1980). The idea also spread to America, where a series of Settlements were established in cities such as New York, Chichago and Boston. By the turn of the century, the Settlement movement had spread throughout the British Empire, Western Europe, China and India (Young and Ashton, 1956). Since then, the fortunes of individual Settlements have ebbed and flowed according to policy changes, funding opportunities and changes in the nature of statutory social work. However, key developments include:

History of the Settlement movement

1884	First Settlement established in London.
1886	First Settlement established in USA.
1884-1914	Spread of the Settlement movement throughout United Kingdom, Europe, USA and beyond.
1914-1918	First World War
1918-1939	Renewal of Settlement activities and the development of international links. While the initial post-war period was a time of expansion, Settlement work began to be affected by the economic downturn of the late 1920s and 1930s, the demise of international relations and, ultimately, the outbreak of the Second World War. The International Association of Settlements (now the International Federation of Settlements and Neighbourhood Centres) was established in 1926.
1939-1945	The war was a period of immense difficulty for the Settlement movement. While Settlements in occupied countries were forced to close, Settlements elsewhere worked tirelessly to support their local communities with the hardships engendered by war, rationing, air-raids and conscription.
1945-1960	The post-war period was a time of crisis for many Settlements, both in terms of the immediate challenges of readapting to civilian life and in terms of changes in welfare provision. In many Western countries, the war led to an expansion of public welfare, forcing many Settlements to reappraise their role. Only those Settlements able to adapt to the changing policy context survived.
1960s	Settlements in many countries faced crisis or stagnation as a result of the economic stability of the 1960s. In the UK, the Settlements seemed out-of-date, unnecessary and irrelevant. Funding was tight and competition was emerging from more dynamic state and voluntary organisations.
1970s	This period witnessed a re-emergence of the Settlement movement in response to the growing awareness of the continued existence of poverty, an increasing emphasis on community development, the impact of the civil rights movement, reductions in state welfare and an international economic recession.
1980s	The 1980s were a difficult time for many Settlements due to mass unemployment, financial difficulties and problems recruiting and retaining staff.
1990s	A period of growth and greater international links. By 1995, the International Federation of Settlements represented over 4,500 organisations, ranging from small self-help groups to large agencies with hundreds of staff.

(Johnson, 1995; Matthews and Kimmis, n.d.; Rimmer, 1980)

*Women in conference. Left to right: Miss Dewar, Warden of the Birmingham Settlement;
Miss Danielson, Lady Brookes, Mrs. G. Morgan, president, and Mrs W. Cadbury.*

B. The Birmingham Settlement

Fifteen years after the creation of Toynbee Hall, the Birmingham Settlement was
founded in Summer Lane. Unlike many of its predecessors, it was a women's
Settlement, established by a group of ladies from the Edgbaston, Harborne and
Handsworth areas of the city and tending to focus in its early years on work with
women and children. Its initial title, in fact, was the *Birmingham Women's Settlement,*
although this was changed in 1919 to the *Birmingham Settlement* in order to reflect
more accurately the scope of its work. Despite this, the Settlement continued to
be dominated and influenced by women for many years to come:

● When the Settlement was founded in 1899, its president, vice-president,
secretary, warden, treasurer and committee members were all women. The
first man did not enter any of these positions until 1913, when Russell Jolly
became chairman of the Finance Committee. However, the number of women
occupying positions of authority within the Settlement continued to exceed
the number of men until well after the Second World War.

- From 1899 to 1932, the Settlement's residents were all women, as were the vast majority of its non-resident workers.

- From the very beginning, a significant proportion of the Settlement's subscribers and donors were women.

- With two exceptions, the Settlement's wardens/chief executives have all been women (see appendix A).

These contributions to the Birmingham Settlement contrast strongly with the male-dominated nature of the Settlement movement's founding fathers and are, in many ways, remarkable. Women, at this time and for many years to come, were subject to considerable legal, social, economic and political restrictions which seriously impeded their scope for action and forced them to remain subservient to men

---

Gender Inequalities

- Until the 1880s, married women were not allowed to hold property or money separate from their husbands.

- Women could not vote until 1918, and could not vote on equal terms with men until 1928.

- Until 1875, women were not permitted to serve as Guardians of the Poor Law.

- In education, School Boards were introduced in Birmingham in 1870, but it was a further three years before the first woman was elected.

- Victorian ideology emphasised that a woman's place was in the home. Queen Victoria herself is thought to have announced, "Let woman be what God intended, a help mate for man, but with totally different duties and vocations." Earlier commentators had suggested that "married life is a woman's profession, and to this life her training – that of dependence – is modelled," and "no woman can or ought to know very much of the mass of meanness and wickedness and misery that is loose in the wide world. She could not learn it without losing the bloom and freshness which is her mission in life to preserve" (quoted Haralambos and Holborn, 1990, p.545).

- Unequal pay for men and women and discrimination on the grounds of sex did not become illegal until 1970 and 1975 respectively.

Against this background, therefore, the history of the Birmingham Women's Settlement (as it was first called) is very much a gendered history, providing women with an opportunity to contribute to the local community and challenging existing gender roles.

The Birmingham Women's Settlement: early days.

Origins of the Birmingham Settlement

In the late nineteenth century, most major towns had a proliferation of voluntary organisations, the majority of which worked in isolation from each other with little co-operation and a considerable overlapping of responsibilities (Young and Ashton, 1956). A particularly good example of this is to be found in the numerous associations of women which existed to provide support, education and advice for women and children. During the 1880s, there was a move towards greater local co-ordination of such associations in order to prevent unnecessary duplication, and a Ladies' Union was formed in Sheffield for this very purpose. The idea spread, and in 1887 the Birmingham Ladies' Union was established to co-ordinate the work of more than 40 organisations working with women and children in the Midlands area. Under the motto 'Union is Strength', this Birmingham group became one of the most active of its kind in the country and was responsible in 1890 for calling the national conference which was to culminate in the creation of an umbrella organisation: the National Union of Women Workers. The Birmingham Ladies' Union became the Birmingham branch of this national movement, publicising its work through the quarterly journal *Women Workers*. It is to this group of women that the Birmingham Settlement owes its creation.

The idea of establishing a women's Settlement in Birmingham was first proposed in 1898 at the annual meeting of the Birmingham branch of the National Union of Women Workers. Having listened to accounts of women's Settlements in Liverpool and Southwark, a committee was established with a view to exploring the viability of founding a Settlement in Birmingham as a centre for philanthropy and for systematic training and study with regard to social work and industrial conditions. Consultations with local clergymen and voluntary agencies proved successful and a permanent committee of 12 members was established to raise funds and set up the proposed Settlement. In June 1898, this committee arranged for Miss M.C. Staveley to come from the Women's University Settlement at Southwark to be the first warden, and placed an advert in *Women Workers:*

> "The Women's Settlement Committee are anxious to hear of a house which would be suitable for a Residence. It should have accommodation for a Warden, two or three Residents and a Servant. A large room which could be used for meetings and parties etc. would be a great addition. The house must be in a poor district, but the committee would like to find one in as airy a situation as possible, and it should be near a tram or omnibus route. Rent about £40."

> (Quoted Rimmer, 1980, p.25)

Summer Lane

It was not long before a suitable property was acquired at 318 Summer Lane with accommodation for 5 residents. The rent was £50 per annum and the Settlement began its work in its new home on 29th September 1899. Although the landlord was initially reluctant to lease the property for any longer than a year at a time, he agreed to let number 317 to the Settlement in 1901 and, in 1905, sold the Settlement the five houses from 316 to 320 Summer Lane for the sum of £3,400 (Rimmer, 1980). Extensive repairs were required, but the Settlement at least had its own premises from which to establish and expand its activities. A second base was later acquired on the 'new' housing estate at Kingstanding, and a branch of the Settlement operated there from 1931 to 1974. Despite many changes and alterations, the Birmingham Settlement remains on its initial site in Summer Lane, keeping close to its roots and to the community it has served over the last hundred years.

The Birmingham Settlement at the turn of the century.

Organisational Structure and Development

From these humble origins, the Birmingham Settlement has developed into a major social agency with a budget of several millions and considerable influence and expertise. While this has involved considerable innovation and commitment from the individuals associated with the Settlement, it has also required radical organisational changes. Voluntary work cannot exist in a vacuum, and none of the Settlement's pioneering work would have been possible without an administrative and bureaucratic structure to support, oversee and facilitate its activities.

From the very beginning, the Settlement's principal officer or chief executive was known as the warden, a title which Samuel Barnett had assumed at Toynbee Hall in London (see appendix A for a list of the Settlement's wardens). However, overall control of the Settlement's affairs was vested in an Executive Committee (which met monthly) and a larger General Committee (which met quarterly). In 1899, these included members of some of Birmingham's leading families, the names of whom constantly recur in the Settlement's records as benefactors, supporters and well-wishers.

Committee members of the Birmingham Women's Settlement, 1899

President
Mrs. C. G. Beale

Vice Presidents

Mrs. Bracey★	Mrs. C. Pelham Lane	Mrs. Ebenezer Parkes
Mrs. G. Cadbury	Mrs. C. E. Matthews	Mrs. Perowne
Mrs. W. Kenrick	Lady Smith	Lady Georgina Vernon

Hon. Treasurer
Mrs. Hunt★

Hon. Secretary
Mrs. Walter Barrow★

General Committee

Miss Archer	Mrs. Percy Hudson★	Mrs. Hume Pinsent
Mrs. Bassett★	Miss Joyce	Miss Saunders
Miss Creak	Miss Ethel Johnson	Mrs. Sonnenschein
Miss Cohen★	Mrs. Johnstone★	Miss Sturge
Miss Dale	Miss Johnstone★	Miss Landon Thomas
Mrs. Fiedler	Miss R. Kenrick	Mrs. T. S. Walker
Miss Fiedler	Mrs. Wilson King	Mrs. C. J. Wainwright
Mrs. Frankland★	Miss Edith Lloyd	Miss E. Williams
Miss Gittins	Miss C. Martineau★	Mrs. John Wilmot
Mrs. Godlee	Mrs. Muirhead★	Miss Young

★ Members of Executive Committee

As the Settlement expanded, it developed a House and a Finance Committee, engaged auditors to oversee its accounts and appointed trustees in whose name the Settlement's property was vested. However, changes in the Settlement's constitution became inevitable during the 1930s once the decision had been taken to expand the Settlement's work into Kingstanding (see chapter 6). From

1934, the Settlement's traditional structure was replaced with a Joint Finance Committee, a Development Committee and an overall Council. Summer Lane and Kingstanding were described as "branches" of the Settlement, each with its own Executive Committee, warden, treasurer and secretary. At the same time, the Council was enlarged to include members of both Executive Committees as well as representatives from a number of local agencies and organisations. These included:

- The University of Birmingham
- The Birmingham Citizen's Society
- The Roman Catholic Archdiocese of Birmingham
- The Free Church Council
- The Birmingham Rotary Club
- The Diocese of Birmingham
- The Birmingham Council for Community Associations

(This tradition continues today, with representatives of the City Council and several academic institutions sitting on the Settlement's Board of Directors).

The new Council also included the wardens of both branches of the Settlement, who had never been members of the old Committee and had not therefore been involved in overall decisions about policy. From this time onwards, the new organisational structure of the Settlement begins to be mirrored in its annual reports, with separate contributions from the Council, the Summer Lane Executive Committee and the Kingstanding Executive Committee.

Although this new structure was more democratic than the system it replaced, the disruption of war prompted a partial return to previous ways of working. During the 1940s, the Summer Lane Executive Committee merged with the Development Committee, the number of meetings was halved and joint meetings of the Kingstanding and Summer Lane Executive Committees took place at Summer Lane. These changes were once again reflected in the Settlement's annual reports, which tended to focus on the overall achievements of both branches together rather than in separate sections as before. While these measures were designed to keep both branches of the Settlement in greater touch with each other, they also created considerable tension, with Kingstanding's warden feeling that her branch had lost its independence and was not receiving sufficient attention at the Summer Lane meetings. To some extent, this was a manifestation of a deeper tension which has always existed between Summer Lane and Kingstanding, with the latter feeling itself to be the poor relation of the former.

In 1950, the Settlement's constitution was revised again. Kingstanding regained its independence and the system essentially returned to its pre-war structure, with an overall Council and separate Executive Committees for Summer Lane and Kingstanding. At the same time, club members over the age of 15 were permitted to sit on the Settlement's Council, thereby increasing the autonomy of the clubs and adopting a more participative method of working. Once introduced, this basic structure remained largely unchanged for the next twenty years.

By 1970, the Kingstanding branch had become increasingly untenable due largely to financial difficulties and the decision was taken to amalgamate the two branches into an overall Management Committee. The next major change was not until 1986, when the Settlement became a limited company, divesting itself of the trustees which it had retained since 1899. This was essentially a legal

The Birmingham Settlen

BIRMINGHAM SETTLEMENT

| EMPLOYMENT AND TRAINING | ADVICE | CENTRAL SERVICES | CARE AND SUPPORT SERVICES | CAPACIT BUILDIN |

BIRMINGHAM SETTLEMENT SALES

EMPLOYMENT AND TRAINING

Women's Training:
Skills based training for women returners and single parents.

Employment Opportunities:
For the long-term unemployed through the Intermediate Labour Market and other schemes.

Employment Support:
Job search advice, information and practical support, through one to one counselling and training plans.

Homebased Care:
Individual care for people living in their own homes, training local residents to provide care services in the community.

Volunteering:
Developing skills, experience and confidence through voluntary work placements.

ADVICE

National Debtline:
A telephone helpline, providing confidential advice an guidance for people tackling the problem of multiple deb

Money Advice Centre:
Free, confidential and independent advice to people Birmingham with debt problems.

Money Advice Training Unit:
Providing training nationally, to increase the quality a availability of money advice.

Business Debtline:
Assisting traders in dealing with debts and cashflow pro lems arising from self-employment.

Fuelsavers:
Advice and practical solutions for individuals and loc businesses to improve energy efficiency.

CCHAT:
Homebased advice and support on benefit issues for loc residents who through disability or circumstances are unab to gain help elsewhere.

change and, outwardly at least, business went on much the same as before. Technically, however, the Settlement was now a charitable company, with members guaranteeing to pay a maximum of £1 towards its liabilities if called on to do so and accorded the right to receive the annual report and to attend and vote at annual general meetings. This, with a Board of Directors in place of the Management Committee, is how the Settlement continues today. Organisationally, it is divided into a series of sub-sections, each with its own remit, associated projects and staff.

organisational structure

Birmingham Settlement

CENTRAL SERVICES

Chief Executive's Office:
Overall management of all aspects of the Settlement's work.
Strategic planning and development.

Financial Services:
Sound financial management to ensure transparency of accounting, and full accountability for funds received.

Personnel:
Payroll and central personnel functions to support staff across all projects.

CARE AND SUPPORT SERVICES

Fundraising:
Enables the Settlement to develop innovative responses to need and to deliver specifically targeted services.

Day Centres:
Provides support for older people and their carers in a stimulating environment, enabling them to maintain independence in their own home.

Children's Services:
High quality, safe affordable childcare enabling parents on low incomes to pursue work and training opportunities.

CAPACITY BUILDING

Capacity Building:
Developing the potential for individuals and community groups to key into decision making processes, and to maximise employment and training opportunities for local residents.

Sustainable Strength:
Equipping women from disadvantaged inner-city areas to enter avenues to social and economic opportunity

Research:
An in-house research programme tackling social issues, working in partnership with Birmingham University.

Reference: (Birmingham Settlement, 1998a, pp.28-29)

Chapter 2:

Birmingham and Newtown, 1899–1999

This chapter describes socio-economic changes in Birmingham through time, placing particular emphasis on developments in Newtown. To this end, it traces:

- The emergence of Birmingham as an industrial centre and major city.
- The expansion of its boundaries and population.
- The growth of Newtown.
- Social, economic and cultural changes in the twentieth century.

The Growth of Birmingham

Now England's second city, Birmingham was once a rural village surrounded by the neighbouring settlements of Aston, Erdington, Witton, Edgbaston and Selly Oak. The earliest written record is a brief entry in the Domesday Book of 1086, in which Birmingham is recorded as having "land for 6 ploughs. In the demesne is 1, and there are 5 villeins and 4 borders with 2 ploughs. It was and is worth 20 shillings" (quoted Birmingham City Council, 1989, p.1). Nearby Aston, today part of Birmingham's inner city, was approximately double the size and worth five times as much.

Sometime between 1154 and 1166, the local lord of the manor, Peter de Birmingham, purchased a charter from the Crown. This enabled him to hold a market every Thursday, and was the first of its kind in the area. With this advantage, Birmingham was able to develop into a prosperous market town, boosted by its central location, its access to riverways, its proximity to the raw materials of the Black Country and its freedom from traditional guild restrictions.

As it grew, Birmingham also began to attract craftsmen, artisans and manufacturers from the metal industry, gradually earning a reputation as an industrial centre 'echoing with forges.' Trade proliferated, and the town became known for its gun trade, brass, metalwork, jewellery and general industrial diversity. Based initially in workers' own homes, Birmingham's industries later came to include a range of factory-based businesses such as BSA at Small Health, Cadbury's at

Bournville and the Lucas works in Newtown. Whereas the old labour-intensive trades continued to be situated in the crowded city centre, many of the new factories settled in the suburbs, clustering along Birmingham's newly emergent canal and railway network. In recognition of such rapid growth, Birmingham became a Borough in 1838 and, in 1889, a city.

Since this time, Birmingham has continued to grow, becoming the second largest city in the country. This has involved a series of demographic, social, economic and cultural changes, all of which have impacted on the work of agencies like the Birmingham Settlement seeking to alleviate the problem of poverty in the inner city. While these changes are difficult to monitor due to administrative reorganisations within the city, a brief overview is provided below to place the Settlement's work in its historical context. Since many of the individual issues highlighted are discussed in greater detail in subsequent chapters, this overview concentrates mainly on broad shifts in Birmingham's population, boundaries, industry and ethnic make-up.

Expanding Population and Boundaries

As Birmingham's industries expanded, so too did its population. Its 24,000 people in 1751 had trebled by 1800 and have continued to grow ever since (Gardiner and Wenborn, 1995). When Birmingham became a Borough in 1838 it comprised just over 8,000 acres and included only the parishes of Birmingham, Bordesley, Duddeston, Edgbaston and Nechells (Birmingham City Council, 1989). However, growth was particularly marked in the nineteenth century, with an increase in population from 71,000 in 1801 to 401,000 in 1881 (Sutcliffe and Smith, 1974). This was the result of an influx of people seeking work in Birmingham's flourishing industries, the oldest of which were based in the inner city. As new recruits arrived and prosperity increased, more affluent citizens moved out into the suburbs, where they could live in more salubrious and less crowded conditions. This process of industrial growth and outward migration produced a 'ripple effect', with the town (and later the city) expanding outwards in a series of concentric circles. In time, these came to form three distinct 'rings', with an inner ring of back-to-back houses and industrial workshops, a middle ring of tunnel-back houses and, later, an outer ring of new municipal estates constructed to house the overflowing population and reduce pressure on the central areas.

As Birmingham's population grew, its boundaries expanded into the surrounding countryside, swallowing a series of smaller settlements in the process. By 1870, a local writer could describe how each year "the neighbouring hamlets are approached by Birmingham's streets and ere long will merge into her arms... the great and multitudinous assemblage of one people – one vast manufacturing community – one Birmingham" (quoted in Briggs, 1952, p.135). The first major expansion came in 1891 with the addition of Harborne, Saltley, Balsall Heath and Little Bromwich. However, the largest extension of all came in 1911, when nearby Northfield, King's Norton, Yardley, Handsworth, Erdington and

Aston became part of the city under the Greater Birmingham scheme. Perry Barr, Castle Bromwich and Sheldon were added in the 1920s and the most recent change came in 1974, when the Royal Borough of Sutton Coldfield became part of Birmingham. As a result of this expansion, Birmingham today is a city of some 39 wards, comprising nearly one million people (Birmingham City Council, 1993).

The Example of Newtown

Nowhere is the outward expansion of Birmingham better illustrated than in Newtown itself. The first documentary reference to the Summer Lane area dates back to 1260, when 'the Lane' was nothing more than a dirt track leading from Birmingham to Walsall. Folklore has it that it was known as Summer Lane because it was only passable in the summer months when the sun turned the ground into a hard, compact surface over which to travel. Owned initially by the Priors of the Hospital of St. Thomas of Canterbury, Newtown then was little more than a rough pasture used for hogs and perhaps goats. Following the Dissolution of the Monasteries under Henry VIII, the lands of Summer Lane passed into the hands of the Colmore family, where they were to remain undeveloped for over two hundred years (Lay-Flurrie, 1982).

Summer Lane, 1931.

As Birmingham's population expanded, the profits to be made from developing Summer Lane into a residential area became increasingly difficult to resist. Early buildings included the 'Asylum' (a workhouse for over 300 poor children opened in 1797), the General Hospital (see chapter 4) and a number of individual houses for wealthy owner-occupiers seeking to escape the overcrowding of the town centre. It was these houses which were later to become the base of the Birmingham Settlement until their eventual demolition in the 1960s (Lay-Flurrie, 1982).

By 1810, the first court had been built to house the workshop and workers of M.H. Moggridge and Co., a japanners business which put a black finish on metal goods. Thereafter, development was rapid, with a series of houses, workshops, schools, shops and churches being constructed around Summer Lane during the first half of the nineteenth century. In the haste to house Birmingham's surplus population, as many dwellings as possible were squeezed into every available space, creating considerable housing problems for the future. By the 1850s, the basic pattern of streets and housing conditions was established that was to remain for over one hundred years until the radical redevelopment of Birmingham's inner city which followed the Second World War (see chapter 6 for more details).

Housing

One of the results of a rapidly expanding population was a high demand for housing, especially in the inner city area where many of Birmingham's traditional industries were based. Although the complexities of Birmingham's housing policy are discussed in greater detail in chapter 6, a key feature of the twentieth century has been the emergence of municipal housing in place of the jerry-built back-to-back homes of the early nineteenth century. At the time, this was seen as a major social achievement, since the back-to-backs were typically poorly designed, badly constructed, overcrowded and insanitary.

Prior to the First World War, progress in resolving Birmingham's numerous housing difficulties had been slow. There was increasing recognition of the scale of the problem, but little had actually been done by way of devising an effective solution. Between 1919 and 1939, however, there was greater action, with the construction of some 50,268 municipal houses for around 200,000 people (Briggs, 1952). After the disruption of the Second World War, progress was even more rapid, with the wholesale redevelopment of entire areas of the city. In Summer Lane, for example, the old back-to-back houses were replaced with high rise tower blocks and the neighbourhood was redesigned into a series of zones which divided housing, industrial areas and open spaces into distinct geographical units, often separated by major trunk routes. Despite the good intentions of the originators of this redevelopment, the new tower blocks were worse in many ways than what had gone before, destroying the area's community spirit without resolving the underlying social issues which had created so desperate a housing problem in the first place.

The new tower blocks, Newtown/Perry Barr, 1967.

By the 1990s, there were 27 tower blocks in Newtown, interspersed with a wide range of medium and low-rise housing. Almost 90 per cent of the area's 4,620 homes were owned and managed by the City Council, with the majority of the remaining 10 per cent inhabited by owner-occupiers who had taken up the opportunity offered to them under the Right-to-Buy campaign of the then Conservative Government. Ironically, some of these privately owned houses are now the most run-down of the entire local housing stock. While a series of regeneration schemes has begun to improve the condition of local authority housing, many of the owner-occupied properties have fallen into a state of disrepair which the owners cannot afford to put right. To make matters worse, these dwellings cannot be sold due to their condition and the reputation which Newtown has acquired. An initiative designed to provide people with a sense of ownership and responsibility for their property has therefore trapped owner-occupiers in a position of enforced poverty.

Since the early 1990s, the ongoing deterioration of the housing stock coupled with growing disaffection among local people has resulted in a number of regeneration schemes which have been successful in improving the physical infrastructure of the area without necessarily resolving the longer-term social issues which continue to influence Newtown (see chapter 6 for more details). While the housing market today is more varied than at the start of the decade, numerous problems and issues remain.

The old and the new, Lozells/Newtown, 1967.

Local residents' disaffection with Newtown

Question: What do you dislike about living in this area?

Area rundown/buildings not maintained	35%
Dirty/litter	35%
Vandalism/violence/fear of crime	34%
Lack of shops nearby	22%
Traffic/noise	9%
Dislike neighbours	8%

(MORI, 1992)

Industry and Employment

Despite the wealth of Birmingham's industrial heritage, the twentieth century has witnessed a number of profound changes in the city's economy, industrial structure and employment patterns. By the late nineteenth century, Birmingham had gained a reputation as a city of a thousand trades and, despite the growth of factor based businesses, many of its industries were still based primarily on small workshops. In 1870, there were thought to be less than 20 firms employing more than 500 people, with as many as 7,000 smaller workshops (Berg, 1994). However, this was soon to change, threatening Birmingham's traditional prosperity and facing it with the spectre of mass unemployment for the first time in its history.

During the twentieth century, technological developments and the globalisation of the economy have resulted in profound changes in the organisation and structure of British industry. With increasing mechanisation, for example, many firms required fewer skilled workers and began to amalgamate with other similar companies in order to gain a commercial advantage through economy of scale. New industries in Birmingham included the manufacture of bicycles, motorcycles and cars. As the century has progressed, Birmingham's traditional manufacturing industries have been increasingly challenged by competition from abroad, the development of more high-tech industries in the south of England and the general decline of manufacturing. The latter has been the result of a number of factors:

The decline of manufacturing

- A world-wide recession following the oil crisis of the 1970s.
- Competition from newly industrialising countries in South-east Asia where labour and production costs are lower than in Britain.
- A lack of investment and modern plant in some British businesses.
- Problems between management and labour in others.
- A lack of government intervention.

(Chinn, 1994)

This decline began somewhere between the 1950s and the 1970s, but reached its peak during the 1980s. Between 1978 and 1989, local employers laid off 107,205 workers and employment in manufacturing fell by 43 per cent (Chinn, 1994). This was the first time that Birmingham had faced significant unemployment and the proportion of those without a job rose from 2 per cent of the workforce in 1966 to 21 per cent in 1981. Although this was a general trend across Birmingham, the situation was worst in the inner city, where unemployment topped 40 per cent.

In Newtown itself, a skills audit conducted in 1988 found that around half the respondents were unemployed. Of this total, well over two-thirds had been out of work for more than a year. Those in employment were found to be in low paid jobs, with 72 per cent of men and 84 per cent of women having incomes of below £100 per week. By 1991, official statistics placed unemployment in Newtown at 32 per cent (as compared with a city average of 14 per cent), although unofficial sources suggest that the true figure may well be much higher (see Birmingham City Council, 1992a for all statistics quoted).

While subsequent regeneration schemes have sought to resolve this situation, unemployment remains a major social issue. In March 1999, there were 2055 unemployed people in the ward of Aston, 5.4 per cent of the total number of unemployed people across the city as a whole (personal communication, West Midlands Employment Information Unit).

Ethnicity

Birmingham in the 1990s is a multicultural city made up of communities and individuals from a wide range of ethnic backgrounds. Although the main changes in the city's ethnic make-up date from after the Second World War, Birmingham has a long heritage of ethnic diversity.

Birmingham's ethnic diversity

"For centuries Birmingham has been a city of immigrants. Its people came from the squire-dominated villages of the Midland Counties; from the famine-ravaged Ireland of the 1800s; and from poverty-stricken Southern Italy. During the 1920s and 1930s, these Brummies were joined by Scots, Welsh and Northern English all seeking a life away from the depredations of the Depression. Since 1945, this mixture of cultures and experiences has been given new vitality by the addition of people from the Caribbean, from East Africa and Yemen, from Pakistan, Kashmir, Bangladesh and India, from China and Vietnam, from Poland and Cyprus and by another wave of emigrants from Ireland."

(Chinn, 1994, introduction)

In addition to this multicultural heritage, immigration was particularly common during the 1950s and 1960s when Britain encouraged migration from former colonies to meet its manpower needs during the post-war recovery and boom. In 1951, Birmingham had an immigrant population similar to that of Liverpool, Manchester and Leeds. By 1966, however, it had a much larger proportion of such immigrants than these three cities:

The Rate of Immigration

% Population born overseas	1951	1961	1966
Birmingham	4.6	8.9	11.1
Liverpool	5.3	4.6	4.1
Manchester	5.9	8.4	9.5
Leeds	4.1	4.5	6.7

Source: Sutcliffe and Smith, 1974, p.208.

Many of these newcomers to Birmingham settled in the inner city, where housing was cheap and readily available, a fact reflected in the high proportion of members of ethnic minorities who still live in these areas. Today, Birmingham has one of the largest concentrations of 'black' and minority ethnic residents in any city in the UK.

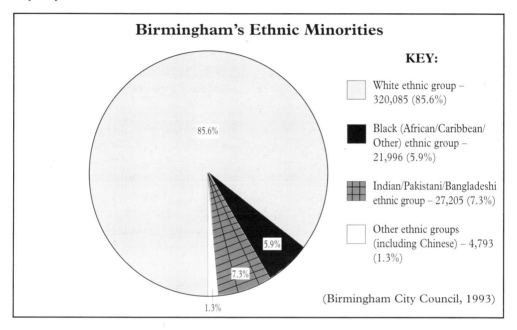

Birmingham's Ethnic Minorities

KEY:

White ethnic group –
320,085 (85.6%)

Black (African/Caribbean/
Other) ethnic group –
21,996 (5.9%)

Indian/Pakistani/Bangladeshi
ethnic group – 27,205 (7.3%)

Other ethnic groups
(including Chinese) – 4,793
(1.3%)

(Birmingham City Council, 1993)

In Newtown, the process of immigration was somewhat slower than in some areas of the city, with changes in the ethnic make-up of the area most apparent in the late 1970s and early 1980s. In the 1990s, however, ethnic minorities account for well over half the population in the ward of Aston (Birmingham City

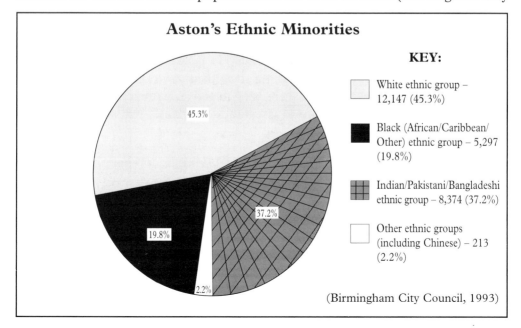

Aston's Ethnic Minorities

KEY:

White ethnic group –
12,147 (45.3%)

Black (African/Caribbean/
Other) ethnic group – 5,297
(19.8%)

Indian/Pakistani/Bangladeshi
ethnic group – 8,374 (37.2%)

Other ethnic groups
(including Chinese) – 213
(2.2%)

(Birmingham City Council, 1993)

Council, 1993). Particularly large groups include the Bangladeshi and Afro-Caribbean communities, which are more highly concentrated in this area than in most other parts of the city. For a complex range of historical and social factors, many ethnic minorities in Birmingham have traditionally been among the worst-off groups in term of socio-economic status (Birmingham City Council, 1996a, 1996b, 1996c, 1996d, 1997).

Newtown in the 1990s

Since information concerning particular parts of Birmingham is generally collected only at ward level, a statistical overview is only available via the 1991 census results for the ward of Aston:

Aston

The 1991 census found that Aston had a population of 26,819, over 50% of whom were from minority ethnic communities. Of the total number of residents:

- 12.2% households were lone parents with children aged 0-15 (5.4% for Birmingham).
- 73.0% households had no car (45.1% for Birmingham).
- 53.5% houses were rented from the local authority (26.4% for Birmingham).
- 32.9% economically active residents were unemployed (14.6% for Birmingham).

(Birmingham City Council, 1993)

Perhaps the most telling statistic of all, however, came from a survey carried out in Newtown by MORI in 1992, in which 31 per cent of local people (nearly one in three) said that there was nothing they liked about the area they lived in (MORI, 1992). Overall, feelings were very negative, with residents expressing their dissatisfaction with a range of issues and services. Priorities for change included:

Priorities for change identified as 'crucial'

Making the area safer	56%
More police on the beat	51%
Improving shopping facilities	50%
Improving housing repairs	50%
Making the area look more attractive	32%

- More training for jobs   28%
- More play areas for children   26%
- Redeveloping disused land   22%
- More child care facilities   18%
- More leisure facilities   15%
- Improving advice services on benefits and debt   12%

(MORI, 1992)

Interestingly, many of these are issues with which the Birmingham Settlement has been grappling throughout its hundred-year history and recur time and time again throughout the following pages.

Chapter 3:

'Want' – Financial and material deprivation

Poverty is frequently (if mistakenly) equated with lack of money, and the issue of access to financial and material resources is crucial to the work of the Birmingham Settlement. As a result, this chapter focuses on the Settlement's attempts to alleviate financial poverty, placing this work in its historical and social policy context. Key features include:

- Changing definitions of poverty.
- An overview of the Poor Law and the growth of the Welfare State.
- Poverty in Newtown.
- The Birmingham Settlement's responses to these issues. These range from the distribution of financial aid to the provision of legal advice, and from money advice to community banking.
- The Settlement's own finances.

The Nature of Poverty

Whenever people think of poverty, they inevitably associate it with financial and material deprivation. This is perhaps understandable in a society which has witnessed widespread famines in countries such as Ethiopia or Sudan and, more recently, the plight of ethnic Albanians in Kosovo. To view poverty solely in these terms, however, is to focus on one of its manifestations, not on its underlying nature. Although there is no commonly accepted definition of the *term* poverty, there is a growing recognition that the *experience* of poverty is not simply a matter of lack of money, but of social exclusion, powerlessness, stigma and lack of choice (Becker, 1997; Novak, 1996). As a result, it pervades every aspect of people's lives, limiting the opportunities of those who experience it across a range of activities which the majority of people would take for granted: education, employment, health, housing and leisure to name but a few. Any organisation working with people in poverty, therefore, needs to address all of these issues if its work is to be successful.

This being said, poverty has not always been conceived in these terms. In the late nineteenth century, for example, the ruling classes saw poverty in an absolute sense. According to this definition, people in poverty were those with insufficient resources to meet basic physical requirements. This conceptualisation assumes that there can be an objective definition of 'subsistence' (the minimum standard required to sustain life) and that the needs of the poor do not change over time. Drawing heavily on the work of social reformers such as Booth and Rowntree, the notion of absolute poverty was later adopted in Beveridge's plans for the Welfare State and came to form the basis of National Assistance (now Income Support). The modern social security system is therefore founded on attempts to combat poverty by keeping the recipients of welfare benefits at the minimum level of subsistence (Blackburn, 1991).

In the second half of the twentieth century, the notion of absolute poverty came to be challenged and ultimately superseded by that of relative poverty. Associated with the work of Peter Townsend, this concept focuses on social as well as physical needs, recognising that poverty can only exist relative to the general standard of living at any one particular time and in any one particular place. According to Townsend, people are impoverished when they:

> *"lack the resources to obtain the type of diet, participate in the activities and have the same living conditions and amenities which are customary, or at least widely encouraged or approved in the society in which they belong."*

> (quoted Blackburn, 1991, p.10)

This definition sees poverty not merely as an inability to subsist, but as an exclusion from social participation, emphasising the way in which financial poverty is linked with and exacerbated by poor access to other resources (see below). It is for this reason that the work of the Birmingham Settlement (and the structure of this book) focuses on such varied aspects of people's everyday lives, addressing the effects of poverty in their entirety. Despite this, however, financial and material deprivation remain an important part of poverty and it is in this area that a history of the Birmingham Settlement's work should begin.

> *"Income is a key resource for families... Families with low incomes are least able to afford, or have access to, good housing conditions. They have little choice about the type of accommodation they live in, or where they live. Families in poverty are more likely to be living in rented accommodation that is insecure, overcrowded and in poor structural condition than higher-income families. Moreover, poor families are more likely to live in less hospitable areas, with poor access to safe play areas and health, education and leisure services. Poverty-level incomes do not enable families to buy the foods that are thought to be important for health, or pay for enough heating to keep homes warm and free from damp and condensation. Families in poverty cannot afford family outings or goods that make life more bearable and are important for mental and physical health. Families on low incomes can often afford only poor-quality equipment and furnishings that are badly designed, wear out or break quickly. For families using credit facilities,*

*goods may wear out or break even before they are paid for... Above all, poverty
is an experience – an experience of 'doing without' – that touches every part of
life."*

(Blackburn, 1991, pp.11-12)

The Poor Law

In the late 1990s, the concept of relative poverty has probably become more
widely accepted than that of absolute poverty. This has not always been the case,
however, and the work of the Birmingham Settlement has spanned this change
in the definition of poverty, taking action to address both absolute and relative
poverty at different stages in its history. In its early years in particular, this was
a massive task, and one not made any easier by a harsh and outdated system for
dealing with the problem of material deprivation. From Tudor times until the
middle of the twentieth century, the principal mechanism for relieving the plight of
those in poverty was the now notorious Poor Law. Under Elizabethan legislation, the parish retained responsibility for 'paupers', levying rates from which to
finance the payment of 'outdoor relief' to the destitute. As Britain became more
urbanised and industrialised, however, this system became increasingly unwork-
able, prompting the need for reform.

Under the Poor Law Amendment Act 1834, access to outdoor relief was
severely restricted and help was provided largely through the workhouse, entry
to which was conditional upon passing a test to deter all but genuine cases of
need. In actual fact, poor relief continued to be paid in practice after 1834,
especially in industrial areas where the workhouses simply could not cope with
the volume of people living in poverty. Nevertheless, the workhouse was the
main source of 'help' and those who did not want to enter an institution often
found themselves with no support at all. This was common, for the workhouses
were hated and feared the world over. As the nineteenth century progressed,
some of these institutions became more humane, developing hospitals and schools
for deserted children, the sick and the elderly. However, the fact remained that
the workhouses were places associated with and based on punishment and a loss
of independence (Chinn, 1995), and the vast majority of people would rather
have starved than receive assistance in the workhouse.

Reform and the Welfare State

To rectify some of the shortcomings of this system, a liberal government devised
two major pieces of legislation in the early twentieth century. The first of these,
the Old Age Pensions Act 1908, introduced a non-contributory, means-tested
pension for older people. The second statute, the National Assistance Act 1911,
implemented a contributory and non-means-tested scheme to provide cover
against sickness and unemployment for some, initially limited, groups of workers.
However, these measures were not sufficient to meet the demands created by the

widespread unemployment of the inter-war period. Policy debates were complex, but a compromise was eventually reached with the introduction of extremely strict tests to ensure that people were genuinely seeking employment, an additional means-tested benefit known as the 'doles' and extensive outdoor relief. Pauline and Bernard Mannion describe how this system operated in Summer Lane:

> *"It was extremely hard to manage in the late 1920's and early 1930's when the Means Test was in operation. This allowed only just enough money on which the family had to exist. The unemployment pay was very poor and when the time came for the husband to apply for extra help, the income and outgoing were assessed before he was even given a hearing. All luxury things in the home had to be sold before he was entitled to any help... Then he might get vouchers which were only for food or coal. And he was forbidden to either sell them or exchange them for anything else... An unemployed man drew something like 21/- a week and 3/6d for his wife, extra coppers were added to this according to how many children he had. It was a never ending struggle against the odds, trying to feed and clothe a family on this, and some families had up to ten children. If a widow married a young widower the number of children could be even more, but somehow, most survived to tell the tale."*

> (Mannion and Mannion, 1985, pp.48-49)

However, these measures simply postponed the inevitable, and the Poor Law was finally abolished with the introduction of a comprehensive contributory social security system under the National Insurance Act 1946 and the National Assistance Act 1948. This, with various modifications, is essentially the same system that operates today with benefit levels still based on the notion of keeping recipients of state welfare just above the level of subsistence. This has only recently begun to change, and it remains to see what impact the current government's welfare to work reforms will have.

Poverty in Summer Lane

In Summer Lane itself, financial poverty has been widespread throughout the hundred years of the Settlement's existence. Shortly before the Settlement was founded, the Reverend Mantle visited the homes of unemployed men in Summer Lane and was appalled by the starving, cold, impoverished people he met:

> *"In the same court I visited a plasterer who has been out of work six weeks. There was not a spark of fire in the grate, and the woman had gone to a neighbour's house to earn 2d. by cleaning the floor in order to purchase bread. 'It goes against the grain,' said the man, 'to ask for help. I haven't got enough cheek for that; but we've pawned everything, the wife's clothes and my own, our bed-linen and all that they would take. At night we throw our clothes over us to try and keep out*

the cold.'... In another 'pearler's' home the desolation and suffering was most distressing. The husband was lying ill in the Workhouse Infirmary... Two sisters had each taken a child to relieve this unfortunate woman, who was shivering in her rags as she told me her sorrows, bursting into tears as she described how one thing after another had gone for food."

(Mantle, 1891)

At the turn of the century, 6.5 per cent of the population of Birmingham was receiving outdoor relief, with St. Mary's being identified as one of the most needy areas in the city (Tillyard, 1906). Although the liberal reforms of 1908-1911 eased the problems of some local people, the distress of many more remained unalleviated and authors writing about the area in the inter-war period have always commented on its grinding poverty (Dayus, 1994; Mannion and Mannion, 1985). A recurrent theme is usually the central role played by Jinny Bighton (sometimes written as 'Brighton' or 'Brigton'), the local pawnbroker, in providing people with the money they needed to survive. It is claimed that Jinny would lend money on anything of any value and rumour has it that she once accepted a man's wooden leg as a pledge to help out a family that had nothing else to offer (Mannion and Mannion, 1985).

Despite a general improvement in the overall material circumstances of Summer Laners in the second half of the twentieth century, there are frequent references in the Settlement's annual reports to a "new generation of the poor" (Birmingham Settlement, 1983, p.5). These people were no longer faced with the utter destitution of previous years, but nevertheless had to struggle to maintain their homes, their friends, their jobs, their hopes and their dignity in the face of ever-increasing despair and degradation.

Perhaps the most vehement criticism of all, however, came from Joseph Priestley during his journey across England in the autumn of 1933. Impressed by Birmingham's city centre, Priestley went for a ride on a tram into some of the inner city residential areas. His exact route remains unknown, but the desolation he described is typical of areas such as Summer Lane:

"Then followed one of the most depressing little journies I ever remember making... In two minutes, its [Birmingham's] civic dignity, its metropolitan airs, had vanished; and all it offered me, mile after mile, was a parade of mean dinginess. I do not say that this was a worse tram-ride than one would have had in Manchester, Liverpool, Glasgow, any of our larger cities, or smaller ones either for that matter... I only know that during the half-hour or so I sat staring through the top windows of that tram, I saw nothing, not one single thing, that could possibly raise a man's spirits."

(Priestley, 1977, p.85)

It was this state of affairs, brought about by financial and material deprivation, that the Birmingham Settlement, in all areas of its work, has been trying to resolve.

The Settlement's response

Provident Collecting

In response to the financial and material deprivation it witnessed, the Birmingham Settlement initiated a range of projects to alleviate the plight of its impoverished neighbours. The first of these, as old as the Settlement itself, was Provident Collecting. Under this scheme, visitors called every Monday morning, collecting an average of 3 or 4 pence per week to invest in what was essentially a penny bank. In its first year, the Settlement visited 92 houses in the Lower Tower Street area and by 1902 was collecting money from over 300 savers. Demand increased rapidly, and the Settlement found itself having to appeal for further visitors in order to expand this aspect of its work. For many people in Summer Lane, this was the first opportunity they had ever had to save money, and they grasped the chance as soon as it was offered to them. Whereas in the past they had been dependent on moneylenders and pawnbrokers to make ends meet, they now had a means by which they could save for the future and put aside a small sum to tide them over when times got tough (Mannion and Mannion, 1985). By 1905, Settlement workers were pleased to see that the people they visited had become so used to saving that they continued to do so in periods of economic hardship or when they moved out of the area altogether. By the outbreak of the First World War, the Provident Society was visiting 11 districts in the area, had branches in 5 local factories and was receiving an annual total of nearly £700 courtesy of some 17,862 deposits.

In 1916, a sum in excess of £1,000 was collected for the first time and the volume of work was such that urgent reorganisation was required. In 1919, the Provident Society was affiliated to the Provident Fund of the Citizen's Committee, a city-wide scheme, with the Settlement retaining responsibility for collections in the Summer Lane area. This arrangement was short-lived, however, and in 1921 the Settlement decided to continue its Provident work in conjunction with the Birmingham Municipal Bank. The sums saved and the number of districts covered continued to increase until, on the eve of the Second World War, there were 25 collectors visiting 1,000 subscribers and amassing a little over £2,000 every year. The society continued to prosper throughout the war and it was only in 1954, when the Settlement's own finances reached something of a crisis, that the decision was taken to terminate its work. By this stage, of course, there were more financial services available to local people and the majority of customers were content to transfer their accounts to the local branch of the Municipal Bank.

The Provident Society was one of the longest-running of the Settlement's projects, spanning over 55 years of its history. Its success lay not only in the opportunity which it offered to ordinary, working people to save, but also in the social contact it provided. As early as 1901, the Settlement's annual report noted that the weekly Provident visits were "a valuable means of establishing

A Provident collector at work, 1931.

friendly relationships" with local people (Birmingham Settlement, 1901, p.5), while in 1907 it was acknowledged that regular contact through the Provident Society was "an easy and natural way of entering into touch" with the Settlement's neighbours and "getting a knowledge of their needs" (Birmingham Settlement, 1907, p.9). Throughout the Settlement's records, the relationships which the Provident Collectors developed with local inhabitants are emphasised almost as much as the amount of money saved. This is particularly the case during the Second World War, when many families came to rely on their visitor as "a personal friend," seeking advice on personal and social problems during visits (Birmingham Settlement, 1945, p.4). It is interesting to note that the only group of people to object to the termination of the scheme in 1954 were older people who had come to rely on the Provident Society as a means of receiving a weekly visit. As a result of the relationships they developed with the people they visited, the Provident collectors came to gain a working knowledge of the local area and to provide a useful social service, providing support to those in need and referring to other agencies where appropriate. Even today, members of the Settlement's clubs and day centres refer fondly to "the Settlement ladies" or to "the bank ladies" who visited them so regularly.

Financial Aid

At the same time as the Provident Society was raising the profile of the Birmingham Settlement in the local community, a second project was working to provide much more immediate financial and material aid. Working in conjunction with the Charity Organisation Society, the Settlement established a sub-committee which met weekly to plan assistance for older people and other adults in financial distress. Although the work of this committee is rarely described in detail in the main body of the Settlement's annual reports, information contained in its accounts suggests that regular sums of money were paid from a pension fund to a number of older people to enable them to subsist. This practice continued until 1931 when provisions for older people had improved and when the last of the pensioners supported by the Settlement died. Financial aid was also granted to 'special cases', examples of which include clothes for pensioners or for younger people about to start work, help during illness, Christmas dinners, medicine and loans to purchase essential items of equipment or to redeem them from the pawnshop. Unlike the older people, who tended to receive ongoing support over a number of years, the 'special cases' tended to be one-off payments to people in need designed to restore their independence.

Working closely with the Charity Organisation Society, the Birmingham Settlement soon acquired a reputation across the city as an agency with considerable experience of poverty issues. In the years to come this reputation was to increase, and in 1907 the Settlement's relations with the Charity Organisation Society were strengthened when the latter, together with the City Aid Society (initially the Lord Mayor's Relief Fund), took possession of 319 Summer Lane as a branch office. These organisations worked closely with the Settlement until 1916 when they merged to form a new agency: the Citizen's Society (later the Birmingham Council of Social Service and now the Birmingham Voluntary Services Council). Thereafter, the Charity Organisation Society office on Summer Lane became a district office of the Citizen's Society and its work with the Settlement continued until 1927 when the central branches of the Citizen's Society were amalgamated into one office in Corporation Street and the branch at Summer Lane closed. Even then, Settlement students continued to visit cases in the Summer Lane area and to spend time at the office in Corporation Street to gain experience, thereby maintaining the Settlement's links with one of its oldest projects.

Economic Distress

In between the foundation of the Settlement in 1899 and the decision by the Citizen's Society to leave Summer Lane in 1927, many local people came to rely on the financial and material aid distributed by these agencies. In particular, there were three main periods of severe economic distress when the Settlement became inundated with requests for assistance:

- In 1905, unemployment was rife and workers from the Settlement, the Charity Organisation Society and the City Aid Society were at full capacity.

- The next major crisis came in 1914 with the outbreak of the First World War. With many reservists living in the area, Summer Lane found itself in a state of emergency when these men were suddenly called up. Within 10 days of the declaration of war, the situation in Summer Lane had reached emergency proportions and immediate action was required. Working closely with the National Union of Women's Suffrage Societies, the Settlement and the Charity Organisation Society opened their office morning and afternoon, pressing all the experienced workers available into service as visitors and interviewers. During the first three weeks of the war, 310 applications for help were received, with almost half coming from the wives or parents of soldiers. In this short space of time a total of nearly £50 was distributed to buy food and fuel, a sum which proved sufficient to weather the initial crisis until War Office pay began to be paid and the situation started to stabilise.

- The final crisis came in the immediate post-war period when unemployment was once again widespread. During this time, the Settlement was involved in distributing aid from a variety of funds to meet the needs of ex-servicemen and their families, to support the unemployed and to provide food and clothing for those in need. Although this volume of work decreased significantly as conditions improved in the mid-1920s, the Settlement still dealt with well over 400 applications for material aid in 1926, the year before the Citizen's Society relocated to Corporation Street.

War Work

In addition to the distribution of aid to families facing poverty as a result of the outbreak of war, the Settlement also involved itself in a number of short-term projects designed to improve financial and material conditions during war time. In 1914, for example, the Settlement established a sewing meeting to make clothes for Belgian refugees. The initiative proved so successful that the Settlement was able to pay local women for the work they did and, for a time, experimented with harnessing the talents of local people in a toy-making business. This, however, proved too expensive and the experiment was discontinued in 1915. Next, the Settlement responded to the harsh winter of 1917-18 by donating food and warm clothes to local older people and by opening up a Communal Kitchen in conjunction with the Food Economy Committee in order to distribute food. Finally, Settlement students were involved in a number of research initiatives, the findings of which were later to influence national policy and debate. Examples include an inquiry into the home conditions of soldiers on service, pensions and the price of coal and of food.

This was clearly a difficult time for the inhabitants of Summer Lane and the Settlement's resources were stretched to the limit – by 1918, the warden was reporting that just surviving was in itself a major achievement in light of the obstacles facing the Settlement. That the Settlement not only survived, but also continued to provide such significant support to its neighbours is testimony to its resilience under pressure and to the dedication and commitment of its workers.

> *"The Settlement still survives. With so heavy an adverse balance against us that seems in itself an achievement."*

(Birmingham Settlement, 1918, p.5)

Maintenance Payments

Both before and after the war, the Settlement grappled with an issue which was clearly placing local women in a position of financial hardship. By 1913, it had become apparent that many women legally separated from their husbands were either unable to extract regular maintenance payments or were subject to physical violence when they tried to claim their entitlements. Although the law enabled Magistrates to order maintenance payments to be made through an officer of the court, this practice had not been adopted in Birmingham and many local women had no choice but to try to collect their maintenance on their own, sometimes using their children as intermediaries (Rimmer, 1980). To rectify this situation, the Settlement wrote to the mayor requesting that an officer be appointed to collect and distribute money on these women's behalf. Signed by the Bishop, the Catholic Archbishop, the Principal of the University and the chairmen of the City Aid and Charity Organisation Societies, this letter proved successful and an official was duly appointed. In spite of this initial success, this was an area to which the Settlement was to return on a regular basis, and records show that a large proportion of the work undertaken by the Poor Man's Lawyer (see below) was connected with cases between husband and wife.

The Poor Man's Lawyer

Mention of the Poor Man's Lawyer above requires further explanation. Although this may not seem entirely appropriate in a chapter focusing on financial and material deprivation, this project clearly had financial implications for the people who used it, giving them access to free legal advice and frequently resulting in financially beneficial outcomes in court. The Poor Man's Lawyer movement began in 1891 when a barrister, Frank Tillyard, began to give free legal advice to poor applicants at the Mansfield House Settlement in Canning Town (Pimlott, 1935). Tillyard subsequently came to the University of Birmingham in 1904 as head of the Faculty of Commerce, and it is unlikely to have been coincidence that a Poor Man's Lawyer Association was founded in the city just four years later in 1908. The Birmingham Settlement was chosen as one of its centres and a lawyer visited Summer Lane every Tuesday evening to give advice both to local people and to those from further afield:

> *"It is safe to say that the Poor Man's Lawyer Association is rendering a real service not only in this district but, judging from the number of applicants who come even from remote suburbs, real service to the City at large."*
>
> (Birmingham Settlement, 1924, p.11)

After closing for a brief period during the war, the Settlement's Poor Man's Lawyer centre re-opened in 1923 and its impact was immediate. Between February and November 1924, the Poor Man's Lawyer provided advice and assistance to over 1,200 applicants during his two-hour weekly slot at the Settlement, the majority of which were concerned with landlord and tenant issues or disputes between husband and wife. Where legal proceedings were necessary, cases were referred to one of the solicitors in the Poor Man's Lawyer Association, who offered their services free of charge and were often successful in winning significant compensation, especially in cases of street accident or industrial injury. The volume of work remained high throughout the 1930s and the scheme was introduced at the Kingstanding Settlement in 1934 to offer the same service to people in that area of the city.

After another brief closure during the early years of the Second World War, the Poor Man's Lawyer began again in 1943, but disappears from the Settlement's records after 1949, the same year as the passage of the Legal Aid and Advice Act. By this time, however, much of the project's work had been taken over by new initiatives (see next page) and its role was somewhat outdated. Clients then needed not just advice but also representation, and the closure of the Poor Man's Lawyer, although an important break with the Settlement's past, was not as detrimental to local people as it might once have been.

The Citizens' Advice Bureaux

A similar project to the Poor Man's Lawyer was that of the Citizens' Advice Bureaux (CABs) opened by the Settlement in both Summer Lane and Kingstanding at the start of the Second World War. These were part of a wider initiative, overseen nationally by the National Council of Social Service and, locally, by the Birmingham Citizen's Society. In Birmingham, 29 CABs were opened across the city in direct response to the outbreak of war, two of which were administered by the Settlement. Building on the work of the Personal Service Bureaux which had been opened briefly at both Summer Lane and Kingstanding on an experimental basis to provide non-legal advice, the Settlement's CABs performed similar work but were organised on a much more thorough basis. At the peak of war-time austerity, the Settlement CABs were open 7 days a week, 24 hours a day (Rimmer, 1980), and were the only ones in Birmingham to open at nights and at the week-end.

All in all, the CABs and the Poor Man's Lawyer had much in common and their work frequently overlapped:

- Both schemes defy simple categorisation, yet owe their place in a chapter devoted to financial and material issues to their role in providing advice and assistance with regard to financial issues. Whereas the Poor Man's Lawyer dealt mainly with tenant-landlord disputes, matrimonial cases, street accidents and industrial injury, the CABs, initially at least, focused primarily on rationing and housing matters.

- Neither project has generated detailed records, but both were clearly very important to local people. While occasional references in the Settlement's annual reports suggest that these were long-standing projects, there is little detailed or regular description of the type or volume of work they continued to undertake.

The CABs

"Queries are being presented at all hours. Some of them are quite straight-forward while others, particularly domestic problems, take a great deal of time to deal with satisfactorily. At 7.30 one night, for instance, 3 families evicted from the same house arrived asking for help. They comprised 5 parents and 13 children from 7 months old. After a great deal of telephoning, the Welfare Department's Officer arranged accommodation in various Hostels and Shelters, and the last family – of eight – left the Settlement at 11.45 p.m."

(Birmingham Settlement, 1952, p.13)

During the mid-1950s, the work of the CABs disappears from the Settlement's annual reports altogether, and records kept by the Birmingham CAB suggest that they closed in 1957-1958 (Wadsworth, 1971). However, the city's CAB movement as a whole survived, relocating first to 161 Corporation Street and later to Dr. Johnson House in the city centre. In 1999, Birmingham's CABs continue to prosper and to provide advice services from a number of offices across the city.

The Legal Advice Centre

After the closure of the Settlement's CABs, the next major development was the foundation in 1968 of a new project: the Legal Advice Centre. Building on the work of the Poor Man's Lawyer, it was staffed by barristers who voluntarily gave their time and offered free legal advice to people on low incomes. Open from

7pm to 9pm on a Monday evening, the centre assisted 600 people in its first year alone, the majority of whom were referred by the Citizens' Advice Bureaux. This was actually the first such centre in the city and one of the first in the country, pioneering the idea of a basic legal service for people who could not afford to pay the fees of a solicitor. Similar to the Poor Man's Lawyer scheme, the only major difference was that the Legal Advice Centre took action on behalf of clients wherever possible rather than referring them to other lawyers. Like the Poor Man's Lawyer, it was very popular, and by 1971 had a team of twelve lawyers dealing with over 1,000 cases a year. Of these, matrimonial disputes and consumer contract problems were the most numerous, although the Centre was also consulted about issues such as hire purchase, insurance, wills, road traffic offences, housing and neighbour/industrial disputes.

New centres were soon established in other parts of Birmingham, and a conference held by the Birmingham Settlement for the various agencies offering legal advice led to the foundation of a city-wide co-ordinating body, the Birmingham Voluntary Legal Services Committee. In 1975, the decision was taken to re-locate the Legal Advice Centre to the CAB premises at Dr. Johnson House, where the project was effectively run by the lawyers themselves with administrative support from the Settlement. This partnership came to an end two years later when the Settlement relinquished all formal responsibility and the Legal Advice Centre became fully independent. This is a classic example of the way in which the Settlement has acted as a nurturing agency, founding new projects, supporting them to grow and enabling them to develop as separate organisations in their own right. Other examples of this will later emerge in areas such as infertility treatment and housing management (see chapters 4 and 6).

The Money Advice Centre (MAC)

The year after the foundation of the Legal Advice Centre, the Settlement set up what was to become one of its most important and enduring projects: the Money Advice Centre. In many respects, this project was the direct result of the Legal Advice Centre, since the need for such an initiative was first identified as a result of the large numbers of clients seeking legal advice for their debt problems. With little experience of these issues, lawyers from the Legal Advice Centre approached the Settlement's warden, who sat with the clients concerned and began to work through their problems with them. With funding from the West Midlands County Council, this developed into a separate project which was to revolutionise the way that financial issues were addressed by voluntary and public sector agencies.

Believed to be the first initiative of its kind in Europe (and quite possibly the first publicly-funded money advice project in the world), the Money Advice Centre sought to offer specialist advice on all matters relating to money and to provide counselling to debtors unable to negotiate suitable arrangements with their creditors. Particularly common themes included debt, income tax, social security, hire purchase and consumer contract problems. Initially slow to take off, the Money Advice Centre received no more than a trickle of cases in its first two years and its immediate closure was considered. By 1971, however, the volume of work had increased and the Settlement dealt with 200 cases in the year. Contrary to popular misconceptions about poverty as the product of individual pathology, the Centre quickly discovered that many of its clients found themselves in debt through no fault of their own:

> *"We found that many people hit by debt were not poor managers or bad budgeters, but people the victims of circumstances. Much debt seemed directly the result of rehousing. On rehousing, rents increase, hire purchase is acquired, surplus on wages vanishes. It only needs a short period of sickness and unemployment for breakdown to take place."*

(Birmingham Settlement, 1971, p.7)

In a consumer society with readily available credit facilities, moreover, it was all too easy to descend into a downward spiral of debt from which it was difficult to escape:

> *"These days, with advertising and door to door salesmen constantly reminding us of available luxury and household goods, many people are confronted by the fact that they have overestimated the extent to which they can afford credit and then find themselves before the County Court or constantly worried by debt collectors. They then try to pay one debt at the expense of another and so the situation escalates. Moreover, the level of skill required to cope with County Court proceedings or to negotiate an agreement with creditors is high. People need skilled advice to place their affairs on a sound budgeting basis and they need someone with skill to act as 'go between' for them with their creditors. More than this people need to be able to get advice as to what is a reasonable level of credit they can manage, which bargains or agreements are best and so on. The Centre tries to provide this service."*

(Birmingham Settlement, 1972, p.18)

As its work expanded, the Settlement developed considerable expertise in the field of money advice and was keen to share its knowledge with others. This was motivated in part by a genuine desire to help, but also by an awareness of the urgent need to attract funding, for the Money Advice Centre was expensive and there were fears that it may have to close. To publicise its work, temporary branches were set up in areas such as Chelmsley Wood, Winson Green, Kingstanding, Balsall Heath and Redditch to provide support to people in debt in these parts of the city and to save them from having to travel long distances to access the Summer Lane centre. (In years to come, centres were to open throughout the country as a direct result of the Settlement's pioneering example, although this could not be foreseen at the time).

Next, the Settlement held the first ever national conference on consumer debt at the University of Aston in November 1974. It was attended by 200 delegates from all over the country, and the resulting publicity provided the funds needed to place the Money Advice Centre on a firmer footing. Grants were provided by the West Midlands County Council and the Esmee Fairbairn Foundation, and a bank manager seconded to the project for three years from National Westminster Enterprises (a company formed by the merger of the

The Money Advice Centre, 1998.

National Provincial and Westminster banks). This released the project leader, John Blamire, for development work, and he was able to promote the concept of money advice through radio and television appearances, the publication of books on debt counselling and budgeting and talks given in towns throughout the country. With this publicity and with the addition of a client account to enable the Settlement to distribute money to creditors, the Money Advice Centre became increasingly popular. Between March 1978 and April 1979, the project received 3,256 telephone calls and opened 612 new cases, gathering positive feedback from the people it had helped:

> *"From your letter I drew enormous courage and decided to sweep into action and am more than grateful for your concise breakdown and encouragement to view things positively."*

> *"I was grateful that you came to court with me. It was such a relief to have someone there as I was dreading the whole experience."*

> *"I feel that I can now continue without further help from yourselves so you can safely close the file on me. Once again let me say thank you for the help you gave me when I was desperate."*

> (Birmingham Settlement, 1979, p.8)

As the Settlement moved into the 1980s, the work of the Money Advice Centre was increased by an unfavourable economic climate, sharp rises in rent and fuel, changes in Supplementary Benefit and the greater use of TV advertisements by finance companies. Debts inevitably increased, and the Settlement found itself dealing with ever-larger amounts of money. Whereas a debt totaling £8,000 per person would have been an exception in 1981, it was commonplace by 1984 and some debts reached as high as £27,000 (excluding mortgages). One response to this situation was to undertake an advisory role for defendants appearing in the County Courts without representation. This work began in 1981-82 with money advisors liaising closely with the Citizens' Advice Bureau to interview clients and to advise the courts as to the background of the debt cases it viewed. This arrangement was formalised in the years to come with the appointment of a part-time solicitor to the staff of the Money Advice Centre to conduct legal proceedings on behalf of clients in all courts, not just the County Courts. Another response was to make existing advice sessions more accessible to people from ethnic minorities through outreach work, drop-in surgeries and close liaison with agencies working with 'black' communities. Cases continued to increase through the 1980s and 1990s, and by 1998 the centre was dealing with over 2,000 enquiries per year (Birmingham Settlement, 1998b).

The Money Advice Centre is now one of the key features of the Birmingham Settlement and its development over the last 30 years or so has paved the way for a number of related and complementary projects.

MAC Training and Development

The first such initiative to emerge from the Settlement's pioneering work with regard to money advice involved training and development. As its work became more widely known, the Money Advice Centre received numerous requests to provide speakers for training sessions for other organisations. In response, talks were held in towns throughout the country and the first ever UK training course in debt counselling and income maximisation was developed by the Settlement. Run in conjunction with Selly Oak Colleges, the course was repeated in subsequent years and a shorter version devised to aid the training of social workers, housing officers and staff at Citizens' Advice Bureaux.

After this success, the Money Advice Centre's training and development role increased dramatically:

- In 1980, the Money Advice Centre contributed to 25 training courses across the UK and provided input into the training of the new Special Case Officers appointed by the Department of Health and Social Security (DHSS) to assist difficult Supplementary Benefit Cases.

- With funding from the DHSS, the Settlement played a key role in the creation of a sub-committee of the National Consumer Congress to consider the problems of low income and debt.

- 1983-84 saw the introduction of a placement scheme for interested professionals to observe the Money Advice Centre's work.

- 1985 witnessed the creation of a new post of Money Advice Development officer, apparently the first such position in the country.

- Settlement workers also contributed to TV and radio programmes, government proposals for welfare reform and conferences organised by agencies such as the National Consumer Congress, the Housing Centre Trust, the Institute of Housing and the Consumer Credit Association.

- Delegates attended an international conference in Germany and successfully lobbied the Department of the Environment for funds to establish a new resource to prevent homelessness.

- As the demand for training increased, further workers were appointed, additional courses set up and new books/training packs published to deal with the increasing volume of work and to support those individuals and agencies interested in developing skills in money advice.

As the work of the Money Advice Centre continued to expand, a new initiative was established to meet the growing number of requests for training. Set up in

1987, the Money Advice Centre Training Unit was a self-funding project designed to take on the training and development work previously handled by the Centre itself. By 1990, it was providing a comprehensive programme of 20 different courses at the Settlement and running in-house courses throughout the country for agencies such as the CAB, The Institute of Housing, local authorities, the probation service and the finance industry. Sales of the unit's specialist handbooks also rocketed, with over 2,000 copies sold of the four most popular titles in 1995: An Introduction to Debt Counselling, Home Owner and Debt, County Court Procedures and Bailiffs Law. In 1999, the Training Unit continues to be an important part of the Settlement's work, raising awareness nationally and providing training in order to increase the quality and availability of money advice.

The MAC Research Project

A second initiative arising out of the Money Advice Centre was the Money Advice Research Project. Funded by the Esmee Fairbairn Trust and supervised by the University of Birmingham, the research project began in 1977 with the employment of a research assistant to investigate the hitherto neglected topic of debt. Information gathered from Money Advice Centre clients, Settlement workers and the National Association of Citizens' Advice Bureaux suggested that a 'typical' service user's problems were triggered not by irresponsible behaviour, but by a single unpredictable event such as sickness or unemployment. Further research began to shed light on the incidence and nature of debt and the influence of factors such as social class, family size and income. The findings generated interest from bodies such as the Scottish Office, the National Consumer Council and the DHSS/SSRC working party on transmitted deprivation, and a new research project was commissioned in 1980 by the West Midlands County Council to evaluate the potential of CABs to provide debt counselling training. Building on this legacy, the Settlement's subsequent work has also had a research focus and some of the more recent Settlement publications have dealt with issues such as debt, income and the extension of money advice services to 'black' communities. This pattern of initial innovation combined with training and development has been a key feature not only of the Money Advice Centre, but also of the Settlement's work as a whole over the last hundred years.

The Right to Fuel

Also stemming from the work of the Money Advice Centre was a growing awareness of the plight of people whose gas and electricity had been disconnected. This was first apparent in the early 1970s, when the Settlement's warden drew attention to the antiquated nature of the existing system for collecting payments and dealing with fuel debt:

"*We are concerned... that despite the vital necessity of gas and electric supplies to family wellbeing in the seventies, regulations controlling the handling of bills and supply credit date back to 1904. It is possible for the Electricity Board to demand a deposit before a supply is connected. It is possible for the Board to disconnect a supply without reference to an independent tribunal. Even hire purchase companies must enforce their rights through the courts. The Electricity Board can disconnect supply ad lib. We are not arguing that supplies should never be disconnected, but in view of the crucial importance of power supplies to the modern home, there should at least be some independent decision as to disconnection and power to order alternative methods of collection of supply debts by earnings or social security attachments perhaps, or by installation of meters rated at some reasonable level above the rate charged.*"

(Birmingham Settlement, 1973, p.8)

In the following year the warden repeated his concerns with a plea for urgent action:

"*In all our work we are still concerned with social reforms. We feel that more safeguards are needed before gas and electricity supplies are disconnected... The effects of disconnection, ...are, in their cost to society, out of all proportion to the amounts involved. It should not be the Board's right to withdraw so essential a service without reference to some independent tribunal to assess the social cost and impose or advise some other method of collection.*"

(Birmingham Settlement, 1974, p.5)

This time, the response was more decisive and a meeting organised by the Birmingham Settlement that year attracted community workers, social workers and county court officials from across the country. The outcome was the launch of a campaign to reform the outdated electricity and gas payment regulations, and a parliamentary Bill was drafted by Donald Hamilton, a leading figure in the Legal Advice Centre and a member of the Settlement's management committee (Rimmer, 1980). Although the Bill was rejected by Parliament, the campaign was taken up by the British Association of Settlements in 1975 under the "Right to Fuel" initiative. The Settlement's warden, Peter Houghton, was elected chairman and the campaign gathered enormous national momentum. In response, the government introduced a range of measures which included a new Code of Practice and an electricity discount scheme to help poorer people with their winter fuel bills. The Settlement's warden was also appointed by the Secretary of State for Prices and Consumer Protection as a member of the Electricity Consumer Council when it was set up in 1977 (Rimmer, 1980). After these achievements, the Settlement's active involvement in the "Right to Fuel" movement ceased for a time when the campaign's headquarters moved to Bradford during the early 1980s.

Fuelsavers

Fortunately for the Settlement, the absence of "Right to Fuel" was only temporary, and the campaign returned to Summer Lane in the late 1980s. Since then, the issue of fuel poverty has become one of the core features of the Settlement's work and has continued to this very day through the Settlement's own Fuelsavers project. Boosted by City Challenge Funding and by the publication of research into fuel poverty funded by the Joseph Rowntree Foundation, Fuelsavers seeks to provide local residents with information on energy efficiency through home visits, surgeries, presentations, advice booklets and contacts with tenant and resident groups. In recent years, the project has provided every Newtown household with a thermometer to check that all homes are adequately heated, distributed free low-energy light bulbs and campaigned to ensure that the people who missed out on improvements funded by City Challenge or who couldn't read the promotional literature received equal access to services. Between April 1996 and March 1997, Fuelsavers provided energy advice to 614 house-holds, carried out 135 follow up visits, addressed 4,260 problems through advice sessions and made 70 presentations to 949 people (Birmingham Settlement, 1997b). In addition to this, the Settlement was also home, temporarily at least, to Community Energy Research, an initiative set up by the West Midlands Heating Group to provide an independent energy service for organisations concerned with tackling the problems of fuel poverty.

Local Energy Advice

In July 1993, the Birmingham Settlement was chosen by the Energy Saving Trust as one of 30 successful tenders to establish pilot Local Energy Advice Centres (LEACs). City-wide in its scope, the Settlement's LEAC provided detailed advice and information regarding potential energy saving courtesy of a computer system which incorporated the latest thinking on energy efficiency from the Building Research Establishment. Subsequent evaluation by the Department of the Environment suggested that the Birmingham centre was performing well, reducing the average annual fuel bills of its clients by £35 in the summer months alone. Unfortunately, this success was short-lived, and the Centre closed shortly afterwards due to funding problems. Despite this, the Settlement's reputation in the field of fuel efficiency enabled it to secure funding from National Energy Action in order to provide fuel advice to the business sector and to members of the general public in the Handsworth and Lozells areas. Unlike previous projects, this initiative was targeted specifically towards the Sylheti, Mirpuri and Afro-Caribbean communities, helping to resolve a previously unmet need. More recently, the Settlement has subsumed all previous energy initiatives into its Fuelsavers project, providing advice and practical solutions for individuals and businesses in order to improve energy efficiency.

Housing/National Debtline

A further product of the Money Advice Centre was the Housing Debtline opened in the Spring of 1987. The first national helpline in the United Kingdom for people with debt problems, the service received over 4,000 calls in its first six months. An independent survey carried out by consultants Geoffrey Allen Associates in May 1988 showed that 90 per cent of callers were satisfied with the debtline and more than 1,000 families saw the Settlement as instrumental in helping them avoid eviction. Prompted by the growing number of people contacting the Money Advice Centre in mortgage or rent arrears, Housing Debtline's initial aim was to prevent the homelessness so often caused by this type of indebtedness. However, the complex and multi-faceted nature of debt meant that advice was often given on a range of financial issues, and the telephone advice line became more of a generic debt counselling service. In recognition of this, the project changed its name to the National Debtline as the volume and diversity of its work increased.

From an early stage, the debtline's key feature was its role in encouraging people in debt to find solutions to their own problems, and callers were provided with emotional support, encouragement, practical advice and self-help information packs. Support from National Westminster, the Money Advice Trust and Birmingham Midshires enabled the installation of a new telephone system and database in 1993 and five additional advisers were recruited. Regular media

The National Debtline.

appearances, both locally and nationally, continue to publicise the National Debtline, and the Settlement is frequently inundated with calls from people in desperate need of support following each of its appearances. In 1999, the service deals with some 67,000 calls every year and provides advice to people in debt in England, Wales, Scotland and Northern Ireland. It has an excellent reputation nationwide and a recent evaluation suggests that it continues to offer a high quality, effective and much-needed service:

The National Debtline

- 63% of callers stated that they had worked out a budget, contacted creditors and negotiated payment arrangements for their debts.

- 62% stated that their debts had either been reduced, paid in full or written off.

- 88% stated that they had found the information packs easy to follow.

- 85% said that the information they received was both helpful and accurate.

(Caller Survey, Birmingham Settlement, 1995, p.9)

Business Debtline

As the work of the National Debtline expanded in the early 1990s, it became increasingly apparent that there was a need for an equivalent service aimed at small businesses. During 1990-91, around a fifth of clients at the Money Advice Centre were small traders and self-employed people with problems which were often more complex than those of consumer debt. While these people had access to various funding and advice sources when they set up their businesses, they had very little support when trying to deal with their debts. To resolve this imbalance, the Settlement undertook a feasibility study through its Money Advice Centre and Research Unit to investigate the problem further. The result was the launch in October 1992 of the Birmingham Settlement Business Debtline.

With a business adviser seconded from the National Westminster Bank, Business Debtline sought to provide a telephone helpline and casework service for the self-employed and micro businesses in Birmingham. This was the only such initiative in the country at the time, and in its first eighteen months dealt with over 1,800 telephone enquiries and 200 personal cases. Franchises were soon established to introduce business debtlines in other areas of the country, and the service's achievements far exceeded expectations. In 1998 alone, individual casework with small traders resulted in 78 per cent of their businesses being saved, 93 per cent retaining their homes and 72 per cent retaining their jobs

(Birmingham Settlement, 1998b). In 1999, there is also evidence that small businesses in debt are starting to come forward at an earlier stage, seeking support when their difficulties first begin rather than at the eleventh hour with a serious crisis. This, of course, is a true measure of success, because it means that the Debtline has established sufficient trust to enable its clients to take preventative action before their problems become too large to resolve. As with other Settlement initiatives, there is also a strong emphasis on self-help, with the project designed to help those in need regain their financial independence and retain control over their own affairs in the future.

CCHAT

A final outcome of the Settlement's money advice work has been the development of the City Challenge Home Advice Team (CCHAT). Previous initiatives such as the Fuelsavers project had already made substantial use of outreach work to raise awareness and establish contact with those unable to access office services, and this technique was exploited to the full by CCHAT. Funded by City Challenge and carried out in conjunction with the Birmingham Citizens' Advice Bureau and Personal Service Debt Counselling, CCHAT provides financial advice to people in their own homes, dealing with issues such as rent arrears, benefit take-up and applications for charitable grants. In 1996, the team carried out 600 visits, raising an average additional income of £845 per household and focusing particularly on dwellings with older people, young children and single parents. To sum up its impact, there is no greater testimony to its achievements than the experience of families who have received its services:

> *"A single parent with 6 young children was referred to us after her youngest child was diagnosed as terminally ill. In helping her apply for Disability Living Allowance we noted that she was not receiving income support or child benefit for her two youngest children; we therefore assisted her application. Through successful applications for charitable grants we helped her purchase a washing machine, beds and equipment for her sick child. Additional assistance resolved problems with her housing benefit claim and so averted possession action for rent arrears which had accumulated. With the assistance of the CCHAT Team our client received charitable grants of £1,100 and claimed an additional £2,500 in benefits."*

(Birmingham Settlement, 1996, p.15)

Newtown/South Aston Credit Union

Another of the Settlement's projects working directly with financial and material deprivation was the Newtown/South Aston Credit Union. Established in 1987 in co-operation with the Birmingham Credit Union Development Agency, it offers people who live and work locally the chance to contribute regular amounts of money to a common fund and to apply for loans at low rates of interest. Its aim was to keep money in the neighbourhood and to provide alternative and cheaper forms of credit, enabling people to save and borrow at the most favourable rates available without the need to resort to expensive moneylenders. By 1989, the Credit Union's membership was well over 200, with nearly £20,000 amassed in savings and over £18,000 distributed in loans to members. Closer links with other credit unions both city- and nationwide were to follow, and a Settlement delegate attended the annual conference of the Association of British Credit Unions. Technically separate from the Settlement but still supported by it, the Credit Union today has over 350 active members, with savings of nearly £75,000 and more than £36,000 loaned out to participants (personal communication). There are currently four collection points, with plans underway to introduce two more and new branches in two local schools run for and by the children themselves. What is most remarkable about the Credit Union, however, is its similarity to the Provident Scheme which was introduced at the Settlement when it first opened in 1899. After a century of social change, the wheel has turned full circle.

The Newtown South Aston Credit Union.

The Aston Reinvestment Trust (ART)

The final initiative to address the issue of financial poverty was the Aston Reinvestment Trust (ART). Arising out of the work of the Aston Commission (see chapter 6), ART was set up in April 1995 with funding from Birmingham TEC, City Challenge and the Birmingham Business Resource Consortium. A separate company chaired by the Settlement's president, ART was designed to promote the re-establishment of community-based banking. Although Aston is thought to have been the location of the first ever Building Society in the world (in a pub next to St. Chad's Cathedral some 225 years ago), its financial institutions declined considerably in the 1980s and 1990s due to long-term unemployment, business failure and poverty. By 1989, there was only a handful of such institutions left, leaving many people on low incomes with no source of credit other than through loan sharks, pawnbrokers or moneylenders, paying anywhere between 60 and 500 per cent interest.

To overcome this credit trap, ART was established to act as an investment broker for loans to Aston-based small businesses and to arrange loans and working capital for non-profit organisations. More recent areas of interest include affordable housing and energy saving, both of which build on long-standing traditions within the Birmingham Settlement of working with housing issues and fuel poverty (see above and chapter 6). In the course of this work, ART not only raises and lends its own funds, but also works with other lenders to attract additional support from other sources. By 1999, it had lent some £440,000 from its own funds, helped secure additional funds of £1,096,000, created 48 jobs and preserved a further 123 (Aston Reinvestment Trust, 1999). City-wide in its remit, ART continues to place particular emphasis on work in the inner city and is based on the same site as the Settlement in Summer Lane. Examples of its work to date include support for the following organisations:

Organisations supported by the Aston Reinvestment Trust

Scenario Audio Visual Services – a conference production company.

Expresslock Limited – protects goods in delivery vans with an instant locking mechanism.

KPM Turnkey – a three-year old Newtown company providing finishing and machinery services to the metal castings industry.

Art of Minds – a new start business in Hockley providing mobile child care schemes.

Vand'Air – a Hockley company renovating and repairing air power tools for businesses.

Betel of Britain – a registered charity helping people to recover from addiction. ART's involvement enabled Betel's trading arm to buy a second van for its used furniture and removal business.

High Tech Stoving – an Aston company providing a painting and plating service to businesses that manufacture engineering components.

(Aston Reinvestment Trust, 1998, 1999)

The Settlement's Own Finances

Last but not least, no discussion of financial and material issues would be complete without reference to the Settlement's own finances. Throughout the last hundred years, the availability of funds has frequently been the key factor in whether a new project has succeeded or not and those initiatives which failed often did so not because they were unpopular, but because there was not enough money. In its early years, the Settlement relied entirely upon voluntary subscriptions, donations and students' fees to finance its activities, with appeals to obtain the money required for large-scale, one-off pieces of expenditure such as building work. As its role expanded, however, the Settlement needed more money and was forced to adopt a number of schemes for raising funds and publicising its projects. Examples included garden sales, drawing room parties, jumble sales and the 'Magnetic Shilling Tea Scheme' (a tea party for 12 guests at one shilling a head. These guests would then hold their own tea parties, creating an ever-expanding network of social links and making a significant contribution to the Settlement's finances).

A fundraising event at the Settlement, 1996.

As the century progressed, the Settlement began to receive an increasingly large proportion of its income in the form of grants from charitable trusts, the local authority, national bodies and government funds, supplemented wherever possible by appeals and fundraising campaigns. This work was greatly facilitated in the 1970s by the efforts of the 'Friends of the Settlement' in Edgbaston and Sutton Coldfield, and by the opening of a 'nearly new shop' in the latter area. This period also witnessed an increase in 'special events' with the inauguration of the House to House collection, the Autumn Market, the annual Flag Day and regular auctions advertised in the Settlement's annual reports.

In recent years, trends in voluntary sector finance have changed, with the Settlement and organisations like it taking on a much greater role in direct service provision. This has led to a growth in contracting, with both positive and negative outcomes. Whereas the Settlement today has become much bigger as it has started to provide more services, its role as a provider under contract to others has placed constraints on its traditional role as an agency committed to innovation and developing new initiatives. As a result, the latter is now funded primarily through income from fundraising and donations. At the same time, this revenue is supplemented by ever-closer links with the private sector, which has a very strong relationship with the Settlement and accounts for some 14% of its finances, and by new funding opportunities available from the European Union. However, a crucial source of funding also derives from the Settlement's shops, which now operate in five areas of the city as a separate company, *Birmingham Sales Ltd.* While the £60,980 which the shops earned in 1998 is not a large proportion of the Settlement's total income, this money represents core funding and can therefore be used flexibly without being ringfenced for a particular project. In the year ending 31st March 1998, the Settlement's total incoming resources amounted to over £2.3 million, with an expenditure of £2.13 million (Birmingham Settlement, 1998a, p.11).

Despite these ongoing efforts to raise money, the Settlement's finances have rarely been secure and its annual reports bear witness to the immense difficulties of keeping the organisation above water. Despite estimating in 1899 that its annual running costs would be £250, the Settlement spent over £470 in its first year, building up an immediate overdraft (Rimmer, 1980). Thereafter, hardly a year has gone by when the Treasurer has not lamented the state of the Settlement's finances, and the situation has become critical on a number of occasions. During the 1920s there was a deficit of nearly £400, and this had risen to £1,627 by the late 1940s. Desperate measures were taken to reduce expenditure in the 1960s, most noticeably through the inclusion of adverts in the Settlement's annual reports, the deliberate reduction in length of these documents and the omission of the annual list of subscribers and donors. Despite this the Settlement's finances remained in the red as it recorded a deficit of £4,400 in 1971, prompting a reorganisation of the Settlement's work and the closure of the Kingstanding branch. Debts totalled more than £27,000 in the mid-1980s and one of the bleakest periods in the Settlement's history was reached in 1989 when its annual report highlighted the serious impact of chronic underfunding on many of the Settlement's projects.

In the early 1990s, the Settlement expanded enormously, although it was some time before its financial and managerial systems were developed sufficiently to be able to take stock of this rapid growth. In the space of five years, the Settlement virtually doubled in size, due largely to an increase in direct service provision

Birmingham Sales Ltd.

and the advent of the City Challenge regeneration scheme (see chapter 6). This has been aided by the diverse range of sources from which the Settlement currently draws its funding, although the flexibility this provides can also generate significant workloads for those involved in the crucial work of fundraising. In 1999, the Settlement's 24 projects receive funds from 18 different sources, including the private sector, the public sector, the European Union, trading income, fundraising and the Settlement's shops.

The brief overview above shows that funding has been an almost constant thorn in the Settlement's side throughout its hundred year history, and it is somewhat ironic that an organisation dedicated to helping those in poverty should itself face such financial insecurity. On the one hand, this may be seen as a positive thing, demonstrating the Settlement's vitality and its ability to operate at full capacity, never standing still and always seeking to expand its work. At the same time, however, subsequent chapters will highlight the adverse effect which lack of money has undoubtedly had on some of the Settlement's most innovative and interesting projects. It is for this reason that the Settlement has embarked upon an ambitious appeal as a part of its centenary, seeking to raise £500,000 in addition to its normal annual fund-raising programme. This money will be used to place the Birmingham Settlement on a sound financial footing for the new millennium and to ensure that it can continue its work for at least another century of poverty and opportunity (see Conclusion).

Summary

Looking back at the Settlement's responses to financial and material poverty over the last hundred years, there has been both change and continuity. In terms of change, the nature and definition of poverty has undergone a radical transformation and with it the work of the Birmingham Settlement. Projects to distribute material aid to people on the fringes of starvation are no longer necessary following the introduction of the Welfare State, and the Settlement's work in recent years has been primarily of an advisory and supportive nature. A classic example of this is the Settlement's pioneering work with regard to money advice, developing a new initiative to meet a newly identified need following the rediscovery of poverty as a social issue in the 1970s. At the same time, however, there is much that remains almost exactly the same, with the Settlement working with similar issues and in a similar way throughout its hundred-year history. Although the absolute poverty of the turn of the century is no more, massive inequalities in wealth persist and the people of Newtown remain just as impoverished relative to the society around them as they were in 1899 when the Settlement first opened its doors. Nowhere is this more clearly illustrated than in the continued and ongoing need for financial initiatives such as the Money Advice Centre.

In addition, there are further elements of continuity which have underpinned the Settlement's work with regard to financial issues. On one level, schemes such as the Legal Advice Centre or the Newtown/South Aston Credit Union mirror initiatives much earlier in the century such as the Poor Man's Lawyer or the Provident Society. Much more fundamentally, however, both traditional and more recent projects alike all have one thing in common: an emphasis on self-help and self-sufficiency. Whether it be by providing financial assistance, opportunities to save, money advice, energy advice, training or whatever, the Settlement has always sought to support people in poverty through periods of distress and to equip them with the skills and resources to survive future difficulties on their own initiative. This is something which dates right back to the founding ideals of men such as Denison, Toynbee and Barnett and something which has characterised every aspect of the Birmingham Settlement's work from that day to this. This concept is perhaps best illustrated by a phrase popularised during the 1980s in connection with fundraising on behalf of the Third World:

> *"Give a man a fish and you feed him for a day. Teach him to fish and you feed him for life."*

Equipping people for life was the aim of Samuel Barnett in London in 1884, of the founders of the Birmingham Settlement in 1899 and of the Settlement today in 1999. While much has already been done, much remains to do, and the work of the Birmingham Settlement, on the eve of its own centenary and of a new millennium, may only just be beginning.

Chapter 4:

'Disease' – Health

Money is a major health resource and poverty has been shown to have a negative impact on the health of those who experience it. This chapter aims to:

- Examine the issue of health inequalities.
- Trace the development of the NHS.
- Outline the Settlement's response to health issues in a changing social policy context. These range from the direct provision of health care to community care services for older people or counselling services for those experiencing difficulties conceiving.

Poverty and ill health have always been inextricably linked. Ever since the first systematic studies of the impact of poverty on health in the 1830s and 1840s (Chadwick, 1842), poor people have consistently been found to suffer more ill health, disability and premature death than people in higher social classes (Blackburn, 1991). While the health and life expectancy of the general population have increased dramatically in the twentieth century, moreover, research suggests that inequalities in health not only persist, but are actually widening (Townsend et al., 1992). The exact nature of the link between poverty and ill health is complex and has been examined in more detail elsewhere (Blackburn, 1991). However, the fact remains that any organisation committed to working with people in poverty must inevitably take action to address their health needs if its work is to be successful.

The Origins of the NHS

Although much of the Birmingham Settlement's more recent work has not had a specific health focus, the opposite was true at the turn of the century. This, in part, was the result of the need to compensate for the limitations and inadequacies of health care provision at the time. Prior to the creation of the National Health Service in 1948, Britain's health system was an ad hoc, complex and fragmented mixture of public, private and voluntary provision. In particular, there were three main agencies or professions involved:

- General Practitioners, at this time, were private professionals who charged a fee which many working class people could not afford to pay. Although some workers combined together to purchase the services of a GP through friendly societies, this excluded the unemployed, married women, children and the elderly. These same groups were also denied access to adequate treatment when the National Insurance Act 1911 introduced free GP services for the employed working classes administered through health panels.

- Voluntary hospitals, assisted by charitable donations, provided cheap or free services to the poor. However, admission even to these hospitals could be selective, with the very poor and those with infectious diseases denied access altogether (Abel-Smith, 1964). As they moved into the twentieth century, moreover, many of the voluntary hospitals began to introduce charges, with patients taking out insurance policies to cover potential payments. Other voluntary agencies were also involved in providing community health services. Working in conjunction with local authorities, they tended to concentrate on issues such as child welfare, maternity, aftercare, district nursing and mental or physical handicap (Baggott, 1998).

- Local authority municipal hospitals developed out of the Poor Law infirmaries of the nineteenth century and were often as overcrowded and unhygienic as the original workhouses. In addition to this, local authorities ran specialist hospitals to cater for people suffering from conditions such as tuberculosis, mental ill health and a range of infectious diseases. Although such hospitals charged fees, these could be remitted in cases of low income (Byrne and Padfield, 1990). Gradually, the local authorities also came to provide a range of environmental and public health services with powers and responsibilities concerning the water supply, the sewage system, food and hygiene inspection, pollution control, public housing, vaccinations and community health services. A key figure in this respect was the Medical Officer for Health, appointed following the Public Health Act 1875 to be a guardian of public health.

Unco-ordinated, inefficient and inadequate for the health needs of the majority of the population, this system came under increasing criticism from the First World War onwards. Wide-ranging reforms were to follow in the 1940s, culminating in 1948 with the creation of the National Health Service. Although this new system has not been able to resolve the inequalities in health described above, it does provide free GP and hospital services for everyone and has resulted in a massive increase in the overall health of the population. While all is far from perfect, Britain's health care system today is the envy of the rest of the world, with an international reputation for its quality and excellence.

Birmingham's Health Care

Ironically, the first hospital in Birmingham, the General, was located on Summer

Lane itself from its foundation in 1765 to its closure and relocation to Steelhouse Lane in 1897. By the latter date, however, it had become outmoded and its site, in one of the worst slums in the city, was considered unsuitable:

> "The hospital in Summer Lane, having done a century's work, was worn out. It was insufficient in accommodation, out-of-date in character, and its surroundings had become insanitary. A higher and healthier, and at the same time, more central site was selected, and upon this was erected the new hospital."

(Lloyd, 1911, p.156)

While it was not long before a number of hospitals sprang up in various parts of the city specialising in various complaints, their services were often denied to poorer people, who needed 'hospital notes' (recommendations from subscribers) in order to receive treatment (Abel-Smith, 1964). Although other health services became available following the advent of district nursing in 1870, the appointment of Birmingham's first Medical Officer for Health in 1872 and the introduction of health visitors in 1899 (Briggs, 1952; Rimmer, 1980; Vince, 1902), these measures too were insufficient to meet the health needs of the city's poor. That this was the case is demonstrated by contemporary health statistics, which suggest that both infant mortality and overall death rates were highest in the inner city wards (Briggs, 1952; Vince, 1902, 1923). Of these, St. Mary's was identified in 1913 as the worst ward in the city (Vince, 1923, p. 141). Despite massive changes and improvements in the provision of health care, moreover, the situation is little different today, with Birmingham's inner city areas continuing to suffer higher mortality rates than more affluent sectors of the city (Birmingham Health Authority, 1997). On the eve of the Birmingham Settlement's centenary, therefore, inequalities in health are just as prevalent as they were back in 1899 when the Settlement first opened its doors to the public.

The Settlement's response

The Crippled Children's Union

One of the Birmingham Settlement's first attempts to address health issues centred around its links with other voluntary organisations. During its first year, the Settlement was approached by the secretary of the Crippled Children's Union and asked to visit local children with disabilities. Weekly visits began and action was taken to access appropriate health and educational services on the children's behalf. Many had unattended medical needs, and Settlement workers ensured that they received hospital and convalescence care. Others required equipment or support to attend school, and this too was duly provided. For those too weak to do so, lessons were arranged in their own homes and later in the Settlement itself. By 1904 there were 168 disabled children on the Settlement's books and the volume of work was such that it was felt necessary to appeal for further assistance and equipment. Two years later, the Settlement began to run weekly 'Crippled Children's Happy Afternoons' with games, arts and crafts in the clubroom. In spite of their disabilities, the children were able to skip, swing and play rounders, and the author of the annual report marvelled at the physical obstacles they overcame in order to continue with their play. Although detailed references to these initiatives disappear from the Settlement's records after 1907, there is every indication that this work continued for many years to come (Rimmer, 1980).

Basket-weaving

Building on its work with disabled children, the Settlement was also involved in the creation in 1901 of a weaving school for disabled girls unable to gain mainstream industrial employment. Established in conjunction with the Crippled Children's Union, the school was managed by a Settlement resident, Miss Prest, and was responsible for the production of high quality woven goods. At the same time, the Settlement ran its own basket-weaving classes under the leadership of Miss Barrow and Miss Southall. Products from the school and the class were sold in the drawing rooms of the Settlement's supporters and provided a much-needed income for those disabled people previously unable to find work. Although the Settlement's involvement with this project finished when the weaving school relocated to premises at Five Ways in 1907, the experience of working with young people with disabilities paved the way for future health-related work.

The Medical Care Committee

In 1909, the Settlement established a new Medical Care Committee in order to meet the health needs of local children. A joint initiative with the Charity Organisation Society, the Committee visited the parents of children who had been identified as needing assistance during medical inspections in local schools. During these visits, medical advice was offered, loans were given to buy equipment such as spectacles, country holidays were organised and funds raised to meet the costs of hospital care for those who required it. The project was soon boosted by a series of lectures on child hygiene provided by Dr. Oats and by weekly surgeries held at the Settlement by Dr. Caroline O'Connor. Between May and November 1909 over 200 children were aided in this way and a long waiting list began to develop. By 1910, the committee was dealing with 40 to 50 cases during each weekly sitting, while in 1911 the volume of work was such that the work of the Medical Care Committee had to be shared between 5 sub-committees. In seeking to explain the work of the committees, the Settlement sought to give a practical illustration:

"A good example of what a Committee of this kind can accomplish may be found in the case of a little girl who had badly deformed feet. She was sent to the General Hospital to be treated for her general health. When she was considered strong enough, and at the request of the hospital, she was sent to the Orthopaedic Hospital for operation. The Infirmary was then requested to receive her for the skilled care that could not be given at home, and finally a short stay at Moseley Hall completed the cure."

(Birmingham Settlement, 1911, p.19)

In the late 1990s such care would be considered a basic human right; in the early twentieth century it was nothing short of miraculous. Put simply, the Settlement offered this child, and many like her, a quality of life that she could never have hoped to receive on her own.

In 1912, a Christmas party was held for 100 children who had received assistance from the Medical Care Committee. These gatherings became known as 'spectacle and adenoid' parties and were repeated on a regular basis throughout the next couple of years. Despite gradual improvement in health services across the city, the volume of work continued to increase and, on the eve of the First World War, over 700 cases were coming to the attention of the Medical Care Committee every year. Although the Committee survived the outbreak of war, its work was hampered in the following year by the decision of the Charity Organisation Society to withdraw its support. This decision was taken on financial grounds, but left the future of the Medical Care Committee very much in jeopardy.

Initially it was decided that the Settlement would take sole responsibility for the project and subsequent reports suggest that the committee continued to work on the old basis throughout the war. In 1918, however, the warden reported that "the development of the medical system of the city and the increasing knowledge of the mothers have greatly reduced the number of cases of the Medical Care Committee." While she acknowledged that some families still needed ongoing support, she also emphasised the difficulties faced by the Settlement in trying to continue its work in the war conditions: "The Settlement survives. With so heavy an adverse balance against us that seems in itself an achievement" (both quotes Birmingham Settlement, 1918, p.5). From then on, references to the Medical Care Committee disappear from the Settlement's annual reports, and it seems likely that general improvements in health care coupled with the numerous demands made on the Settlement in the immediate post-war period made the committee's work nonviable. Despite this, the contribution of the Medical Care Committee was an important one, and its work was praised by Dr. Auden, the School Medical Officer and father of the poet W. H. Auden, in his report to the city's Education Committee. In his opinion, voluntary effort had an important role to play in encouraging and assisting parents to follow the advice of the school doctor, and it seems clear that the Settlement's work in this field enabled the provision of medical care otherwise unavailable to the impoverished families of the area.

The School for Mothers

In the same year that the Medical Care Committee was established, the Settlement embarked upon another project designed to meet the health needs of the local population. Working with the Edgbaston Branch of the Birmingham Women's Temperance Association, the Settlement founded a Mother's Guild or School for Mothers. The 'guild' or 'school' was in fact an infant welfare clinic which provided free consultations with local medical practitioners during weekly sessions and visited expectant mothers to advise about child care. This project was particularly valuable since it was set up at a time when the health needs of young children in inner city areas were becoming an increasing concern to the city authorities. The project could also not have been better placed geographically, since the infant mortality rate in the area around the Settlement was one of the highest in the city (Vince, 1923). Demand was such that it soon became necessary to establish a Visitation Committee to arrange regular visits to young families in the area. To support this work, Settlement workers arranged and attended a series of lectures and classes on subjects such as hygiene, home nursing and first aid. A savings club was also established to encourage expectant mothers to save in preparation for their confinement, and a similar initiative – the Hospital Contributory Scheme – was set up many years later in 1930 for people to save money in case they needed it in an emergency to purchase hospital care.

In addition to this, a series of classes was devised to teach new mothers how to make and adapt baby clothes and to devise their own equipment. Short of money, Settlement workers were forced to rely on their ingenuity in order to make these classes a success. Necessity is the mother of invention, and the Settlement's annual reports describe how banana crates supplied by George Cadbury were "converted into smart and hygienic cots at a cost of 1/5 each" (Birmingham Settlement, 1910, p.19). At the same time, the Settlement purchased Virol (a yeast extract to feed babies) at cost price, decanting the mixture into what became known as 'Settlement Bottles'. Limited though these initiatives may appear, their impact was very real and in 1911 the Settlement's annual reports emphasised the "readiness and gratitude" with which its visits and advice were received (Birmingham Settlement, 1911, p.20). The following year, it reported a drop in the number of infant deaths from diarrhoea from 30 to 3. While the report attributes this almost entirely to a favourable climate and the support of sympathetic doctors, hospitals and charitable organisations, it seems clear that the Settlement's work in this area was quite literally life-saving.

Temperance

In 1913, the School for Mothers relocated to a more central site in Gosta Green and its work continued independently of the Settlement. However, the link established with the Birmingham Women's Temperance Society was maintained, and the Settlement turned its attention to the issue of alcohol consumption on a number of occasions. In 1909, for example, members of the Young British Women's Temperance Association approached the Settlement's warden to request assistance in their preparation for the Temperance Collegiate Association. The Association's exams required a knowledge of alcohol and temperance issues relating to history, economics, chemistry, pathology, hygiene and physiology (Ring, 1911), and the Settlement responded by establishing a series of classes to prepare interested students as temperance workers. With a syllabus designed by doctors and other experts with knowledge of the subject, the students performed well in their exams and the classes were repeated over the course of a number of years.

The Horse and Jockey

Building on this work, the Settlement embarked upon an ambitious new venture in 1912 with the advent of a temperance public house. Following the withdrawal of the license of the Horse and Jockey in Lower Tower Street, the Settlement took possession of the building and reopened it "under entirely new management" (Birmingham Settlement, 1912, p.12). Instead of beer, the Horse and Jockey sold tea, coffee, cocoa, lemonade and ginger cordial at the rate of half a penny per cup or glass. Open daily from 12pm to 2pm and from 4pm to 10pm, it had its own billiard room and offered free access to newspapers, magazines, draughts and dominoes.

Unfortunately for the Settlement, this experiment failed. Despite initial interest, custom quickly declined and the pub was forced to close temporarily until new workers could be found to take on its running. At this stage, the most regular customer was an elderly man who had been to prison 45 times, although his subsequent disappearance suggests that he may have been about to start his 46th spell of detention (Matheson, 1912)! With one customer less, the Horse and Jockey soon re-opened, but in 1914 the annual report lamented that "business unfortunately remains far quieter than we could wish" (Birmingham Settlement, 1914, p.25). Permanent closure was considered and the decision to continue the project for another year was taken only on the grounds that "we think it is wise to keep open a place of amusement for lads and men in the hope that we may eventually succeed in making it attractive to a fresh set of customers" (Birmingham Settlement, 1914, p.26). This hope was not to be realised, and the Horse and Jockey closed for good in March 1914.

Although the idea of a temperance public house may seem eccentric in the late 1990s, the Horse and Jockey was an important experiment in an area long associated with the social problems caused by heavy drinking. In the early 1900s, there were over 100 pubs and more than 30 off licenses in the area around the Birmingham Settlement, and a council committee established that there was 1 pub for every 77 yards of street space around Newtown Row and Brearley Street (Mannion and Mannion, 1987). Arrests for drunkenness on the eve of the First World War were most frequent in the central areas of the city, with St. Mary's ward coming second highest on the list (Mannion and Mannion, 1987). The backlash against this state of affairs was strong, and a number of different attempts were made to combat the evils of excessive alcohol consumption through Band of Hope classes, Salvation Army meetings and temperance societies. Despite this, the pub trade in Summer Lane continued to thrive, boosted no doubt by the desire of local inhabitants to find temporary solace from their poverty and to occupy their leisure time in one of the only ways they could afford:

> *"There is no doubt about it, a lot of people suffered through the demon drink in the 1920s and 30s... The pubs did supply that 'something' that was missing from their hum drum life, they were places to escape to where there was company, warmth, a chance to air their views, with maybe a sing-song or two, to round the evening off. It gave men the chance to get away for a time from the poverty that stared them in the face in their miserable homes. Matters could only get worse if the Mother of the family took to drink, then it was usual to see a pram parked outside a pub with older children sitting on the doorstep, waiting for Mother to come out and give them their meal. It was not such a regular occurrence as when the father had the habit, many a Sunday dinner was missing because Dad had spent his wages on Friday night in one good blow out. But, we must not judge these people too harshly, their lives and living conditions, their lack of even the smallest comforts was enough to drive anyone to drink, it was the only way they could forget it for a short time."*

(Mannion and Mannion, 1987, p. 6)

'Liquor Control'

Unperturbed by the failure of the Horse and Jockey, the Birmingham Settlement continued to campaign against the excessive consumption of alcohol with two notable successes. In 1914, the warden joined with the heads of 29 other Settlements to send a memorial to the Prime Minister drawing his attention to the dangers of alcohol and requesting government intervention. A Liquor Control Board was subsequently established and the Birmingham Settlement's warden was offered a position on the women's advisory committee of this body. With specific instructions to investigate the alleged increase in drinking among women, the committee made use of Settlement workers to collect evidence in Birmingham. The second of the Settlement's successes came in 1935 when the Birmingham Settlement made clear its opposition to the proposed extension of licensing hours from 10pm to 10.30pm. The campaign was taken up by the then warden, Edith Batten, who authorised extensive research into the views of local people. It soon became clear that very few people wanted the hours extended and Miss Batten's evidence proved the decisive factor when the case came to court. As a result of the Settlement's contribution, the brewers lost and closing time remained at 10pm (Rimmer, 1980).

Campaigning against excessive alcohol consumption

"To the Right Honourable H. H. ASQUITH,

We, the undersigned, representing the Settlements of the United Kingdom, beg to call your attention to the dangers of either popular drinking or popular jubilation in "slum areas" owing to the present facilities for obtaining intoxicating drink. We understand that this danger has been recognised in both France and Germany and the sale of intoxicants curtailed.

In the interest of the families who are left behind and of the men themselves when they return [from the war], we do most humbly pray that Parliament will consider the matter with a view to safeguarding the good name of the English Working classes by imposing a restraint that will be no hardship to the sober among them and that will protect them from the disgrace of excess among the large class of unrestrained men and women who are unfortunately to be found in every large town.

Your Memorialists are all residents in very poor neighbourhoods and have there-fore had personal experience of the difficulty on which they venture to address you."

(Birmingham Settlement, 1914, p.39)

The Summer Lane Mortuary

As described in chapter 6, the houses in Summer Lane were usually two or three storeys high with one room on each floor. There was little enough space for a large family at the best of times, but this was all the more so when a person had died and his or her coffin had to remain in the house for mourners to pay their respects before burial. Often, there was nowhere for it to go other than in the main downstairs room and families would carry out their daily activities and have their meals in the same room as the deceased. Settlement students even recall local children using the coffin as a table and eating their food directly off it (Rimmer, 1980). This was to change in 1931 when the Settlement presented a mortuary to the neighbourhood (thanks to the generosity of two of its supporters, Mr. and Mrs. Sydney Walker). Based on Summer Lane itself, the mortuary was intended to prevent families from having to retain their dead at home until burial and the attendant health risks. Mrs. Walker in particular was very proactive in explaining the purpose of the mortuary to the Settlement's members and the 1930-31 annual report suggests that the gift was greatly appreciated. Interestingly, however, the mortuary was rarely used, as many families preferred to keep their dead at home as they always had done in the past:

"When there was a death in the family the coffin was kept in the house for at least a week so that all could come and pay their respects. If you were lucky enough to have two rooms downstairs, the coffin would be put in the parlour, but in the majority of cases there was only one room, then the body would lie there, while they had their meals... It was not until 1930 or thereabouts that a public mortuary was built in Summer Lane for the benefit of those who only had one room, so that the body could be kept there until the funeral... The mortuary was opened by Mrs Walker, the wife of the benefactor. The funny thing about it was that the mortuary hardly ever got used as the custom to keep the dead at home was so firmly entrenched that things went on as before, until the only bodies that were in there were suicides or the men from the Model Lodging House."

(Mannion and Mannion, 1985, p.50)

Changing Priorities: Work with Older People

As health care provision has improved in Britain in the second half of the twentieth century, the Birmingham Settlement has inevitably had to review its work in this field and divert its attention to other areas. With the introduction of the NHS, for example, it was no longer necessary for the Settlement to continue schemes which provided medical care to children or to run infant welfare clinics. Such work has now been taken over by the State and a comprehensive health care system, free at the point of delivery, is now available. Nevertheless, one of

The Day Centre Gardening Project, 1998.

the Settlement's key features throughout its hundred year history has been its ability to respond to policy changes by identifying new needs and developing initiatives to fill gaps in existing service provision. A classic example of this is the Settlement's work with older people, which has played a major part in its history from the Second World War onwards. This particular aspect of the Settlement is multi-faceted and does not fit neatly into any of the categories around which this book has been structured. However, it has been included in the current chapter as a result of the positive health effects which it undoubtedly had and the contribution it made to maintaining the independence of those frail older people who would otherwise have had to enter residential or nursing care.

Work with older people.

Visiting Service and Community Care

In 1948, the Birmingham Settlement was approached by the Birmingham Council for Old People (now Broadening Choices for Older People) and the Birmingham Council of Social Service with a view to establishing a visiting service. Concern was mounting about the number of older people who had lost family during the war or whose children had left the area, and the Settlement was asked to take responsibility for visiting and assisting some 300 older people in and around Summer Lane. Some of these people required help with common activities of daily living such as shopping, cooking, pension collection and visits to the hospital, while others had medical needs which required more urgent attention. Most, however, were simply lonely and isolated, benefiting considerably from the regular human contact which the Settlement was able to offer.

During the course of this work, the Settlement saw the need for new services such as meals on wheels or day care and set about exploring how to provide them. By taking the lead in this area, the Settlement was working far in advance of city-wide or national developments. At this time, local authority services for older people were based around the provisions of the National Assistance Act 1948 and were very much geared towards residential care. As a result, opportunities for preventative services in the community were virtually non-existent (Means and Smith, 1998). It was this situation which was to lead to rapidly increasing public expenditure on institutional care in the mid-1980s and the subsequent introduction of the NHS and Community Care Act 1990 in an attempt to reduce the traditional bias towards residential care and to enable frail older people to remain at home in the community for as long as possible. The Birmingham Settlement's work in the provision of community care services from the 1950s onwards was therefore extremely innovative, anticipating future national policy by many years.

Day Care

With financial support from the Birmingham Council for Old People and Birmingham Rotary Club, the Settlement opened a Day Room for older people. This had first been proposed in 1948 in plans drawn up with St. George's Church in Tower Street and the British Red Cross, but did not come to fruition until 1956 when the distress of the war years had eased. To all intents and purposes, the Settlement day centre was probably one of the earliest in the country – the first day centre in the United Kingdom is thought to have been set up in Bartley Green by the Birmingham Council for Old People in 1955 (Birmingham Council for Old People, 1996).

The first day centre to meet at the Settlement was a group of 12 older people who came to the Settlement one afternoon per week. By 1958, however, the Day Room was open four times a week with mid-day meals provided on two of these days and a bus donated by the Birmingham Soroptimists to collect those people too disabled to make their own way. The physical environment of the building had also been transformed, with the addition of a new dining room, a kitchen, a bathroom and a ramp to facilitate access. The Day Room then carried on in much the same format until 1973 when it relocated to a more central site at the St. George's Church Centre. Thereafter, it continued to function as before, but began to attract slightly younger and more active service users who were encouraged to participate in the running of the club and to visit older, frailer members.

Best of friends: the Settlement Day Centre.

In 1980, the Day Room returned to the Settlement after several happy years at St. George's and has remained there ever since. Boosted by the acquisition of its own tail-lift ambulance and the extension of its activities to 5 days a week, the Day Centre remains as popular as ever and now welcomes up to 35 people every day. In addition to the company, hot meals and activities which it organises, it also has an important role in liaising with health and social services in order to support members to maintain their independence in the community and to identify any potential problems at an early stage. The Day Centre is now also able to provide culturally sensitive meals to those who require them and to offer NVQ training to social care and nursing students from local colleges.

Over in Kingstanding, events were moving very much in the same direction. Following the introduction of a visiting service similar to that taking place in Summer Lane, a new day centre, the Sunshine Club, was established in 1957 to provide entertainment and social stimulation through activities such as coach trips, film shows, group holidays and Christmas parties. By 1958, it had a membership of 120 with an average attendance of 90, although an initial lack of transport meant that only those older people physically capable of making their

The Queen's Silver Jubilee at the Day Centre.

own way to the Settlement were able to participate in the club. Three more day centres were added in Kingstanding in the 1960s and by 1969 there were nearly 6,500 individual attendances at the Settlement's older people's clubs every year. With such a large membership, more and more ambitious activities were possible and the club's annual holidays became a regular feature. As was the case in Summer Lane, the older people at Kingstanding became increasingly involved in running their own services, electing a committee of members to plan club activities. Even after the Kingstanding Settlement closed down, its day centres and Sunshine Club continued not only to function, but also to develop further. A fourth day centre was soon added, and a new older person's club was effectively established as members of a Mum's Club set up for young mothers and their children in the 1930s grew older and became increasingly frail. In 1999, groups of older people from Kingstanding still continue to meet together, although they are now brought by minibus to attend the day centre at Summer Lane.

Looking back at over 40 years of day care services for older people, perhaps the greatest testimony to their popularity and importance comes from the service users themselves. In 1966, the Settlement's annual reports changed their format for one year only, replacing the traditional description of numerous projects with a series of case studies concerning people the Settlement had supported. Of these, most related to work with older people. The following is one of the more unusual examples, but demonstrates the impact of the Settlement's work on the lives of older people in need:

"Mr. B. has been a patient in a mental hospital for the last twelve years receiving treatment for depression. He had lost touch with the ordinary world and was frightened of being alone. The minibus went to take him to the Day Room. He was still quite active and could get there by himself, without difficulty; but without the regular call of the minibus he would never have gone. He is now one of the regular helpers of the more crippled members and is always ready for a chat. Most significantly, he now goes along by himself. The minibus is making other calls."

(Birmingham Settlement, 1966, p.9)

Meals Services

After the successful introduction of day centres, the Settlement's next major innovation in its services for older people was the advent of meals on wheels. In 1962, the National Assistance (Amendment) Act gave local authorities greater scope to provide meals services (Means and Smith, 1998) and both the Kingstanding and the Summer Lane Settlements were asked to cook and deliver meals to local older people. Shortly afterwards, the decision was taken to cook the Summer Lane meals in Livingstone House (one of the local authority's residential homes), with the Settlement continuing to co-ordinate the distribution of the finished product. By 1970, Summer Lane was delivering four days a week to over 60 people, with around 30 deliveries per day. Some people received two meals a day, and the most needy four. Over in Kingstanding, meals were distributed to over 60 people on two days of the week. Both branches of the Settlement had long waiting lists, but were unable to expand their service due to a shortage of volunteer drivers and inadequate kitchen facilities.

The Settlement Day Centre.

The Settlement's meals on wheels were clearly gratefully received, and a survey carried out in 1971 in conjunction with Selly Oak Colleges found that 45 per cent of service users needed Settlement meals more often. The Settlement was also alarmed to discover that the food it delivered represented the only well-cooked meals that many older people had all week. Both meals services continued to grow thereafter, until the Settlement's finances became too tight and the City Council took over responsibility for the Summer Lane meals in March 1975. However, the twice-weekly service at Kingstanding continued for another five years until the Council once again intervened. With the loss of its meals services, the Settlement had more time and resources for its day centres and concentrated its activities on these projects.

Biannual Surveys

In 1971, the Settlement embarked upon a new initiative designed to shed light on the needs of local older people. Concerned that its visiting service was too limited in its scope, the Settlement sought to take stock and reappraise its role:

> *"The Settlement has previously in both Centres acted as the focus for panels of visitors. This has always been difficult because of the relatively few visitors available in both neighbourhoods and because we felt that the way the service was provided gave only a limited service to the neighbourhood. Comparatively few regular visits were made to isolated individuals and little was done to bring the elderly more into contact with the life of their area. The 'friendly visit' was too infrequent and too much an isolated act to really help the person."*

(Birmingham Settlement, 1972, p.10)

In response to these concerns, the Settlement began a twice-yearly survey of people over 60 in the tower blocks of South Newtown. Over 500 pensioners were visited and the project was designed to ensure that "every elderly person in the neighbourhood is contacted, knows where they can obtain help or advice and is aware of the statutory and voluntary services available to them" (Birmingham Settlement, 1972, p.11). After the survey was completed, those individuals in need of further assistance were invited to the Settlement's day centre, offered a regular visiting service or referred to social services. A similar scheme was soon set up in North Newtown by the Newtown Community Centre and St. George's Church, and plans were made to extend the survey to the Warren Farm area of Kingstanding.

Despite the success of the Settlement's biannual surveys, the project was not to be a long-term venture, culminating in 1976 with the opening of the South Newtown Community Project or 'Community Flat' at 47 Mosborough Crescent (see chapter 6). Although the flat catered for people of all ages, it continued to be used by various pensioners' clubs throughout its history, maintaining the Settlement's focus on services for older people. What is remarkable about the

The Settlement Day Centre.

Settlement's biannual surveys, however, was the extent to which they anticipated future policy developments, preceding by more than twenty years the annual health checks which GPs are currently required to carry out on all patients aged 75 and over. Once again, this is a classic example of the Settlement's ability to develop services to fill gaps in existing service provision until city-wide or national policy is sufficiently advanced to be able to develop statutory alternatives.

Transport

A final element of the Settlement's work with older people concerns transport. Although this may seem out of place in a chapter on health, research has emphasised the important but much neglected role of adequate transport in maintaining social contacts and general wellbeing. Throughout the history of the Settlement's day care and meals projects, transport has been a recurrent problem which has limited the expansion of much-needed services. A classic example arose in 1972-73 when there were difficulties with Community Transport, an agency which the Settlement used to help bring service users to and from its day centre:

"Problems of transport have been to the fore recently, as Community Transport... have been waiting the greatly overdue delivery of new vehicles. As a result, the Settlement minibus has been the only available vehicle, and at times it has been needed in two places at once, as it sometimes has to be used for Meals on Wheels. Transport is such a vital part of our work that these difficulties have to be resolved, taking up a good deal of time and energy that could have been used in other equally important work."

(Birmingham Settlement, 1973, p.23)

The Settlement Day Centre.

Although this incident was disruptive, it was only a single manifestation of a recurring and ongoing problem. In response, the Settlement initiated the Shared Transport Service (STS) in 1980. Based on close working relationships with the Centre for Policy on Ageing, Birmingham Social Services Voluntary Liaison, Birmingham Voluntary Services Council and Community Transport, STS was essentially a brokerage service which matched organisations with under-used vehicles to other groups needing transport. Free to agencies whose transport was used in the project and available upon subscription to other agencies, STS also offered an updated information pack on transport, a quarterly newsletter, information sheets on relevant legislation and discounts for mechanical repairs and vehicle hire.

Concerned about the lack of transport facilities for people with disabilities, the Settlement also began to experiment with the notion of a 'Dial-a-Ride' scheme for those unable to use public transport. Responding to concerns expressed at a meeting of "Transport for Disabled People" regarding the under-researched nature of the need for and provision of transport for people with disabilities, the Settlement suggested a pilot Dial-a-Ride scheme to run during the summer of 1982. This would then be evaluated in order to establish its suitability for a more permanent project. The Settlement's proposal was accepted and the subsequent experimental transport service was monitored with interest. A second pilot was carried out in December of the same year and an evaluation by students at the University of Aston made recommendations for future projects based on the various strengths and weaknesses of the Settlement's scheme (Webb and Phillips, 1983). This was later used to inform the creation of a 'Ring and Ride' service in Birmingham by the West Midlands branch of the National Advisory Unit for Community Transport. To facilitate this process, the Settlement took the decision to transfer both operational responsibility and funding for the whole STS project to Community Transport, thereby preventing unnecessary duplication and freeing up resources to introduce the proposed Ring and Ride service.

Today, Ring and Ride is one of the trading arms of West Midlands Special Needs Transport Limited, a registered charity which provides accessible transport for people of all ages in the West Midlands who have a mobility problem and no transport of their own. Currently, there are 40,000 active users of this service making around 1,800,000 trips per annum via a fleet of 100 specially adapted mini-buses and an additional 45 buses used on contracts and back-up (personal communication, West Midlands Special Needs Transport Limited).

After responsibility for STS passed to Community Transport, the scheme continued to operate independently of the Settlement until lack of support from participating agencies forced its eventual closure in the mid-1990s. Despite this, the issue of community-based transport is now back on the political agenda in 1999 with projects in a number of cities looking to develop integrated transport schemes similar to that introduced by the Settlement in the early 1980s. In Birmingham, funding from Centro and the European Regional Development Fund is likely to culminate in some form of regional transport resource to help agencies work together, share good practice, develop funding strategies and stimulate employment. Although the Settlement is no longer involved in transport projects, its work in this field was once again ahead of its time, addressing important issues which were neglected by policy-makers elsewhere for many years to come.

Mid-life

Building on its experience of working with older people, the Settlement soon sought to extend its services to slightly younger people between the ages of 35 and 60. This idea was first proposed in 1981 when the Settlement became aware that over 30 per cent of the population fell between these ages, but that there was no age-group organisation for people in middle-life. These people did not fit into services for young people or for older people and faced their own unique problems connected with the experience of ageing. From the offset, the Settlement identified five key issues and set about exploring how best to respond:

The problems of mid-life

● Problems of health and the need to change diet, exercise and body care patterns to meet the requirements of a less youthful physique.

● Problems to do with the family – children in their difficult teens, parents in old age, loss of children and the need to live with your partner in new ways.

● Problems of work and interest – women re-entering the labour market and wanting to do so with reasonable prospects; men appraising their careers and past-times and needing change with all that entails in retraining and risk.

● Problems of money as the level of commitments and the need to seriously plan savings for retirement reach their peak.

● Problems of how to use increased leisure time.

(Birmingham Settlement, 1981, p.13)

In the end, the Settlement chose to establish a Mid-Life Centre development group which met to examine the problems, needs and opportunities of people between 35 and 55. This was recognised from the beginning to be an area about which very little was known and even less provided, and progress was initially slow. In 1982, a quarterly journal, *Meridian,* was inaugurated to provide a discussion of mid-life and to disseminate information. In the same year, the first ever national consultation on the topic of middle age was held by the Settlement to discuss issues such as career changes, employment problems, health care, finance and alternative lifestyles. A small library was also established and a series of training courses and leaflets were introduced in order to raise awareness.

After this, the next stage was to establish a counselling and information service to help people come to terms with the lifestyle changes inherent in the ageing process. A limited company, *Midlifestyle,* was also formed to develop and market courses on various aspects of middle age. Perhaps its greatest achievement came in 1984-85 when it succeeded in attracting support from the Crest chain of hotels in organising a series of 'midlifestyle weekends' for people aged 30 to 50 at a number of venues throughout the United Kingdom. It was also around this time that the Settlement began to collaborate with the Department of Administrative and Social Studies at Teesside Polytechnic in order to set up the Centre for the Study of Adult Life, researching personal change in adulthood and feeding findings back into the Settlement's work.

Women and Mid-life

Although the Mid-Life Centre continued to function up until the early 1990s, its focus changed considerably in the mid-1980s with special emphasis given to women's needs. This work began in 1986 when the Settlement liaised closely with the media as part of the preparation for a Radio 4 programme on the subject of the menopause. At the same time, it was becoming increasingly apparent that the Settlement's counselling service was being used predominantly by women, and proposals for a specialist women's project were considered:

"In 1986 the Settlement began to investigate setting up a special Women's Mid-Life Centre. The Settlement was faced with many often desperate women experiencing the menopause, trying to adjust to the end of their role as mothers as their children left home, trying to re-enter work with outdated skills and trying to cope with separation and divorce. There were also women having problems caring for elderly dependents and single women troubled by their status both as a single person and as a non-parent. A hidden problem had been unearthed, women seem to posses a 'hidden disability' where they become stuck in despair and powerlessness as they feel obsolete with the loss of their nurturing role. Women have a need for support through the physical and emotional changes accompanying menopause and periods of loss in the 30-55 age group. The Settlement has made detailed proposals for a Women's Mid-Life Centre to help women gain the confidence to make positive changes in their lives, and to raise awareness among the public about problems in this age group with a view to remedy. The proposals have attracted support from the Family Planning Association Women's Therapy Centre, psychologists, health promotion officers and many other of the support services in Birmingham. With the appropriate financial support the Centre will begin extended operations on a local level."

(Birmingham Settlement, 1987, p.21)

In the end, the launch of the Centre was delayed until 1989, although when the time came, funding from the National Westminster Bank and later from the Department of Health enabled the project to get off the ground and expand its initial work extremely quickly. In order to support women through the changes of mid-life, the centre provided practical advice and support through individual counselling, group-work, training sessions, information sheets and a quarterly newsletter, *Midlife Matters*. The latter in particular attracted considerable media attention as the first magazine to deal specifically with the opportunities and difficulties facing women in mid-life. As the Centre continued to develop, members became involved in assertiveness training, a course in complementary medicine, lectures on physical and emotional health and a self-help group, as well as more recreational activities such as demonstrations by the Body Shop and organised social events. Despite this, the Mid-Life Centre was unable to attract sufficient funds and was forced to close in March 1994. Although it was hoped to resurrect the centre as soon as funding opportunities presented themselves, this was not to be and the Centre, with all its experience and information, was never to reopen.

Body Care

Despite the eventual closure of the Mid-Life Centre, the Settlement's expertise was not wasted, and was used to inform further health-related projects for middle-aged people. A good example is the Exercise for Health Advice Centre, which was opened in Summer Lane in March 1984. With funding from the Sports Council and the West Midlands Regional Health Authority, the Settlement was able to convert the old youth block into a gymnasium and the project was officially opened on 9th March 1984 by Denis Howell M.P.

Claiming to be the first of its kind in Britain, the project's stated aim was to "help the middle aged unemployed to cope with the physical and mental stress of unemployment" (Birmingham Settlement, 1984, p.15). To do this, the centre offered its clients individual tuition and a gently graded exercise programme to be carried out under instruction. Fitness courses, keep fit sessions and nutrition and general health advice were soon added, together with classes in audio-visual relaxation, slimming and stop-smoking. The project soon changed its name to Body Care and was used by over 700 members. Unfortunately, the scheme proved too expensive to continue and, in 1986, was single-handedly responsible for a deficit of £5,000. Although the initiative was scrapped when external funding ran out, Body Care's contribution should not be underestimated and its ideals persist to this day through City Council schemes such as Passport to Leisure.

The Gateway Club

Although the Settlement's post-war work in the field of health has concentrated primarily on older and middle-aged people, a number of its projects have focused on different groups of people altogether. The first of these was the Kingstanding Gateway Club, an experimental day care service set up in 1967 for young people who were described then as mentally handicapped, but who would now be referred to as people with learning difficulties. Although this was a new initiative, it built on foundations already laid by individuals such as Ellen Pinsent, who was a member of the Settlement's executive committee in 1899 and a pioneer in the movement for the education of the mentally handicapped (Rimmer, 1980). In addition to this, the Gateway Club was also based on a close relationship with the Junior Training Centre for the Mentally Handicapped, which had used the Lower Hall of the Kingstanding Settlement for its activities until its relocation in the mid-1960s to a purpose-built centre. As a result of these links, the Gateway Club was able to begin almost immediately and membership of its fortnightly sessions exceeded 30 throughout its first year. Aware of the complexities of the work it was undertaking, the Kingstanding Settlement offered training sessions for all helpers and affiliated the club to the National Society for the Mentally Handicapped. Soon the club was meeting on a weekly basis and its work was boosted by the donation of a minibus by students from the University of Birmingham.

Although the focus of the Gateway Club was primarily social, it also offered the families of service users regular respite from caring and must undoubtedly have played an important role in helping people with learning difficulties remain in the community rather than enter residential care. With the closure of the Kingstanding Settlement in 1974, the Club relocated to a local church, since the Local Authority at the time was not prepared to take on its running. This is greatly to be regretted in light of the government's failure to develop viable community-based alternatives for the long-stay hospitals where people with learning difficulties had traditionally resided. This was a long-standing issue, and pressure for reform was ultimately to culminate in a highly critical and extremely influential report by the Audit Commission (1986). This in turn was to pave the way for a government review of community services and the subsequent introduction of the NHS and Community Care Act 1990 (Means and Smith, 1998). Viewed from this angle, therefore, the Settlement's provision of a community-based day care service for people with learning difficulties should be seen as another major innovation foreshadowing future national policy developments.

The National Association for the Childless

Shortly after the Gateway Club disappeared from its records, the Settlement was involved in the creation of a new health-related project. In 1976, the National Association for the Childless (NAC) was established by Peter and Diane Houghton (the Settlement's director and his wife). Themselves childless, the Houghtons saw the need for an organistion to "offer encouragement and advice to childless people about the distress and futility they feel about their situations" (Birmingham Settlement, 1976, p.6). This was initially a personal matter for the

Houghtons, who simply wished to establish contact with other couples suffering from fertility problems. However, a letter placed in The Telegraph generated such an enthusiastic response that an Association was set up with three main aims:

- To campaign for changes in the priority attached to fertility treatment in the NHS.

- To provide a framework of support groups throughout the country to help childless people come to terms with their grief.

- To raise awareness of the problems faced by the childless through a monthly newsletter and other publicity.

(Birmingham Settlement, 1977, p.10)

The range of emotions associated with being unable to have children was described by the Houghtons as 'unfocused grief' in a booklet which they published in 1977. By 1979, some 2,000 copies had been sold and a major publicity campaign had begun to raise awareness yet further. With funding from the Department of Health and Social Security, membership increased and NAC began to produce its own factsheets. A fund was established to support infertility research and counselling training was offered to some 80 or so contact members in localities across the country. TV and radio appearances followed, and an independent organisation, the Childless Trust, was established to set up a clinic for infertility research. NAC was also involved in exploring the issue of inter-country adoption and worked in partnership with a range of social services departments over fostering, adoption and counselling issues. Close links with the drug company Serono enabled regular meetings between the childless and infertility medical specialists, and the Association was successful in campaigning for a government inquiry into the ethics of human reproduction (the Warnock Inquiry). By 1985, NAC's support services had been extended to hospitals in London, Birmingham and Manchester, and there were 4,500 members.

In 1986, NAC celebrated its tenth anniversary with the 'Baby Lobby', a major media event which included a press launch at the Royal Horseguards Hotel, a tea party at the House of Commons with Anna McCurley M.P. and the publication of the largest ever survey of people with fertility problems. Organisational changes were to follow after an investigation by an independent management consultant, and in 1987 Peter Houghton gave up his dual role as Director both of NAC and of the Birmingham Settlement to concentrate on the latter. After this, the next major development was the introduction in August 1990 of a Fertility Helpline to give telephone advice on infertility treatment. Beginning with one counsellor and a single telephone, the service had received

1,043 calls by March 1991 and a further 937 messages on the answer phone. Such demand prompted the need for expansion and a concerted fundraising campaign enabled the helpline to become a national service with three counsellors. This meant a greater reliance on income from companies and trusts, and NAC's sponsorship grew from nothing in the late 1980s to over £80,000 in the early 1990s. Such was its success that NAC began to prepare for independence, and in April 1993 became a separate charity in its own right under the title of iSSUE. This had always been the intention of NAC's founders, and the Settlement's role was largely that of a nurturing organisation, supporting NAC until it was ready to leave Summer Lane and set out on its own.

Since gaining its independence from the Birmingham Settlement, iSSUE has played a leading role in organising Britains' first ever National Fertility week, founding the International Federation of Infertility Patient Associations and participating in the annual National Infertility Awareness Campaign. In the course of this work, it has liaised closely with the media and has secured funding from the Department of Health and the National Lottery in order to expand its counselling service and to subsidise membership for those unable to pay (iSSUE, 1998). Now based in Walsall, iSSUE has an annual turnover of more than £100,000 and is Britain's oldest established organisation offering independent support to those experiencing difficulties in conceiving (iSSUE, n.d.). Although now entirely separate from the Settlement, the growth and emergence of iSSUE is testimony to the Settlement's initial role in identifying a gap in existing service provision, developing a project to respond to previously unmet needs and supporting this initiative until it was ready to become an independent agency in its own right.

Summary

After a hundred years of working with poverty and health issues, it is interesting to note a change in the nature of the Settlement's health-related projects. On the whole, its early initiatives were concerned to compensate for the lack of basic health care services through schemes such as the Medical Care Committee, the Mother's Guild or the Summer Lane mortuary. This was no longer necessary after the creation of the National Health Service, and improvements in the general health of the population enabled the Settlement to move away from the provision of health care towards a more varied approach designed to promote the physical, social, emotional and mental health of local people.

In many ways, this mirrors a more general change in the concept of health itself, with traditional notions of health as the absence of disease giving way to a more holistic perspective which focuses more on general wellbeing than on medical cure. As a result, the Birmingham Settlement has sought to promote health in its widest sense, addressing issues such as transport and community care services for older people and those with learning difficulties, emotional support for infertile couples or those facing lifestyle changes as a result of the ageing process and physical exercise for the unemployed. Despite these changes, however, the Settlement has remained heavily involved in campaigning work throughout its history, whether this be with regard to alcohol abuse, the specific issues of middle age or the emotional distress of people unable to have children. It has also been a major source of innovation, anticipating developments in areas such as community care, transport and leisure services. On the eve both of its centenary and of a new millennium, therefore, much has changed, yet much remains the same.

Chapter 5:

'Ignorance' – Education and training

Education is one of the main priorities of the current government and is crucial to any attempt to combat poverty. This chapter:

- Describes the growth of Britain's education system.
- Highlights persistent inequalities in education.
- Outlines the Settlement's attempts to educate those in poverty. These range from training in 'housewifery' to evening classes, and from adult literacy to residential accommodation for young people in the care of the local authority.
- Analyses projects designed to educate others about poverty. These include the training of social workers, research work and the sharing of the Settlement's expertise.

When Toynbee Hall was first established in 1884 in London, it was intended to be an educational centre which would encourage reciprocity. Just as the settlers would learn from their neighbours what it was like to be poor, so local people would learn from the settlers what it was like to have culture and education. In its early years, indeed, Toynbee Hall was seen by many as an outpost of the existing university system, and it was believed that its founder and warden, Samuel Barnett, intended the Settlements to become colleges for working people (Pimlott, 1935). Building on this tradition, the Birmingham Settlement has always seen education as a core feature of its activities, working to combat the widespread 'ignorance' identified by Beveridge as one of the five 'giants' of the post-war world.

The Origins of the Education System

Prior to 1870, there was no national system of education in Britain, with primary schooling provided mainly by voluntary bodies connected to churches. As a result, provision was extremely patchy, with more than two thirds of Birmingham children remaining untaught (Coley, 1911). To rectify this situation, the Education Act 1870 enabled the creation of School Boards to run and maintain elementary 'board' schools for children up to the age of 11 in areas where voluntary supply was insufficient. These schools were to be financed by a combination of local rates, Treasury grants and school fees of up to 9d a week (Ball, 1986). The act also made women eligible to sit on School Boards, although it was three years before the first woman was elected in Birmingham (Coley, 1911). In 1871, the Birmingham School Board issued byelaws compelling attendance at school from the age of 5 to 13, and this was confirmed by statute as an obligatory rather than an optional policy in 1880. It was not until 1891 that all school fees were abolished.

In 1902, Balfour's Education Act replaced the School Boards with Local Education Authorities and gave these bodies the power to establish their own secondary schools. Further pieces of legislation introduced school medical inspections as well as cheap school meals and free milk for those in need. The age of compulsory attendance was also raised to 14 and additional classes were provided for children between this new school leaving age and 18. The next major reform came in 1944 with Butler's Education Act, which raised the leaving age to 15 and provided universal free secondary education in grammar, secondary modern and technical schools following an Eleven Plus exam. This provided the framework for Britain's education system until the introduction of comprehensive education in the 1960s and the creation of grant-maintained schools under the Education Act 1988 (Hill, 1997). The school leaving age was also raised to 16 under a statute of 1964 (not implemented until 1973) and Local Education Authorities are now responsible for a small pre-primary sector (under 5), primary education (5-11) and secondary education (11 to 16, with many pupils continuing at school till 18). Britain's education system is not without its critics, but has come a long way in a relatively short time and has recently been the central concern of successive governments. When the now prime minister spelled out his three main priorities in the run up to the general election of 1997 he spoke only three words: 'education, education, education.'

Educational Inequality

Despite these radical changes in the provision of state education, practice has often lagged far behind policy and children from lower social classes have repeatedly performed less well than their middle class colleagues (Ball, 1986). When mass schooling was first introduced in 1870, for example, the ignorance of children in Birmingham at least was very great, since many had never been to a school before. Attendance was irregular and the children from poorer classes in particular were known as 'half-timers,' attending school in the afternoon, having been at work during the morning to raise money for their families. Even those children that went to school on a full-time basis were often not in a physical state to profit from their education, with many having worked either before or after school or both.

At a local level, this issue was highlighted by the Industrial Law Committee of 1913-14, which found many examples of wage-earning children. Although the law forbade the employment of children under 14 between 9pm and 6am, the Committee found one district of Birmingham where 16 out of 37 boys investigated were working illegally. They even cited a case study of a boy of 12 who worked in a fruit shop for 56 hours a week. When added to school hours, his working week was over 83 hours (Ring, 1914). This was felt to have a very detrimental effect on children's schooling, as a writer in *Women Workers* reported:

> *"[Wage-earning children] are not able to take proper advantage of the education in school. A boy who has started his working day at 6.30 for the delivery of news-papers, walked several miles, and had a hurried breakfast, will probably arrive late and be half asleep in school hours. The evidence of teachers is unanimous that it is impossible to get good results from such children, and that it is a waste of the money spent on teaching to be obliged to attempt it."*

(A.A.B., 1916)

Another barrier faced by children in the central areas of Birmingham was the high rate of illness and the incidence of malnutrition. Such was the concern about the effects of these on school children that the Birmingham Schools Dinner Society provided breakfasts of cocoa and milk, bread and marg and jam, hot milk, porridge with treacle and bread and dripping. It was considered important to provide such food at the start of the day in order to prepare the children for work, since those from poorer areas tended not to have been given breakfast at home (Vince, 1923). Such was the scale of the problem that in 1906 alone, 250,000 breakfasts were provided in Birmingham schools.

Although material conditions have improved throughout the twentieth century, educational inequalities have persisted. This seems to be the result of a multitude of factors, and sociologists have identified a range of issues which may contribute to the lower educational achievements of children from the lowest social classes:

Inequalities in education

- The material environment.
- Parental attitudes.
- Child-rearing practices.
- Culture differences and community.
- Linguistic development and social learning.
- Sources of inequality within schools themselves.

(Ball, 1986)

Whatever the reasons, the fact remains that there is no such thing as a level playing field in the British education system, with members of the lower social classes performing consistently less well than their middle class counterparts. Despite the concerns of educational sociologists and policy makers alike, inequalities in education persist to this very day, with exam results and entry to higher education both remaining highly correlated with parental occupation and class (Gaine and George, 1999). In some areas, indeed, inequalities may even be getting worse. A classic example is that of university entrance, with fears that changes in the way that higher education is financed will discriminate against young people from working class backgrounds and that access to university education will be based more on the ability to pay than on academic ability. A century after the foundation of the Birmingham Settlement, therefore, the need for educational projects in poorer areas remains just as acute as ever.

In response to these issues and policy developments, the Birmingham Settlement has placed education at the heart of its work. This has often been a dual process, with projects to improve the knowledge and skills of local people on the one hand, and initiatives to educate other people about the problems of poverty on the other. For this reason, the remainder of this chapter is divided into two sections, dealing with each of these issues in turn.

A. The Settlement's response: educating people in poverty

Children with Disabilities

When the Settlement was founded in 1899 it sought not to duplicate the work of local schools, but to fill the gaps it identified in existing educational provision. As a result, one of the Settlement's first educational projects dealt not with the numerous failings of the school system described above, but with the education of children with disabilities. This work is described in more detail in chapter 4 as a result of its input to the children's health needs. However, the project also had an educational focus, supporting the children wherever possible to return to 'board' schools and teaching those unable to do so at home. In anticipation of the opening of a 'Special Cripple School' promised by the School Board, the Settlement ran a daily class on its own premises for disabled children "too delicate to face the rules and work of a big Board School" (Birmingham Settlement, 1902, p.10). Even after a specialist school was opened on Dean Street, the Settlement continued its classes for those children who were ineligible or who had not yet received a place at the new school. A weaving school was also set up at 320 Summer Lane for disabled young women, although this scheme is described in further detail in chapter 4.

Practical Skills

After its initial input into the education of disabled children, the Settlement turned its attention to increasing the knowledge and skills of the young people it had met through its various clubs and societies (see chapter 7). The first such scheme comprised a series of classes in 'housewifery' arranged for girls between 12 and 14 from two local schools. Supervised by workers from the Settlement, these young people came to Summer Lane to study topics such as lighting fires, cooking, the cost of various types of fuel, the importance of fresh air and cleanliness and the practical skills involved in housework. The Settlement felt that this was an important way of preparing these girls for their future responsibilities and one which could begin to ameliorate the appalling housing conditions of the area. It also prided itself on its own innovation, noting that Summer Lane was "the only place in England where practical Housewifery is taught in an ordinary dwelling house and not in a centre reserved specially for the purpose" (Birmingham Settlement, 1908, p.27).

Although the Settlement's housewifery course disappeared from its records the following year, it was replaced with two more initiatives designed to teach practical skills to school children. The first of these was a sewing class held on Wednesday evenings at the Settlement. In 1910 this was recognised as an evening continuation school by the Education Committee, who duly provided a teacher to supervise proceedings. Despite rather uncertain attendance levels, the class continued throughout the early years of the First World War and was only abandoned in 1917 in order to concentrate on other aspects of the Settlement's work. For its time, the class was a novel venture which the Settlement felt had a role to play in the local area:

> *"This class last year was the first experiment of the kind in Birmingham, and we are glad to learn that the Education Committee were so far satisfied that they have agreed both to continue our class and to extend the privilege to one or two other clubs in the City."*

> (Birmingham Settlement, 1911, p.16)

The second initiative was also a sewing class, although this time for pupils from Summer Lane Boys' School. From 1911 onwards, the Settlement received boys whom the headmaster considered untidy, who would remove the offending garments and mend them under the Settlement's direction. Surprisingly, this project proved very popular, and the headmaster was afraid that his pupils would deliberately damage their clothes in order to attend the Settlement (Rimmer, 1980). The novelty of the scheme was such that the *Daily Mirror* heard about the Settlement's classes and published pictures of the boys at work. This sewing class was later absorbed into the more general work of the Settlement's boys' clubs (see chapter 7).

The Kindergarten

In 1907, the Settlement was approached by the People's Free Kindergarten Association, who were looking for premises for some 20 children from 2 to 6 years old. The Association was permitted to rent the Settlement's club room together with part of its garden, and a new project began which was to influence the work of the Settlement for decades to come. Although the aim of the Kindergarten was partly recreational, it was primarily concerned with the education of pre-school children and had an important impact, both on the children and their parents. Activities included gardening, baking, music, craft and the tending of animals, something which the Kindergarten's workers felt encouraged the children to nurture and care rather than to destroy, and made life in the slums more bearable. Regular medical inspections were also carried out to ensure that the children's health needs were met, and local parents were encouraged to attend with their children to learn more about child-rearing and how to foster good habits in their offspring. As the Settlement's annual reports noted, "this co-operation between the home and the Kindergarten is a welcome sign, for it widens the influence of the Kindergarten for good on the child as well as bringing fresh ideas and a happier atmosphere into the home-life" (Birmingham Settlement, 1915, p.31). It was also an important development for the city as a whole, since provision for young children was, at this time, inadequate, prompting Birmingham's Medical Officer for Health to express his concern about the number of children being left alone in insanitary conditions while their parents went out to work (Women Workers, 1905).

When the People's Free Kindergarten Association closed at the end of the First World War, the Education Committee took over the project and established a Municipal Nursery School at the Settlement. This was actually one of the first

Children's projects at the Birmingham Settlement.

such nursery schools established under the Education Act 1918, and its progress was monitored with interest. Waiting lists grew quickly and the Settlement noted with regret that only the restrictions of its buildings prevented the project doubling in size. A weekly evening class for mothers was also established to give the Nursery's superintendent chance to get to know them better and the project took over the ground floor of 316 Summer Lane in order to expand its provision to 90 places. In addition to its educational work, the Nursery also prompted an increase in the children's health through the provision of milk and dinners. Although the project relocated to new premises in Brearley Street in 1939, it was replaced temporarily by a Public Health Department nursery and by a Parents Group which met to discuss the bringing up of children. Even now in the 1990s, the education and care of young children is an important feature of the Settlement's activities and the Kindergarten first established in 1907 continues to exert influence on its work (see chapter 7).

The legacy of the Kindergarten: modern children's projects at the Birmingham Settlement.

The Reading Room and Clean Hands Club

Towards the end of the First World War, the Settlement initiated another educational project by equipping one of its rooms as a Children's Reading Room with books, pictures and comfy chairs. Interestingly, part of the inspiration for this scheme may well have come from the Horse and Jockey temperance pub (see chapter 4) where the popularity among children of the magazines and reading material provided indicated the need for some sort of reading scheme for this age group (Matheson, 1912). Supervised by the Settlement's students, the reading room was designed for children of all ages and was open from 5pm till 6pm most evenings. Membership cards were introduced in 1924 and a 'Clean Hands Club' established to reward those who visited the library regularly with clean hands by allowing them to wear a club badge and to take books home with them. The popularity of the library and the Clean Hands Club was such that a new rule had to be introduced whereby members were only allowed to visit once a week, thereby freeing up time and resources for membership to expand. It was not long before members had read almost every book in the entire library, despite the fact that the Settlement's collection of books was constantly increasing due to the generous donations of its supporters. A children's library was also established at Kingstanding and this proved as successful as its Summer Lane equivalent. Perhaps the greatest compliment of all, however, came in 1929 when an American visitor compared the Birmingham Settlement extremely favourably with other Settlements in terms of its attitudes to reading:

> *"I was impressed by the Library. I have found few real efforts made in English Settlements to stimulate reading, and I welcome any extension of the Library system which may in time make books available for every resident in the neighbourhood."*

Erlund Field, Barnett Memorial Scholar
(Birmingham Settlement, 1929, p.13)

As the children who used the reading room grew older, the Settlement found it necessary to start an adult library as well. Funded by the Carnegie Trust and boosted by generous donations of books, the adult library attracted a range of readers, including adolescents and older people. Regular donors soon organised themselves into a group known as the 'Friends of the Library' and an individual gift of £10 in 1932 proved sufficient to purchase over 50 new novels. An adult branch was also established at Kingstanding with help once again from the Carnegie Trust. Although the adult libraries are rarely mentioned in the Settlement's annual reports in the early 1930s, they were clearly an important part of the Settlement's work. This was also an issue to which the Settlement would later return with its focus on adult literacy during the 1970s (see below).

Overseas Links

The mention of an American visitor above is a good example of one of the many links which the Birmingham Settlement developed with other Settlements and with similar agencies in different parts of the world. This not only enabled the Settlement itself to learn about different ways of working, but also expanded the horizons of local people and provided important educational opportunities. As early as 1903, the Settlement received an academic from Chicago to speak at a conference of the Northern Settlements held in Summer Lane, while in 1923 the warden took 10 senior girls from the Settlement's clubs to spend a week in France. After the Second World War, two young men from another Settlement club went on an exchange to Sweden and three senior girls visited a Parisian Settlement. Around the same time, visitors came to Summer Lane from places such as Scandinavia, Eastern Europe, Western Europe, Burma, Rhodesia, Zanzibar, Ghana, Thailand, Cairo, Sydney, India, Nigeria and Hong Kong. The presence of 'black' visitors in Summer Lane was of particular interest, since there were few 'black' people in the district at the time. Young Americans also came to Summer Lane and Kingstanding to help out in clubwork under the Winant Volunteer Scheme, and the Settlement later established links with the International Christian Youth Exchange. For local people, some of whom may rarely have been outside Birmingham before, these international contacts can have been nothing short of miraculous. Now in the 1990s, the wheel has turned full circle, and the Settlement is arranging a series of exchanges and conferences as part of a joint centenary celebration with Association House in Chicago, reaffirming links established as early as 1903 when the American visitor spoke at the Summer Lane conference.

War Work and Post-war Revival

At the start of the Second World War, many of the Settlement's educational projects gave way to more immediate concerns in the local neighbourhood (see chapter 6). Towards the end of the war, however, the situation had stabilised and there was something of a revival in the Settlement's educational classes. In Kingstanding, for example, a series of groups met for physical training, keep fit, handicrafts, discussion, play reading, needlework, art and toymaking. These classes later received sponsorship from the Local Education Authority and expanded to include basketry, drama, dressmaking and embroidery. Dressmaking, sewing and cookery classes were also established in Summer Lane in conjunction with the Education Committee, who provided the premises and the teacher for the latter.

Perhaps the most successful initiative of all, however, was the training given to young people entering the Economic League Speakers' Contests. These were annual competitions organised on a regional basis and requiring teams of four young people (a chairman, a speaker, a proposer and seconder of a vote of thanks) to talk about current social and economic issues (Rimmer, 1980). In 1945, a team from Kingstanding came third in a debate on post-war housing, while in 1949 a team reached the national finals of a similar competition run by the National Association of Girls' Clubs and Mixed Clubs with a presentation on 'what I would like to say to my Local Education Authority.' After this achievement, Kingstanding appears to have acquired a reputation for its public speaking and the annual competitions became a regular feature.

Adult Literacy

In the latter part of the twentieth century, the Settlement's educational work has focused very much on the issue of adult literacy. This had traditionally been an invisible issue, with many adults too embarrassed or ashamed to seek help. In 1963, however, a young man at the Cambridge House Settlement in Camberwell sought help with his reading problems, and the Settlement there pioneered a literacy scheme to provide individual tuition to those in need. This was publicised through the British Association of Settlements and the extent of adult illiteracy began to become increasingly apparent. By the 1970s, for example, it was estimated that some 25,000 adults in Birmingham alone were semi-literate, often as a result of factors such as childhood illness, the need to care for younger siblings, truancy, lack of parental support and frequent changes of school. Many recent immigrants also had difficulty reading, since English was not their first language.

In response to this situation, the Birmingham Settlement set up a new venture in 1969 to match voluntary tutors with adults seeking private tuition. Support from the City Library and funding from the Barrow and Geraldine Cadbury Trust soon enabled the appointment of a secretary and a part-time organiser, and the project doubled in size. By 1972 there were some 60 pupils across Birmingham with 59 tutors and a waiting list of 13. Working closely with further education colleges, the British Association of Settlements and the National Association for Remedial Education, the Settlement received referrals from a wide range of sources, including hospitals, GPs, the probation service and personal contacts. Once the scheme was up and running, the Settlement seems to have been surprised by the range of people coming forward for help and by the sheer scale of what had previously been a hidden problem:

> *"Pupils vary in age from school leavers to middle-aged. Case histories are equally varied – men competent at their jobs and hoping for promotion but afraid their illiteracy may become apparent, young mothers fearful that their children will discover their inability to read, unemployed youths finding their chance of a job restricted because they cannot read or fill in forms. It is lamentably true that several pupils escaped for several years the carefully arranged programme of schooling laid down for everyone."*

(Birmingham Settlement, 1972, p.19)

> *"The most surprising aspect is that the handicap has been an inviolate secret for so long – even the bridegroom whose bride only discovered his problem at the registry office (this with tragic results) – the gardener safe with one employer for twenty-nine years, suddenly bereft and loath to explain why he was unable to apply for alternative positions – the mothers who do not want their children to know – and the father who would like to be able to read to his children. Each bears testimony to embarrassment and anguish and these are the people we try to help."*

(Birmingham Settlement, 1973, p.12)

Soon, the volume of work was such that some form of city-wide co-ordination was required, and in 1973 the Local Education Authority appointed a full-time organiser. A network of Voluntary Teaching Units was established throughout the city and some of the Settlement's students transferred to units nearer their own homes, leaving the Settlement to focus on the Newtown and Handsworth areas. Estimates of the number of illiterate English-speakers in Birmingham had by this time risen to 50,000 and the Settlement's one-to-one teaching scheme was transferred to the Aston and Handsworth Institute of Further Education in 1977 where it continued to function independently of the Settlement.

Literacy Development and the Right to Read

In November 1973, a British Association of Settlements conference in London estimated that between one and two million adults in Britain had a reading ability less than that of the average nine-year-old. A Birmingham conference followed in March 1974 and a City Working Party on Adult Literacy was established. In May of the same year the British Association of Settlements initiated its "Right to Read" campaign, which was to culminate in a national literacy scheme in conjunction with the BBC and an abortive attempt to introduce legislation concerning adult literacy resources. Contributions to the former were sought from the Cambridge House, Blackfriars, Liverpool and Birmingham Settlements, all of whom had been able to develop considerable expertise in this area (Rimmer, 1980).

Shortly afterwards, a new literacy project was established at the Birmingham Settlement to identify and support those people in the Aston and Handsworth areas who lacked the confidence to access existing literacy scheme. Set up in 1975 with funding from a private trust, the Literacy Field Development Project introduced an experimental daytime class for the unemployed, housewives, pensioners and night-shift workers. It also pioneered a preventative literacy scheme, working with individual families to provide input to children of school age before their reading difficulties became a problem in later life. Although the Development Project was terminated in 1978 following the end of its funding, its preventative work was sorely missed by the parents and social workers who had first alerted the Settlement to the need for such a scheme.

The Special Teaching Project

Also arising from the Settlement's literacy work was the Special Teaching Project. Set up in 1974 on the basis of two years' funding, the scheme provided individual tuition to children excluded from or suffering problems at school. Some of these children were in care, some were from single parent families, many had a record of physical violence, most were illiterate and all had educational or emotional problems of one sort or another. To overcome these issues, the Special Teaching Project offered these children the individual attention of a friendly adult who would demonstrate an interest in them as people and give support with whatever problems the children were worried about. Lessons were not always at the Settlement, but sometimes took place on canal banks, in a strawberry field or in museums, according to the children's interests. The strength of the project seems to have been its informal and relaxed atmosphere, for many of these children had only previously had contact with anxious and fraught parents or adults who they saw as authority figures. This approach clearly worked, and by 1977 the Settlement's annual report was noting that several of the children had referred their own parents to the Settlement and were hoping to join the various projects at Summer Lane. Such was its success in demonstrating the advantages of one-to-one teaching, indeed, that it was able to convince the Local Education Authority to take this way of working on board, enabling the Special Teaching Project to disband safe in the knowledge that its work would be continued.

The Residency

A final initiative relating to the education of those in poverty was the Residency Project. Traditionally, the residence at the Settlement had been solely for students and workers seeking to serve the local community (see below). In 1969, however, the Settlement began to make plans to purchase St. George's rectory in Tower Street, expand the residence and transform it into a residential unit for young people experiencing difficulties in their lives. In the first couple of years, only two or three of this new type of resident came to live at the Settlement – an orphan of 16, a boy of 17 whose home situation had irrevocably broken down and another boy whom the Settlement supported to undertake remedial education. This caused problems as there were no staff specifically to supervise these young people, and the initial stages of the experiment witnessed a series of conflicts with residents unhappy with authority and even a drugs scare. When the Tower Street Rectory was purchased and completed, however, the warden and his wife moved into a flat in the Residency and operated a unit for six boys in the care of the Local Authority. This was an exciting new project, and its aims were neatly summarised by Diane Houghton, the warden's wife:

> "*The motivating idea behind the Project has been the desire to experiment with a form of residential care that might prove suitable for a few of the many young people in their teens who are presently 'at risk' through being homeless, underprivileged and underachieving; yet who could possibly benefit from living in an environment that provides stimulus towards intellectual achievement and creativity, as well as security, understanding, counselling and a chance to form affective ties over a long period. This kind of care is badly needed in Birmingham, both for young people from families where there are few overt signs of stress, and for those from families that have broken up.*"

(Birmingham Settlement, 1972, p.14)

Open 24 hours a day 365 days of the year, the Residency was probably the most arduous and difficult to sustain of all the Settlement's projects. Disputes between young people in care and student residents were not uncommon, the colour TV was stolen and there was even a serious suicide attempt which fortunately did not succeed. Heavy demands were placed on the Houghtons in particular, who in addition to running the Settlement during the day fulfilled an almost parental role with the residents, day and night. By 1974, the energy required by the project could not be sustained and change was urgently needed. Residential workers were appointed to oversee the project and the Houghtons moved out of the Residency, the first time in its history that the warden no longer lived in the Settlement (Rimmer, 1980). In spite of these difficulties, there were many successes and the Settlement discovered early on that with the right support, the less privileged residents could really make something of themselves:

> "Long-term individual therapy is provided, as needed, by the Warden, under guidance from the consultant psychiatrist. The therapy is designed to give the new resident confidence in himself and his abilities, and to help him make tentative steps in the Settlement community... Over the last three years there have been failures: one boy left of his own accord and is now in prison for a criminal offence; a few have been bewildered and frustrated by the comparative freedom given them; others have needed greater intensity of affection than that they could possibly be given. Yet there have been successes: one boy achieved three Grade A's in his A-level exams, and is going to Leeds University in October to read Physics and Philosophy; another has shown promising artistic ability and is now contemplating entering Art School to become a graphic designer; another... is going to Matthew Boulton College in September to study for A-level."

> (Birmingham Settlement, 1972, p.15)

Throughout its existence the Residency was essentially an educational project. There were many recreational activities in the form of the Rare Glare Disco, holidays, hiking, trips and parties, but the underlying aim of the initiative was reciprocal learning or "social education" (Birmingham Settlement, 1973, p.24). As students and young people in care mixed together, they could not help but learn from each other. For the students and staff, it was an important lesson to see that there were people of a similar age to themselves who had experienced none of their opportunities or advantages. This encouraged a willingness to serve others and was a useful preparation for entry into professions such as social work or education. For the young people in care, hitherto limited horizons were expanded beyond belief and new opportunities to increase confidence, self-respect and educational attainment were developed where none had previously existed. Such an experience of shared learning and communal living must have been quite literally life-changing, and some of the emotions which the project awakened are summarised in a poem by a former resident:

"*Enclosed here with years to come no way out except through me.*

Turn your head deep down inside love and emotions you will find.

Bring them forward now.

Wipe out your miseries

Replace them with your true and understanding self.

Accept yourself, be life's burden no more instead be bold.

And step forward with confidence itself,

New horizons lie ahead wake up stop sleeping turn your head."

(Andrew Alison, quoted Birmingham Settlement, 1978, p.14)

The Closure of the Residency – the end of an era

By 1979, the Residency comprised a community of some 25 people, both male and female, from different parts of the country. Such was its appeal that for every one person accepted, ten were turned down. As residents grew older, moreover, the Settlement found a shortage of suitable accommodation for those people leaving care and, in co-operation with the Moseley and District Churches Housing Association, obtained four bedsits to give ex-residents a 'breathing space' as they made the sometimes traumatic transition from care to independent living. In 1982, however, funding problems forced the Residency to close. The project had always been expensive to run, and by the late 1970s was operating with an annual deficit of over £3,000. Concerns about occupancy levels in the early 1980s were initially overcome, but reductions in local authority funding in 1982 led to staff cuts and, ultimately, to the closure of the project. In its final year, it was estimated that the Residency alone accounted for over 70 per cent of an annual deficit of £11,592. Although the Settlement pledged to retain the capacity to restart the project when its services were needed again, this moment never came and the Residency never re-opened. While the Residency's facilities were used in the short-term to house a number of refugee families seeking accommodation, this was truly the "end of an era" (Birmingham Settlement, 1982, p.19) which marked a final break with the Settlement tradition of not only working, but also living, among the people it served. While the Birmingham Settlement continues to maintain many of the ideals of founding figures such as Edward Denison, Arnold Toynbee and Samuel Barnett, the closure of its residential facilities marked a radical break with the past.

B. Educating others about poverty

One of the main aims of the founding fathers of the Settlement movement was to learn about poverty and to use this knowledge to inform the training of professional workers and policy developments. This was also true of the Birmingham Settlement, which from 1899 to the present day, has sought to use its experience of working with poverty to raise the awareness of others. Even prior to its foundation, the Committee which was appointed to investigate the feasibility of establishing a Settlement in Birmingham emphasised the need not only for "a centre for philanthropic work in the neighbourhood of the residence, but also for systematic training and study with reference to social work and industrial conditions" (Birmingham Settlement, 1899, p.3). This was re-inforced in 1903, when the Settlement began to preface its annual reports with a state-ment of its aims. Whereas its second objective was to promote the welfare of local people, its stated priority was to provide a centre for the systematic study of social issues. The report continued to explain the way in which this was to be achieved:

> *"Students are given work, under experienced workers, which will afford them insight into present conditions. Arrangements are made for them to attend some committees, and for visits to educational, poor-law, and other institutions. They are advised as to a course of reading, and lectures and classes are arranged."*

(Birmingham Settlement, 1903, p.3)

Residents

As part of this process, the Settlement provided accommodation for students and interested workers to live on Summer Lane and learn about conditions there through personal contact. When the Settlement first opened its doors in 1899 it had accommodation for five residents, who paid £50 a year if students, £1 per week or £40 per year if resident workers and 25 shillings per week if not giving a full-time commitment to the Settlement. The number of residents increased as improvements were made to the Settlement's buildings and there was rarely a spare room for more than a few weeks at a time. Residents were initially all women and the first male residents did not come to live at the Settlement until 1932 when an expansion of club work with men and boys necessitated male workers living on site. These residents not only helped the Settlement with its own projects, but also "assisted in carrying out the aim with which the Settlements started...: the bridging over of the separation between the dwellings, and therefore the lives of the different classes of the community in our large towns" (Birmingham Settlement, 1904, p.6). Previous students frequently stayed in touch with the Settlement through the Guild of Associates, which was founded in 1907 for this purpose and which continued up until the 1950s.

Resident students studying at the Settlement.

Over in Kingstanding, accommodation was also provided following the acquisition of 612 Kingstanding Road in 1942 and both branches of the Settlement received numerous visits during vacation periods in particular from students from across the country. Although the Kingstanding Settlement closed in 1974, the residential function of the Summer Lane branch continued up until 1982 when it became too expensive to maintain. By this time, of course, the Settlement had established a bold experiment by providing accommodation both to students and to young people in the care of the local authority (see previous section). For more than 80 years, therefore, the Birmingham Settlement was a residential organisation, fulfilling the desire of its founders to bring the educated and the uneducated, the rich and the poor together in one community to live amongst and learn from each other. This was education in its truest sense: not learning from textbooks or lectures, but from daily contact and shared experiences.

Wardens, students and maids, July 1929.

The University of Birmingham

In addition to its residents, the Settlement worked with a range of groups and educational organisations to teach others about poverty. Of all these links, by far the oldest and most important was with the University of Birmingham, which received its charter in 1900, a year after the Settlement was founded. From the beginning there was a close working relationship and in 1900-01 the Settlement held four lectures in a room provided by the University. These lectures were well attended and covered topics such as 'the problem of women's wages', 'special factory legislation for women', 'how Settlements may help industrial development' and 'how to study social questions.' The last of these was chaired by Dr. (later Sir) Oliver Lodge, the Principal of the University, and the lecture was given by Beatrice Webb, a leading British socialist and co-founder of the London School of Economics. The following year, Principal Lodge commended the Settlement as a suitable "practising ground" for students from the University's School of Economics, emphasising the need for professionally trained social workers to replace the "untrained and inexperienced" amateurs who had previously performed this role (Birmingham Settlement, 1902, p.3). After this, a number of female students came to stay at the Settlement and a regular course of Autumn lectures on current social issues was inaugurated at the University. Some 50 undergraduates were also invited to tea at Summer Lane, where they heard about the work of the Settlement and the relationship between the University and the social work of the city.

Social Studies

In 1905, the Settlement's warden was involved in the development of the first ever course of lectures in Social Studies at the University. This was an evening class which led to no formal award, but was soon supplemented by an annual three-day Vacation School for Social Study established by the Settlement in 1907 in response to requests from students at the University. Repeated every Easter, the Vacation School included visits to factories, schools, law courts and the homes of local people, giving the students an accurate insight into social conditions in the poorer areas of the city which many had never visited before. Different topics were selected each year, enabling the 40 or 50 participants to learn about issues such as modern industrial conditions, childhood problems, destitution, punishment, child labour and demobilisation. With a change of warden in 1919, however, the Vacation School disappears from the Settlement's records and does not seem to have taken place again thereafter.

In 1908, the University of Birmingham introduced a one-year Diploma in Social Studies. This was the first initiative of its kind in the Midlands, although similar schemes were already in operation in cities such as Liverpool, London, Berlin, New York and Amsterdam. Like its modern day equivalent – the DipSW – this course was both practical and academic, entailing lectures in the history of English government and local administration, economics, statistics, sanitation, industrial conditions and industrial law as well as visits to various institutions and to people's homes (Women Workers, 1908). The Settlement's warden later became one of the tutors for this course and continued to fulfill this role until the late 1940s when the University finally appointed a full-time practical tutor to relieve the warden of her teaching duties. Up until this point, however, the Settlement was responsible for arranging students' practical work, observational visits and discussion groups, organising trips to almost every type of institution and agency in Birmingham. Financial assistance for those in need was sometimes available via the Guild of Associates, and many students completing the diploma course also spent time at the Settlement's own projects, either as residents or non-residents.

During the 1920s, the University Diploma trained around 20 students each year, more than half of whom gained practical social work experience at the Settlement and 5 or so of whom at any one time were usually Settlement residents (Rimmer, 1980). Some of these were even fortunate enough to gain experience of social work overseas, with one winning a scholarship to go to New York and others travelling with Settlement workers to countries such as France or Belgium. A key figure in these early years was Cecile Matheson (warden 1908-16), whose belief in the need for integrated theory and practice was at least 30 years ahead of her time (Rimmer, 1980). In this way, the Settlement was able to influence generation after generation of trainee social workers, many of whom went on to obtain positions of authority in various projects throughout the country.

Raising Awareness

In addition to its work with the University of Birmingham, the Settlement also organised and ran its own classes, lectures, talks and courses to raise awareness about poverty and train workers interested in this issue. In 1908, for example, the Settlement's warden spoke on Settlements and social work training at several venues in Birmingham and in towns such as Stafford, Oxford, York and Leeds. A course was also devised in 1908 in response to requests from the District Nursing Society to teach trainee nurses about contemporary issues, and the Settlement's lectures were regularly reported in the daily newspapers. The following year saw the beginning of lectures on personal hygiene by Dr. Violet Coghill (lecturer in hygiene and public medicine at the University of Birmingham) to an audience of Charity Organsiation helpers, provident collectors and district nurses. Classes were also held for the Young British Women's Temperance Association (see chapter 4) and the Settlement responded to invitations from various groups of working men and women to speak on a range of legal and social issues.

By 1914, the warden was travelling almost the length and breadth of the country to give lectures on the Settlement's work and received so many requests for speakers that a great many had to be refused. Two years later, the Settlement's warden read a paper at a conference on 'the training of university women for social and administrative posts' and gave evidence to a committee in London considering the whole issue of social work training and work with volunteers. She also addressed a meeting of the Student Christian Movement on a similar topic and lectured at various venues throughout Britain. A series of classes on civic education, social ideals and the problems of post-war reconstruction was also arranged in 1918 with guest lecturers from institutions such as the University of Birmingham, the University of Liverpool and the Geographical Society. While all these activities were important in sharing the Settlement's expertise with other people, they were also beneficial to the Settlement's day-to-day work in Summer Lane:

"This branch of work has its own value in making the special knowledge and experience we have gained available to enquirers and workers over a wide area but it also facilitates the Settlement Work. Not only has it brought us helpers, donors and students but the friendship and interest engendered means that we have correspondents both in every part of Birmingham and also in most neighbouring towns to whom we can apply when our people move or if they have relatives elsewhere for whom they desire our help."

(Birmingham Settlement, 1916, p.17)

World War I

During the First World War, the Settlement began two new educational ventures. To begin with, the Settlement worked with the Workers' Educational Association (WEA) to provide classes in home nursing and first aid, with 31 out of 35 candidates obtaining their St. John's Ambulance certificate in the project's first year. A series of social events were also arranged and the courses proved so successful that they were repeated the following year. More important than the actual content of the classes was the close working relationship with the WEA, which brought the Settlement into contact with a number of women to whom its ordinary work may not have appealed. As the war progressed, however, the WEA classes were discontinued and the Settlement turned its attention to more urgent matters. With the approval of the Ministry of Munitions, the Settlement agreed with the University of Birmingham to run a short emergency course to train women as Welfare Supervisors in munitions factories. The course was run once in 1916 and again in 1917, and was an important contribution to the war effort. A similar training initiative was later to be revived in the 1940s when the Settlement and the University once again combined to train students sent by the Ministry of Labour as Factory Welfare Workers.

Club Leaders' Training

After the war, the Settlement's next major educational project began in the 1920s with the introduction of a weekly training class for Settlement residents and local social workers. Run by the Birmingham Trained Gymnasts' Club, the classes were designed to train participants in the teaching of team games, singing games and dances suitable for clubs and play schemes. The class was formally recognised as part of the University's Social Study course in 1922 and was soon opened up to senior members of the Settlement's clubs on the understanding that they would use the skills gained to supervise their younger counterparts. Although the project soon disappears from the Settlement's records, it was replaced in the 1930s by a Club Leaders' Training Class in response to a request from the Birmingham Union of Girls Clubs. Inspired by the Prince of Wales' appeal for voluntary social service, the training class combined lectures and practical demonstrations in an attempt to raise the standard of youth clubs all over the city. Even after the project ceased to function at Summer Lane, the Settlement's warden and staff continued to speak at similar training courses in Birmingham and elsewhere from time to time.

Social Workers, Clergymen and Teachers

At around the same time as it began to run classes for club leaders, the Settlement embarked upon three separate but similar training courses for three different types of student:

- Like the Vacation School set up in 1908, the Social Study Weekends covered different topics each year, catering for around 150 students and workers at a time. Topics ranged from 'can democracy survive?' to leisure, and from health to social services, with observational visits to various social institutions and housing areas to re-inforce learning and encourage debate. Contributions were made by representatives of various organisations, including the Communist Party and the British Union of Fascists, whose addresses were apparently "stimulating" (Birmingham Settlement, 1936, p.10)!

- Next, the Settlement began weekly lectures for theological students at Queen's College. The course was soon extended to theological colleges across the city and was designed to prepare future clergy and ministers for the social issues they would face after qualification. Lectures covered a wide range of social issues and, like previous initiatives, were supported by educational visits to agencies involved in relevant social work.

- Finally, the Settlement began a short intensive course of talks and visits for students at the University of Birmingham's Education Department who were about to become teachers.

All three of these schemes ran side by side throughout most of the 1930s, enabling the Settlement to influence almost an entire generation of the city's students training to enter what would now be called one of the caring professions.

The Luncheon Club and Family Service Units

Although the Second World War may not seem like an appropriate time to establish a new educational venture, it was actually during this period that the Settlement began its monthly Luncheon Club for local clergy, health visitors and social workers interested in meeting to discuss social issues. A similar scheme, the Fraternal, was also established in Kingstanding, enabling workers on the estate to debate the problems and issues they encountered in an informal setting. As these two groups became more established, they began to organise lectures on topics such as the Education Act 1944, legislation affecting children and the work of the police.

Perhaps the Luncheon Club's most important contribution, however, was the subsequent role it played in setting up the first ever Family Service Unit in Birmingham. During the war, a voluntary organisation known as the Pacifist Service Unit (PSU) had been established in London to undertake air-raid and war relief work. As the air-raids subsided, the PSU became increasingly involved in the general welfare of children and families and further units opened in other parts of the country. These quickly developed expertise in dealing with so-called 'problem families' and were the forerunners of what are now called Family Service Units or FSU's (Rimmer, 1980). During the late 1940s, workers at the Settlement's Luncheon Club had become so concerned about these 'problem families' that they invited a representative from the Paddington FSU to speak to one of their meetings in May 1950. Over 90 people attended, including members of the Local Authority and several magistrates, and the decision was taken to set up a similar agency in Birmingham. Chaired by a member of the Settlement's council and convening in a room provided by the Settlement, a planning committee met to implement the Luncheon Club's decision.

The Birmingham Family Service Unit was established the following year, renting a room from the Settlement on Summer Lane (Birmingham Family Service Unit, 1952). Although it later moved to new premises in New St. John Street, representatives of the Settlement continued to sit on the FSU's committee until the mid-1970s, with a member of the Barrow family (closely connected to the Settlement for many years) as chair and later vice president. Even after the Unit's departure to Small Heath in 1970, links were maintained through the Settlement's social worker who took over much of the FSU's work in the local area. In 1999 there are two Family Service Units in Birmingham, one of which, still based in Small Heath, is the fruit of the Luncheon Club's original labour.

Changes in Social Work Education

During the 1950s and 1960s, there were major changes in the education of social workers. By this time, social work was viewed as a useful activity, but had not yet established itself as a profession in its own right (Jones, 1994). This was the result of a number of factors:

The limitations of social work

- The majority of workers were un- or under-qualified.

- There was little co-ordination in the training and practice of the various branches of social work, with medical social workers, psychiatric social workers, probation officers and child care workers all training on separate courses.

- Unlike their American counterparts, British social workers placed very little emphasis on research.

- Social workers were lowly paid and lacked support services such as car allowances or secretarial assistance.

(Jones, 1994; Rimmer, 1980)

In response to these issues, two reports on the employment and training of social workers were commissioned by the Carnegie Trust and produced by the London School of Economics' (LSE) Eileen Younghusband (1947, 1951). The result of these endeavours was the introduction in 1954 of the first ever generic postgraduate social work course at the LSE (the so-called 'Carnegie Experiment'). Similar schemes, often referred to as applied social studies courses, were established in 1956 at Birmingham and Southampton, combining academic and field-work in a single training programme. A government working party was also set up under the chairmanship of Eileen Younghusband, culminating in the introduction of a two-year Certificate in Social Work at various colleges of further education and the creation of a National Institute of Social Work Training (now the National Institute of Social Work or NISW).

In the years to come, these changes stimulated a widespread expansion in social work training. From a mere 300 social work students in 1950, the number had risen to 3,123 by 1975 (Younghusband, 1978). However, the reforms also led to a two-tier system, with students completing either a two-year 'Younghusband' course at a college of further education or an applied social studies course at a university. These two approaches were unified in 1971 with the creation of the Central Council for Training and Education in Social Work (CCETSW) and a single social work qualification (the Certificate of Qualification in Social Work or CQSW). This was to remain the formal award for qualified social workers until it was replaced in 1989 by the current Diploma in Social Work (DipSW).

As these changes took place, the training of social workers became an increasingly large part of the Settlement's work. The University of Birmingham had always been involved in social work education, but in 1956 introduced a new applied social studies course. Shortly afterwards, the Birmingham College of Commerce (later Birmingham Polytechnic and now the University of Central England or UCE) set up a new 'Younghusband' course, with the first such students arriving at the Settlement in 1964. Since both courses were dependent on prospective social workers undertaking practical work in local agencies, the Settlement was a valuable resource for these and other academic institutions, with students continuing to work in Summer Lane and Kingstanding as they had done throughout the century. During the 1960s, however, the shortage of suitable placements was such that the National Institute of Social Work Training commissioned a national survey of current facilities. The subsequent report made a number of recommendations for expanding the opportunities for students to gain practical experience, one of which involved the creation of specialist units with groups of students studying under one supervisor (Brown and Gloyne, 1966).

The Student Unit

In response to these developments, the Settlement set up a Student Unit in 1971 with funding from the Department of Health and Social Security. An expansion and a more formalised version of the student supervision which had taken place at the Settlement throughout its history, the Unit received its early students from the two-year Certificate in Social Work/Child Care at Birmingham Polytechnic and the Diploma in Pastoral Studies at the University of Birmingham. Some of these students were originally from overseas, and in 1971-72 the Settlement was fortunate enough to receive the Principal of an Australian College of Deaconesses, the Principal of a Theological College in Assam and a Finnish Lutheran Pastor. The aim of the Unit was to provide supervised placements in a voluntary agency setting, with students not only undertaking individual casework with individuals and families but also becoming involved in a range of group activities and the Settlement's other projects. The latter in particular was a mutually beneficial process:

> *"In this year the unit has extended its role away from the pure involvement in the social work section and placed students in the other projects of the Settlement... This has had a remarkable effect. Firstly, it was much appreciated by the students because it broadened their experience and enabled them to see social work skills in new contexts. Secondly, it was very much appreciated by the projects because it had the effects of adding a skill to their work after a period of induction and of inspiring a critical examination of the projects' achievements."*

(Birmingham Settlement, 1974, p.24)

With a change of personnel in 1974, the Student Unit began to attract candidates from further afield, including the University of Birmingham's Diploma in Social Work, the Selly Oak Colleges and other courses outside Birmingham. Participants were also able to involve themselves in a number of practical and research projects, learning valuable skills while at the same time using their abilities to benefit the local community. Early examples included the installation of a warning system in a block of older people's bungalows, a campaign to draw attention to the plight of Indian residents charged by their doctors for inferior medical treatment and a population survey carried out in one of Newtown's 27 tower blocks.

In the course of its work, the Student Unit also sought to develop innovative social work methods, experimenting with the new systemic and teamworking approaches which were beginning to emerge in the mid-1970s. As it progressed, the Unit developed its own social work library and the range of placements it offered expanded considerably. By the 1980s, students from the Unit were able to gain experience of individual and groupwork with single parents, social work in a health centre setting, day care for people with mental health problems, social skills training, work with neighbourhood groups and co-working in family situations. At its peak, the Unit provided training for some 20 students at a time, utilising its links with agencies such as the Birmingham Association for Mental Health, All Faiths for One Race and the Midland Adventurers Contact and Organisation for Youth to provide a range of varied placements.

The Practice Learning Centre

In 1992 the Settlement's Student Unit became a recognised Practice Learning Centre with additional funding from CCETSW, offering training for students on the new Diploma in Social Work (DipSW) course at institutions such as the University of Birmingham, the University of Central England and Selly Oak Colleges. Funded via a block contract with CCETSW, the centre organised placements for these students in the Settlement's own projects until changes in the financing of social work training forced it to reconsider its position in 1996-97. This was primarily the result of CCETSW's decision to replace existing block contracts with a more cost-effective system based on payments for each individual placement. Under these new arrangements, the Practice Learning Centre was less financially secure and had little option but to reduce its activities considerably. Although social work students continue to undertake placements at the Settlement's Practice Learning Centre in 1999, this is now much more ad hoc and varies from year to year according to demand.

The Practice Development Centre

At the same time as it was setting up its Practice Learning Centre, the Settlement launched the West Midlands Practice Development Centre in order to promote anti-racist and anti-discriminatory social work practice. Building on its links with a range of 'black' partner agencies, the Centre arranged placements for a number of students in 'black' managed voluntary organisations where they could increase their knowledge, skills, experience and understanding of working in an anti-discriminatory manner. Requests for placements came not just from Birmingham universities, but also from academic institutions as far afield as Staffordshire, Wolverhampton and Humberside. In addition to this, the Practice Development Centre was responsible for maintaining the Settlement's library, which by this time consisted of some 1,100 books and pamphlets and 35 videos. By 1995, the library had become a regionally recognised resource on 'black' culture and contained a wealth of literature on anti-racist and anti-discriminatory practice. Unfortunately, the Practice Development Centre was disbanded in 1997 when CCETSW funding was withdrawn and the library was donated to the Selly Oak Colleges. However, links with 'black' voluntary organisations still remain, with the much-reduced Practice Learning Centre arranging placements for a number of students in such agencies.

Research Work

In addition to its contribution to the training of social workers, the Settlement has sought to disseminate its knowledge about poverty issues through its research work. This has been a constant theme throughout the Settlement's history, with campaigns such as the Right to Fuel, the Right to Read or the Village in the

City (see chapters 3, 5 and 6). However, the Settlement's research activities were boosted in 1982 by the creation of a Future Studies Centre (FSC). With the donation of a library from a former University of Birmingham student, the FSC was a project initially dedicated to studying the future or "trendwatching" (Birmingham Settlement, 1986, p.23): that is, identifying significant developments in society, finding appropriate responses to them and promoting awareness of alternative options for the future. To this end, the FSC began to publish a quarterly newsletter, *Common Futures,* and to conduct its own research projects. An early success was a Settlement paper on 'Villaging the City' (see chapter 6) submitted to the IXth Conference of the World Futures Studies Federation in Honolulu, although unfortunately not personally!

In 1987, the FSC held its first major conference, with 130 delegates meeting to hear experts from as far away as Germany and the USA discussing the topic 'Can Birmingham grow again?' Unfortunately, however, funding was again an issue and the project was forced to reconsider its own future in 1988 following an abortive attempt to obtain financial support for the *Common Futures* newsletter from a range of publishing companies. Despite concerted efforts from the Settlement, no one would provide the necessary funding without demanding editorial control in return. This, the Settlement was reluctant to do, and a radical shift in focus was required to prevent the project from folding altogether.

The Research Unit

In 1988, a solution was found with the transformation of the Future Studies Centre into a new Research Unit. Although it was anticipated that this project would attract more funding than its predecessor, it was very much a gamble. Despite previous research experience in the local area and with regard to its own work, the Settlement lacked a reputation for more wide-ranging academic research and had to begin almost from scratch, gradually acquiring credibility in what is still a very competitive world. That it has been successful is testimony once again to the Settlement's ability to carve out a new role for itself when previous ways of working have become untenable.

From the very beginning, the new Research Unit sought to provide a full facility for research, development and evaluation as well as offering up-to-date information on current issues likely to affect the Settlement's other projects. Early work focused on the Local Government Act 1988, the effects of contracting on the independent sector, fuel poverty and the provision of training in community development and voluntary sector management skills. As the Research Unit developed, it was able to establish working partnerships with a range of local, national and international bodies. Perhaps the most important of these was once again with the Department of Social Policy and Social Work at the University of Birmingham, which was to culminate in 1994 with the creation of ENACT (Enquiry into Action).

ENACT

A joint venture seeking to promote practical responses and projects arising from research, ENACT was a mutually beneficial partnership which expanded the capacity of both constituent agencies to compete for research contracts. Whereas the Settlement was seen as lacking rigour by some funding bodies and the University as being too 'academic' by some practice-based agencies, ENACT was viewed as an initiative with both practical and academic experience which could successfully bridge the gap between research and practice. More recently, the ENACT partnership has expanded to include other agencies with links in different areas of the country, while the Settlement's Research Unit has addressed issues such as health care for 'black' communities, the availability of credit, employment, illicit drugs and urban regeneration. As a result, the Birmingham Settlement has been able to develop an excellent reputation in the research field, increasing its capacity to disseminate its considerable expertise and continuing its ongoing role in educating other people about poverty.

Summary

Looking back at the Birmingham Settlement's work over the last hundred years, there is considerable continuity, both with the educational ideals of the founding figures of the Settlement movement and with previous Settlement projects. This is particularly apparent in four main areas:

- Men such as Samuel Barnett founded Settlements to enable the educated and uneducated to come together and to learn from each other's experiences. This aim was embodied for the majority of the Birmingham Settlement's existence through its residence and is still maintained through close links with the University of Birmingham and other academic institutions now that the Settlement no longer has students and workers living on site.

- The Settlement has constantly been involved in educating local people to equip them with the skills they need to overcome their poverty and increase their independence. This has again continued throughout the last hundred years, whether it be through housewifery classes, the Kindergarten, the Settlement libraries, overseas visitors, public speaking, adult literacy, the Special Teaching Project or a whole host of other initiatives.

- The Settlement has played a key role in organising, developing and supervising the training of social workers, working in partnership with a range of academic, statutory and voluntary sector agencies and maintaining a close working relationship with the University of Birmingham in particular.

- The Settlement has been extremely active in sharing its expertise with others, carrying out its own research and using its experience of poverty issues to raise awareness and campaign for policy changes. In the course of this work, it has been a constant source of innovation, developing new educational courses, new ways of working and new agencies.

While the education system in Britain has been transformed over the last century, therefore, the work of the Birmingham Settlement has remained true to its own educational heritage and traditions.

Chapter 6:

'Squalor' – Housing and community

Housing has been a crucial issue throughout the history of Birmingham as a whole and has been even more central to the development of Newtown. This chapter places the work of the Birmingham Settlement in its historical context by examining:

- Housing conditions in Birmingham in general and Newtown in particular.
- The redevelopment of the inner city and the legacies of this policy.
- The Settlement's attempts to grapple with housing and community issues. These include projects connected with rent collection, the provision of housing, community development, the environment, crime and community self-help.
- The Settlement's own housing problems.

Of Beveridge's 'five giants', that of 'squalor' is possibly the most relevant of all to the work of the Birmingham Settlement. This is the result of two main factors:

- The housing conditions in Summer Lane and the nature of the local community have been subject to considerable scrutiny, controversy and criticism throughout the Settlement's hundred-year history.

- The rapidly changing nature of the local housing and community has strongly influenced the work of the Birmingham Settlement and the physical environment in which it has operated.

At a wider level, housing has also been a key issue throughout the history of Birmingham and has received detailed attention from campaigning organisations, academics and policy-makers as a result (Birmingham City Council, 1989, 1992a, 1992b, 1992c, 1992d, 1992e; Bournville Village Trust, 1941; Chinn, 1991, 1993; McGregor *et al.*, 1995). Such has been the impact of housing on the work of the Birmingham Settlement and the people it serves that a brief outline of key developments is required to place the Settlement's contribution in context.

Slum Housing

Some 25 years before the Settlement was established, the problem of Birmingham's slum housing had become so severe that drastic action was required from the City Council. At this time, the areas in the very centre of the city contained some of the worst slums in the country (Birmingham City Council, 1989) and were filled with insanitary, dilapidated and overcrowded dwellings, many of which were unfit for human habitation:

> *"It is not easy to describe or imagine the dreary desolation which acre after acre of the town presents to anyone who will take the trouble to visit it... Little else is to be seen but bowing roofs, tottering chimnies, tumbledown and often disused shopping, heaps of bricks, broken windows, and coarse, rough pavements, damp and sloping. In one case a filthy drain from a neighbouring court oozed into their little back yard; in another, the sitting-room window could not be opened, owing to the horrible effluvia from a yawning midden just under it. And in another case, the fireside of the only sitting room had to be deserted owing to the noxious percolation from a privy penetrating the wall within a foot or two of the easy chair."*

> (Councillor White, quoted Birmingham City Council, 1989, p.12; Briggs, 1952, p. 78)

Under the leadership of Joseph Chamberlain, the Council embarked upon an ambitious programme of redevelopment which was later to earn Birmingham the reputation as 'the best governed city in the world'. Using powers granted

Life in the back-to-backs.

under the Artisan's Dwelling Act 1875, an Improvement Scheme was devised to purchase, clear and redevelop some 43 acres of land in the inner city (Briggs, 1952). The scheme cost £1,300,000 and led to the creation of a new thoroughfare – Corporation Street – in place of the old rookeries (Birmingham City Council, 1989). Despite this redevelopment, however, there remained a ring of wards around the city centre where further action was urgently required to resolve the housing problems which continued to exist. One of these was St. Mary's ward, the future home of the Birmingham Settlement.

Back-to-back Houses

When the Settlement was founded in 1899, Summer Lane was an area of back-to-back houses interspersed with public houses and small workshops and factories. Constructed mainly in the early nineteenth century by private builders looking to make a quick profit, the back-to-backs were cheap to rent, but often badly built, overcrowded, in a poor state of repair and inadequately ventilated. Typically, these houses existed in terraces of a double row of homes built back-to-back under a single roof. Either two or three storeys high, they had one room on each floor – usually a kitchen on the ground floor, a bedroom above that and

An entrance to a court, Brearley Street.

A court in Brearley Street, 1931.

perhaps an attic room at the top. At regular intervals, a narrow passage or 'entry' would lead to a yard behind which contained water closets for communal use and a washhouse ('brewhouse') for the weekly family wash. The yard would typically be surrounded on all sides by more back-to-backs and formed the focal point of the local community. Although local byelaws introduced in 1876 forbade the construction of back-to-backs, these houses remained the norm in central areas well into the twentieth century (Birmingham City Council, 1989).

In 1913 a Special Housing Committee established under the chairmanship of Neville Chamberlain once again highlighted the magnitude of Birmingham's housing problems. Despite the 1876 byelaw, the Committee found that some 200,000 people were still housed in back-to-backs, with 51 to 76 per cent of homes in the 6 worst wards of the city being of this type. Over 42,000 dwellings had no separate water supply, no sinks and no drains, while over 58,000 had no separate sanitary amenities. The Committee concluded that "a large proportion of the poor in Birmingham are living under conditions of housing detrimental to both health and morals" (quoted in Briggs, 1952, p.86), but was unable to take preventative action due to the outbreak of the First World War. Thereafter, conditions failed to improve significantly and standards continued to fall far short of the 'land fit for heroes' promised by Lloyd George. Indeed, research conducted by the Medical Officer of Health and by Bournville Village Trust (1941) in the late 1930s emphasised the continuing prevalence of dilapidated, insanitary and overcrowded housing in the city centre. It was clear that something would have to be done, but action was once again delayed by the declaration of war in 1939.

The Second World War

During the Second World War, the city's already inadequate housing stock was diminished yet further. Between 1940 and 1945, 2,000 tons of bombs were dropped on Birmingham causing some 4,863 fires, destroying 12,391 houses and damaging many tens of thousands more (Chinn, 1996). The area around Summer Lane was particularly badly hit owing to its proximity to the Lucas factory works and other local firms participating in munitions production. No matter how terrible the destruction, however, the Second World War proved to be a turning point in the history both of the nation and of Birmingham. Increased government restrictions on every aspect of people's lives, coupled with the communal experience of the Blitz, meant that nothing could ever be the same again, and it is no co-incidence that the immediate post-war period saw the election of the first majority Labour government and a series of wide-ranging social reforms. It is also no co-incidence that this period in Birmingham saw a radical shift in the Council's housing policy which was to lead to the total transformation of some of its worst housing stock.

Post-war Redevelopment

Under the influence of Herbert Manzoni (City Engineer and Surveyor), the City Council announced the creation of 5 redevelopment zones in Summer Lane, Nechells, Ladywood, Bath Row and Gooch Street. Using powers granted under the Housing Act 1935 and the Town and Country Planning Act 1944, the Council compulsorily purchased properties for slum clearance in some 981 acres in these five areas. With personal experience of working in the back streets and courtyards of the area around Summer Lane, Manzoni saw the need for widespread redevelopment based on sound town planning principles. His aim was to create a series of neighbourhoods of about 10,000 people in areas which were strictly zoned (that is, with land divided into areas for housing, industry and open spaces), contained adequate social amenities and combined high-rise flats with two-storey houses and maisonettes (McGregor *et al.*, 1995). To engage the public in this process, the Council invited readers of the Evening Mail to choose new names for the new areas. While Ladywood and Nechells retained their old names, Gooch Street became Highgate, Bath Row became Lee Bank and Summer Lane (technically St. Mary's ward) became Newtown.

Unfortunately for Manzoni, the need to re-house those made homeless by demolition necessitated a far larger population density and therefore higher flats than he had originally envisaged. In the end, Newtown had blocks of up to 20 storeys, while in other areas the flats reached up to 32 storeys (Birmingham City Council, 1989). Although the new tower blocks were initially very popular, moreover, the destruction of the back-to-backs served only to destroy the communal spirit of the courtyards and engender instead a sense of isolation.

The actual buildings may have been more modern and comfortable, but those residents who remained yearned for the neighbourliness of their former homes and resented the anonymous lives which they felt they were being forced to lead in these soulless tower blocks. This was actually exacerbated by Manzoni's zoning principle, which served only to divide local people further through the major roads and trunk routes which now dissected some of the redeveloped areas. Nowhere is this better illustrated than in the example of the Settlement itself, which was initially surrounded by back-to-back houses at the very heart of the community. After the redevelopment of Newtown, however, the Settlement found itself isolated from its previous neighbours in a predominantly industrial

A re-housed family by the new tower blocks, Newtown, 1969.

zone, segregated from some of the main housing areas by major roads. Faced with so sudden a change, it is testimony to the Settlement's resilience and flexibility that it was able to adapt to its new surroundings, developing outposts in the new residential areas through its Community Flats (see below).

> *"The tower blocks were quite alright in the beginning – we thought it would be marvellous. But you lost the friendliness and the neighbourliness of the back-to-backs. If someone was sick, you knew that a neighbour would do the washing and look after the children. You could leave your door open at night and there were no muggings. When the tower blocks came it all changed. Now I'm scared to go out and I don't see anyone anymore. The back-to-backs weren't the nicest of places, but you knew that there was someone looking out for you and it really felt like home."*

(Personal communication from a service user at the Settlement's day centre)

Moving house prior to slum clearance, Lozells, 1967.

Maintaining the flats was also very expensive and their condition quickly deteriorated. Public opinion was quick to turn against the tower blocks, and by the 1970s the redeveloped areas were experiencing just as many housing problems as they had before the war, only without the community spirit and neighbourliness which had hitherto helped individual families survive (Birmingham City Council, 1989). This was then exacerbated by a host of other social issues such as the effects of economic recession, crime, unemployment and financial poverty. By the 1980s, the scale of the problems was such that Birmingham's inner city areas were recognised as "the largest single concentration of deprivation anywhere in England and Wales" (University of Aston Public Sector Management Research Unit, 1985, p.9). Many of these issues have persisted into the 1990s, with the local area trapped in a spiral of decay:

Newtown in the 1990s

- Unemployment in the area was 35% with four out of every ten men out of work.

- Two out of three people had no formal school or college qualification.

- The number of lone parent families was three times the national average.

- Infant mortality rates were among the highest in the country.

(Newtown South Aston City Challenge, 1998)

Official Responses – Regeneration Schemes

In response to some of these issues, Newtown and other areas in the inner city have been the subject of numerous regeneration and redevelopment initiatives from the mid-1970s to the present day:

- **Urban Aid** was a three-year government grant to assist social welfare schemes in inner city areas in the mid-1970s.

- The **Inner City Partnership** sought from the late 1970s onwards to assist the regeneration of the inner city economy, to tackle the problems of obsolescence in local buildings and infrastructure and to improve personal services and encourage people to help themselves. As part of this process, the Partnership supported a number of voluntary initiatives designed to encourage self-help.

- The **Village in the City** was the Birmingham Settlement's own concept for the improvement of Newtown and formed the framework for a series of local projects. It was also considered as a potential mechanism for more widespread redevelopment in the 1990s as part of the **Newtown Regeneration Initiative,** but was overtaken and subsumed by City Challenge (see below).

- In the 1990s, **Estate Action** invested £60 million in structural repairs to Newtown's housing, external improvements and individual refurbishment. Key changes included the installation of concierge systems, more modern heating facilities, double-glazing, insulation and new bathrooms and kitchens.

- **City Challenge** was a five-year project (1993-1998) which invested £37.5 million of public money and sought to attract further investment from other sources in both the private and the public sector. Key aims were to stimulate business development, enhance educational achievements and employment prospects, restore confidence in the area, create a self-sustaining housing market, develop the significance of Newtown to the rest of the city, create an attractive environment, alleviate poverty, reduce ill health and enable local people to have a say in the shaping of the area. As part of this process, City Challenge worked on a number of flagship projects, including the £16 million refurbishment of the Newtown Shopping Centre and the development of a new £16 million state-of-the-art Mail Centre. Although the City's first bid for City Challenge money was rejected, its second bid proved successful.

- The **Single Regeneration Budget** (SRB) is a source of funding managed (in the Birmingham area) by the Government Office for the West Midlands. It is intended to co-ordinate regeneration activities and is available to both the public and the voluntary sectors. Various waves of SRB funding have been used in Newtown and Aston, including an extremely successful voluntary sector-led programme inaugurated by the Settlement and its partners in 1996 (see below).

The Achievements of Regeneration

After decades of regeneration, the achievements of these initiatives are somewhat ambiguous. On the one hand, they have made a massive public investment in the physical environment and infrastructure of Newtown which has changed many parts of the area almost beyond recognition. On the other hand, however, there is a general consensus that physical regeneration alone is not sufficient to resolve the problems of Newtown without the social changes required to create a more vibrant and cohesive community. Schemes such as City Challenge may have gone a long way towards laying the foundations for such changes, but there remains a long way to go.

Newtown Shopping Centre and the ambiguities of regeneration

Of all the changes which have taken place in Newtown between the 1970s and the late 1990s, those connected with Newtown Shopping Centre are probably the best examples of the ambiguous nature of the various regeneration schemes. At one time, the centre was the focal point of the community and had one of the first Sainsbury's supermarkets in Birmingham. Despite this, decline set in in the 1970s and the 1980s, and by 1995 only 7 of the original 120 units were occupied (Newtown South Aston City Challenge, 1998). The area was known popularly as 'Little Beirut', with burnt-out cars in the car park and frequent muggings. This was probably the most visible sign of all Newtown's problems, and came top of local people's priorities for change (M.E.L, 1992; MORI, 1992). For any redevelopment strategy to be really effective, it would have to address the issue of the shopping centre.

During the 1990s, the centre was a key component in the City Challenge programme. A massive refurbishment was carried out, including changes to the traffic system, the replacement of the underpasses with pedestrian friendly crossings, new office accommodation, high-tech security and the opening of new shops such as Aldi, Farmfoods and McDonalds. Even with all these changes, however, the majority of the centre remains virtually empty, many of the offices lie vacant and the inside of the mall is dark and dingy. After massive investment, therefore, Newtown Shopping Centre is physically much safer, better designed and of greater use to the local community, yet remains an unpleasant area which most people with any positive choice would avoid if at all possible. Regeneration, it seems, involves much more than physical investment and is an extremely long-term process which is only just beginning.

Kingstanding and the Changing Community

At the same time as the housing in Summer Lane was being transformed, so too was the nature and make-up of the community. This was initially a gradual process, but the rate of change began to accelerate as the twentieth century progressed. In the late nineteenth century, some of the people displaced from the city centre slums under Chamberlain's Improvement Scheme found new accommodation in Summer Lane. By the 1930s, however, redevelopment plans were being drawn up for the Lane itself and many of its inhabitants were re-housed in Kingstanding. Up until 1927, Kingstanding had been little more than a series of country lanes on the outskirts of Birmingham. In this year, however, it was incorporated into the city as part of Perry Barr and became the site of a new council estate designed to house Birmingham's expanding population and relieve pressure on housing in the city centre. By 1939 it was the largest estate in Birmingham and one of the biggest in Europe, with 4,802 houses on 493 acres (Chinn, 1997a). While the houses had better amenities than the back-to-backs of Summer Lane, the rents were higher, there were few local facilities and the cost of travelling back to their old homes near the city centre was more than most people could afford. It was for these reasons that a branch of the Settlement was opened in the 1930s at 610 Kingstanding Road. If ex-Summer Laners couldn't come to the Settlement, the Settlement would come to them. From lowly origins, the Kingstanding Settlement became an important part of the local community, as this extract from a publication on Kingstanding past and present demonstrates:

> "The Kingstanding Settlement was started in the early 1930s as a direct result of approaches made by people who had been re-housed from the Aston area of the City. These people had already experienced the companionship of the Settlement in Summer Lane and wanted to see a similar project in their new environment. In its earliest days, the Settlement had no buildings and meetings were held in local schools, but with the passing years a large complex of buildings had been provided. These now include two large halls, a completely covered games area, lounges, workshop, small committee rooms and a very large fully equipped kitchen. Much of the Settlement's work is done through the medium of clubs and these exist for all ages from the very young to the elderly. In addition, the Settlement is responsible for the provision (preparation and distribution) of Meals on Wheels in the area. Other services for the elderly include Day Centres, Dinner Club and a comprehensive visiting service... It is now known as the 610 Centre."

(Birmingham Public Libraries, 1968, p.18)

The new estate at Kingstanding.

The Settlement's Response

In response to these developments, the Birmingham Settlement has established a range of projects and initiatives to contribute to the housing needs of local people and to the community as a whole. This work first began at the turn of the century when the Settlement held a small class for its workers on sanitation and opened its offices for monthly meetings of the North Birmingham District Committee of the Sanitary Council. By this stage, the Settlement had already begun to acquire a working knowledge of local housing conditions through other branches of its work, and in 1902-03 carried out a sanitary inspection of all the courtyards and houses within a small local area. The following year, one of its non-resident workers was supported to complete a course in housing management under Octavia Hill, a leading housing reformer and future co-founder of the National Trust. Having undertaken the management of properties owned by a number of landlords in London, Hill carried out extensive repairs, developed green open spaces, encouraged tenant responsibility through prompt payment of rent and got to know the occupants personally through regular visits. Her perseverance was rewarded and her success lay in being able to demonstrate that the provision of high quality housing could be more profitable to the owners than allowing tenants to live in slum conditions. Working closely with fellow reformers such as Samuel Barnett, Hill's methods were taken up in other parts of the country and her example had a considerable influence on the Settlement movement.

Rent Collecting

That this was the case in Birmingham is clearly demonstrated by a new committee established in 1904 to manage the property of Dr. Carter, a private landlord. Settlement workers visited this and other properties to collect rent on the owner's behalf, to carry out improvements and to provide advice to tenants. Although the exact nature of their work is poorly documented, it is clear that the Settlement saw this as an important aspect of its work:

> *"The scheme for house management on the lines followed by Miss Octvaia Hill has been fairly started by a small committee... This very important social work, which if sufficiently developed may prove a considerable factor in the solution of the housing problem, is felt to be closely connected with Settlement aims... The business management of the property is carried on on strictly commercial lines, while the intimate knowledge of the circumstances of the tenants, gained by regular and sympathetic visits of the collector ought to be of much social value. It is hoped that owners of small house property may take advantage of the opportunity thus offered of employing a lady rent collector."*

(Birmingham Settlement, 1905, pp.6-7)

As the years progressed, the regularity of rent payments increased, the standard of cleanliness became higher and incidents of drunkenness and disorder became fewer and fewer. This was an achievement to be proud of, for the poverty of Summer Laners meant that the non-payment of rent was common. It was not a rare occurrence for families in arrears to 'do a moonlight flit', borrowing a hand cart, packing up their belongings and moving into another house nearby under the cover of dark, leaving the bailiffs to search for them in vain at their old home (Dayus, 1994). Settlement workers also found that rent collecting, like Provident visiting, was a useful way of meeting families in distress and frequently took the opportunity to refer those in need to the appropriate channels of relief. The rent-collecting scheme continued throughout the First World War and was augmented in 1915-16 by a series of cookery classes held in the rented properties for the tenants who lived there. In the following year, however, the project came to an abrupt end following the death of the worker responsible for the committee and the decision by Dr. Carter to make alternative arrangements for his properties.

Housing Exhibition

In 1923, some five years after the termination of the rent-collecting scheme, the Settlement again returned to the issue of housing with a one-off exhibition held in conjunction with Lee, Longland and Co. of Broad Street. Lasting for three weeks and visited by over 3,000 people, the exhibition was designed to demonstrate to local people how they could make the best use of their houses. To do this, three small rooms the exact size of those in the Summer Lane back-to-backs were erected in the Settlement Hall and furnished so as to give "a maximum of comfort and space with a minimum of labour and expense" (Birmingham Settlement, 1923, p.9). Trouble was taken to ensure that the furniture displayed could be manufactured at home by any capable handyman, and the Settlement later reported that some of the designs exhibited were copied almost immediately after the exhibition. Although this event seems to have been a huge success, it was not repeated in the years to come and a potentially important opportunity was lost.

COPEC Housing

In the following year, the Settlement involved itself in what was to become one of the voluntary sector's most important contributions to the resolution of Birmingham's housing problems. Between the 5th and 12th of April, 1924, a meeting of Christian churches – the Conference on Christian Politics, Economics and Citizenship (COPEC) – was held in Birmingham under the leadership of William Temple (then Bishop of Manchester and later Archbishop of Canterbury). The Birmingham Settlement, like other Settlements, took part in the conference and held a lunch for some 50 delegates from the Federation of Residential

Settlements. The COPEC conference was very much a landmark in church history, bringing representatives from almost every denomination and from all over the United Kingdom to discuss issues ranging from education to leisure and from the relation of the sexes to the nature of God. However, one of the principal issues debated was that of housing, prompting the formation of the COPEC Housing Improvement Society in 1925 under the influence of a small group of local people. Although this was always a separate organisation, a link was provided by a series of key individuals involved with both COPEC and the Settlement:

● Sir Frank Tillyard was chairman of COPEC, a lecturer for the Settlement's social studies classes and a leading figure in the Poor Man's Lawyer Movement (see chapters 3 and 5). Mrs Tillyard was also a member of the Settlement's committee from 1904 to 1909.

● Florence Barrow, COPEC's honorary secretary, was a resident at the Birmingham Settlement and had previously been responsible for running the Settlement's basket-weaving class for people with disabilities (see chapter 4) and after-care work (see chapter 7). The Barrow family as a whole was very involved in the Settlement for many years, with members serving on the Settlement's council and executive committee, acting as the Settlement's Honorary Solicitor, serving as trustees and making regular donations (Rimmer, 1980).

● Katherine Lloyd was COPEC's first full-time trainee, obtaining a qualification in housing management to supplement the Social Study Diploma she had already obtained from the University of Birmingham. She later became warden of the Kingstanding Settlement (Fenter, 1960).

Seeking to acquire and recondition slum housing in the central areas of the city, COPEC's first property was purchased on Pope Street in St. Mary's ward with money donated by Miss Barrow herself following the sale of her house (Fenter, 1960). Although COPEC came to own houses throughout the central wards, the majority of its properties were concentrated in the Summer Lane area in roads such as Hospital Street, Brearley Street and Tower Street. Once properties were purchased, they were redecorated, repaired, modernised and managed according to the principles already laid down by Octavia Hill and the Settlement's own rent-collecting scheme.

  Although the history of COPEC has been told elsewhere (Fenter, 1960) and although it was technically a separate organisation from the Settlement, the importance of committed individuals such as Florence Barrow and the close working relationship which was established between COPEC and the Settlement should not be underestimated. Moreover, this is a classic example of the Settlement's role as an originator of innovative projects, supporting and nurturing new initiatives which later expand and develop into independent and often very successful agencies. Thus, COPEC later merged with the Hestia and St. Chads Housing Associations to form the Focus Housing Group. Now, in the late 1990s, Focus is the largest charitable housing association in the West Midlands and one of the country's top 20, with 11,000 homes for rent in 26 local authorities, 1,200 'supported' bed spaces for homeless people, 900 'shared ownership' homes and more than 600 staff (Focus Housing Group, 1998). Mighty oaks really do grow from tiny acorns, and the history of COPEC is a lesson to us all concerning the potential for good which individual contributions can have.

Housing Research

Such innovation as that described above must inevitably be based on thorough research if it is to be successful and enduring. Inquiry into contemporary social problems has always been an important part of the Settlement's work, and the sphere of housing policy is no exception. In 1913, for example, the Settlement's warden had been responsible for compiling and presenting evidence to Neville Chamberlain's Special Housing Committee. In the late 1920s, moreover, Settlement students were involved in visiting local houses as part of a survey published by COPEC and presented to the City Council (Barclay and Perry, 1929). This research emphasised the terrible conditions of the houses visited, calling for the construction of new properties, the purchase of old houses for renovation and an increase in the number of sanitary inspectors. Although progress was slow, the request for more inspectors was granted and a number of improvements resulted (Rimmer, 1980). A similar initiative was undertaken in the late 1930s when Settlement students once again participated in a housing survey, this time for the Bournville Village Trust. The results of this survey were published in 1941 in a comprehensive report which not only described the current situation, but also set out what needed to be done *When we build again* (Bournville Village Trust, 1941). While none of these initiatives offered a definitive solution to Birmingham's housing problems, each one contributed to the growing body of evidence that something had to be done and paved the way for the post-war redevelopment which was to transform areas like Summer Lane.

War Work

During the Second World War, the Settlement was extremely active in the local area, suspending some of its pre-war work in order to ensure that it was capable of meeting the needs of its neighbours in an emergency situation. With air-raid shelters in the basement of the Youth Block and in the garden in front of the residence, the Settlement was far ahead of the City Council in providing protection from enemy bombs (Sutcliffe and Smith, 1974) and was used by local people as a public shelter. With these facilities in place, moreover, the Settlement was able to continue some of its previous work in relative safety and to open up its rooms for the children who were not allowed to return to school until air-raid shelters had been provided (Rimmer, 1980). When the bombing became particularly heavy in 1940-41, both the Summer Lane and Kingstanding branches of the Settlement opened up as Rest Centres for neighbours who had lost their homes and belongings, providing accommodation, blankets and emergency refreshments. Settlement workers also served as fire-watchers, air-raid wardens and shelter marshals, risking life and limb for members of the local community. Although very little of the Settlement's war-work was documented owing to a paper shortage and the existence of much more urgent matters, it seems as though the Settlement and its neighbours were drawn ever closer together by the communal experience of the Blitz:

> *"The story of the Settlement in Summer Lane... is commonplace enough when compared with that of any other residential social centre in a danger zone – yet because it is in its way an epic some points about it are worth recording. It is indeed a matter of rejoicing that no resident has suffered injury and no serious damage was done to premises. One Thursday morning the mattresses in the Men's Flat, owing to the successful efforts of the A.F.S. [Auxiliary Fire Service] the night before, ran water when touched. One Tuesday night the Sub-Warden was blown through the partition doorway of the front garden shelter by blast. One Friday night not only were the Settlement shelters full, but the Boys' Gymnasium housed for hours neighbours who had to be evacuated from other parts of the district. We hope that the neighbourhood was glad to have the Settlement, and our only regret is that we could do so little. We, for our part, would like to record our admiration for neighbours and members who made the long hours more endurable by enquiry as to our welfare, by kettles of hot water for Oxo and by quiet, uncomplaining courage. The behaviour of two little old ladies from the Almshouses, silhouetted against the red glow of burning buildings, remains very clearly in memory. Our thanks, too, are due to members who joined the Settlement Fire Service and spent so many hours on watch."*

(Birmingham Settlement, 1941, p.1)

The Night Shelter

As Birmingham began to return to normality in the immediate post-war period, there was growing recognition of the problem of homelessness. This was the result of three main factors: immigration, the resumption of a large number of evictions from private rented houses held up by the war and people coming to Birmingham to find work. By 1946 the number of homeless people in the city was estimated at many thousands and was said to be increasing at a rate of 50 per week (Sutcliffe and Smith, 1970). Against this background, the Settlement began to focus specifically on the plight of the women and children who were homeless. As part of an attempt to persuade the City Council to become more proactive in this area, the Settlement opened its Youth Block as a temporary Night Shelter for a period of twelve weeks beginning in January 1951. During this time, it was used on 279 occasions by 41 women and 20 children, some of whom made their own way to the Settlement, others of whom were referred by agencies such as the police (Rimmer, 1980). Always intended to be a short-term project, the Night Shelter was nevertheless successful in highlighting the extent of the need for such a service.

Homelessness and the Settlement Night Shelter

"As soon as the youth clubs closed at 10.30 p.m. each night, twelve deck-chairs were set up and cocoa and blankets provided. All the women were interviewed by the Warden. More than half had been evicted from furnished lodgings. One boy of ten had spent one night in the male reception ward of Western Road Hospital, formerly the workhouse. The women and children were allowed to stay for up to four nights until better accommodation could be found. The experiment made heavy demands on the Settlement staff and voluntary helpers. It also caused problems for the domestic staff as "the buildings began to smell". A full report was submitted to the City Welfare Committee but it was some time before additional accommodation... was provided by the city. This concern for women and children reflected one of the major interests of the founders of the Settlement."

(Rimmer, 1980, p.105)

The Settlement Social Worker

Following the closure of the Night Shelter, the majority of the Settlement's post-war work has been concerned with issues relating to the redevelopment of Newtown. Anticipating radical change in Summer Lane, the Settlement established a Development sub-committee in the 1950s to consider the future of the neighbourhood and to plan how best to respond to any social problems which may emerge as a result. In the event, this proved premature, and it was not until much later that the redevelopment of Newtown was to impinge on the work of the Settlement, creating a demand for new services to meet newly identified needs. Perhaps the first of these was the Settlement caseworker or social worker who began working in Summer Lane in the late 1960s. While many of the future redevelopment schemes were to focus on physical changes, this was an attempt to tackle some of the social problems identified in the introduction to this chapter as being crucial to any successful attempt to regenerate Newtown.

By 1970, the social worker was assisting 18 families with 75 children, 3 adolescents, 1 single person, 1 unmarried mother, 6 people with physical or learning disabilities and 38 older people. In addition, she was also responsible for tutoring around 20 students on placement per year (see chapter 5) as well as supervising a Special Children's group and pre-school playgroup, a Teenage group and a mother and baby group. Such was the need for this service that the Settlement's social worker was taken on by the City Council and seconded to the Settlement on a full-time basis. Despite this, the Settlement noted that "the project could double in size if staff and funds were available" (Birmingham Settlement, 1971, p.4). A key aim of this initiative was to help people in need to regain their independence:

> *"The social work section exists to give intensive help to families or individuals who are, for some reason, failing or unable to cope with day to day problems... What we aim to do is help families and individuals gain the confidence and independence to manage their own affairs and respond positively to their situations. This is difficult because the demand for help is very great and increasing, and we have to spend most of our time patching up the family quarrel, preventing the child being received into care, coping with social security problems, fighting off debt collectors and so on. Nevertheless we do seem to be able to work more intensively with the cases than it is possible to do in the statutory departments where the number of cases per worker is very much higher. The liaison with other work projects of the Settlement is also valuable and contributes greatly to the help we can give to our people."*

(Birmingham Settlement, 1972, p.12)

Although social work was an important part of the Settlement's work at this time, the project ceased to function on two occasions in the mid-1970s following the departure of the existing social worker and a shortage of new workers to take his or her place. During these periods, the caseload of the social worker had to be absorbed by other projects and placed considerable strain both on the Settlement's staff and on other services for local people. Particularly hard hit were the Student Unit (see chapter 5), the Community Flat (see below) and services for older people (see chapter 4), which tended to bear the brunt of the social worker's absence. However, this situation was resolved in August 1978 with the appointment of a part-time worker funded by Birmingham Social Services to engage in "preventive work" (Birmingham Settlement, 1979, p.19). Rather than intervening after a crisis had occurred, the social worker sought to work with local people to prevent problems from arising in the first place, encouraging self-help and holding regular surgeries in various community locations. As part of the process, the social worker utilised the Settlement's students and took on a role as a link person, establishing close relationships with the police, social services, health visitors, local schools and a number of community groups.

   With the reorganisation of Birmingham Social Services in 1984, the scope of the social worker's activities was expanded and she became much more involved in counselling for the National Association for the Childless (see chapter 4), support to Money Advice Centre clients (see chapter 3) and work with the Student Unit (see chapter 5). After another brief vacancy in 1986, a new worker was seconded from the City, only for the initiative to disappear altogether from the Settlement's annual reports at the end of the 1980s. In 1999, however, close links with Birmingham Social Services Department still remain, especially in conjunction with projects such as the Day Centre (see chapter 4) and Homebased Care (see below).

The Community Flats

In addition to its social work service, the Settlement also became increasingly involved in outreach work following the creation of the South Newtown Community Project in 1976. Inspired by community development work in Kingstanding and by the Settlement's work with older people (see chapter 4), the Community Project was intended to relieve the isolation of those in tower blocks, to promote increased interaction amongst people of all ages and to enable local residents to increase their control over decisions affecting their lives. With funding dependent upon establishing a resource base in the community, the Settlement sought the support of the City Housing Department and was granted use of a three-bedroom, ground-floor flat at 47 Mosborough Crescent. This quickly became known as the 'Community Flat' and was used by a pensioners' club, a number of children's projects, a food co-operative, a hairdressing group and a keep fit class. The City library also set up a branch there, which was soon running story telling sessions for its 300 or so members. Based in the midst of a residential area, the Community Flat was a useful outpost for the Settlement, maintaining a presence in the community and enabling the Settlement to retain contact with some of the people who had been re-housed away from Summer Lane following the post-war redevelopment of the area.

   As the project developed further, advice and support were provided by the Settlement's community worker and social worker, local councillors attended frequently and the local residents' association used the flat as a meeting place. One of the key aims of the initiative was to enable local people to take control over their own lives, and this was encouraged by devolving the management of the flat to a committee made up of two representatives from each user group. This way of working proved so effective that local residents involved in the Community Flat were soon meeting as a sub-committee of the Birmingham Settlement itself and encouraging the development of further self-help schemes in other parts of Newtown. Their efforts were rewarded and similar initiatives were later set up in Clyde Tower and James House. In total, the Community Flats were an important part of the Settlement's work for over 20 years, with Mosborough Crescent surviving longer than its counterparts and continuing to

The Food Co-op at the Community Flat.

function up until the mid-1990s. By this time, however, many of the groups based at the Flat had become increasingly static, with few opportunities for new recruits to join and little turnover in membership. Fresh blood was needed but not acquired, and this, coupled with general financial difficulties, prompted the decision to close the Mosborough Crescent Community Flat once and for all. In 1999, however, part of the ethos of the Community Flats is maintained through a Settlement annexe built with City Challenge funding at Reynolds House in 1996. Housing projects such as the Credit Union (see chapter 3) and Homebased Care (see below), the annexe helps to sustain the Settlement's community presence and acts as a visual reminder of the Settlement's community flat projects.

Newtown Neighbourhood Project

Such was the success of the South Newtown Community Project in encouraging the involvement of local people in community affairs that its methods were adopted in a much larger and more ambitious programme of activity. Conscious of the scale of the problems to be resolved in the inner city, the Settlement established and provided administrative support for regular meetings of the Newtown Neighbourhood Project, a co-ordinating body made up of representatives from the voluntary and statutory sector agencies working in the area. This group had evolved out of a Christian body known as ACORN (Active Christians Operating Round Newtown) and early members included:

Newtown Neighbourhood Project

- Newtown Community Centre
- The Wallace Lawler Centre
- The Police Community Relations
- St. George's Church Centre
- The Community Health Council
- The Newtown Health Centre

- Newtown Recreation Centre
- Area 5 Social Services Department
- St. George's Primary School
- The Community Flat
- The Probation Service
- The Birmingham Settlement

In 1980, a successful application for funds from the Inner City Partnership paved the way for the employment of two community development workers, one based at the Birmingham Settlement and the other based at St. George's Church Centre. Key contributions included the rejuvenation of the *Newtown News* as a popular community newspaper, close liaison with the housing department, the creation of a new park on the site of a derelict churchyard and campaigns on issues such as the regeneration of Newtown Shopping Centre or the need for a Newtown parish council to empower local people. However, one of the earliest and most enduring products of the Newtown Neighbourhood Project was the concept of the Village in the City, which was to shape the future of community development work in Newtown for many years to come.

The Village in the City

In 1979, research conducted by the Birmingham Settlement had begun to suggest that Newtown was not a homogeneous district, but six distinct areas or 'villages' separated from each other by busy roads, derelict land or changes in housing type. The achievement of the Newtown Neighbourhood Project was to turn this into a framework for community development, building on the success of the Community Flat in order to develop similar self-help schemes in each of the six 'villages' in Newtown. Over the next few years, numerous projects were initiated, with many of them making extremely relevant and important contributions to the local area. Examples included the community room opened at William Cowper Junior School or the employment of home/school liaison teachers by four local schools (Rimmer, 1980). With funding not always guaranteed, however, there were many casualties, and it was not uncommon for projects to disappear from the Settlement's records altogether having only recently been established. While it is not possible to describe each of these in detail, some of the more important schemes developed by the Settlement deserve specific mention.

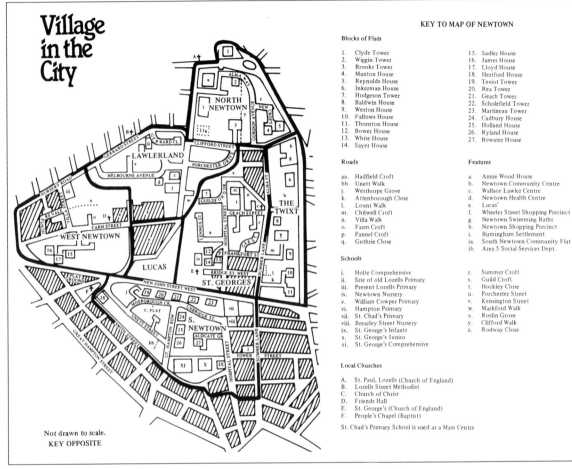

Village in the City

KEY TO MAP OF NEWTOWN

Blocks of Flats

1.	Clyde Tower	15.	Sadler House
2.	Wiggin Tower	16.	James House
3.	Brooks Tower	17.	Lloyd House
4.	Manton House	18.	Hertford House
5.	Reynolds House	19.	Teviot Tower
6.	Inkerman House	20.	Rea Tower
7.	Hodgeson Tower	21.	Geach Tower
8.	Baldwin House	22.	Scholefield Tower
9.	Weston House	23.	Martineau Tower
10.	Fallows House	24.	Cadbury House
11.	Thornton House	25.	Holland House
12.	Bower House	26.	Ryland House
13.	White House	27.	Bowater House
14.	Sayer House		

Roads

		Features	
aa.	Hadfield Croft	a.	Annie Wood House
bb.	Unett Walk	b.	Newtown Community Centre
j.	Westhorpe Grove	c.	Wallace Lawler Centre
k.	Attenborough Close	d.	Newtown Health Centre
l.	Lount Walk	e.	Lucas'
m.	Chilwell Croft	f.	Wheeler Street Shopping Precinct
n.	Villa Walk	g.	Newtown Swimming Baths
o.	Farm Croft	h.	Newtown Shopping Precinct
p.	Pannel Croft	i.	Birmingham Settlement
q.	Guthrie Close	ia.	South Newtown Community Flat
		ib.	Area 5 Social Services Dept.

Schools

i.	Holte Comprehensive	r.	Summer Croft
ii.	Site of old Lozells Primary	s.	Guild Croft
iii.	Present Lozells Primary	t.	Hockley Close
iv.	Newtown Nursery	u.	Porchester Street
v.	William Cowper Primary	v.	Kensington Street
vi.	Hampton Primary	w.	Markford Walk
vii.	St. Chad's Primary	x.	Roslin Grove
viii.	Brearley Street Nursery	y.	Clifford Walk
ix.	St. George's Infants	z.	Rodway Close
x.	St. George's Junior		
xi.	St. George's Comprehensive		

Local Churches

A.   St. Paul, Lozells (Church of England)
B.   Lozells Street Methodist
C.   Church of Christ
D.   Friends Hall
E.   St. George's (Church of England)
F.   People's Chapel (Baptist)

St. Chad's Primary School is used as a Mass Centre

Not drawn to scale.
KEY OPPOSITE

Rimmer, 1980, pp. 142-143

The Site Improvement Scheme

Perhaps the first such project was the Newtown Area and Settlement Site Improvement Scheme, set up in August 1979 with funding from the Manpower Services Commission and a number of charitable trusts. Seeking to restore and improve areas of land in and around the Settlement with teams of people experiencing long-term unemployment, the Improvement Scheme embarked upon a number of projects. In its first year, the scheme concreted the Settlement's car park, planted a vegetable garden, renovated St. George's churchyard and redecorated the Church hall. Next, it began work on the Settlement's own buildings, constructed a new greenhouse and harvested nearly a ton of potatoes and dozens of lettuces from the garden completed the year before. Produce from the garden was later sold to help the Settlement, although the project disappears from the Settlement's records shortly after 1983. Although only short-lived, the Improvement Scheme was valuable while it lasted, enabling the Settlement to undertake much needed renovation work on its own buildings and harnessing the skills of local unemployed people to improve the appearance of the neighbourhood.

FANS and the Area Caretaker

Around the same time that the Improvement Scheme disappears from the Settlement's records, a number of new projects were beginning to take shape. The Friends and Neighbours Scheme (FANS) was a group of 20 or so volunteers from the west area of Newtown in three tower blocks – James House, Sadler House and Lloyd House. These volunteers sought to break down the isolation of the tower blocks, visiting older tenants, cleaning and shopping for those unable to leave their flats and organising social events. After a sustained fundraising

The Area Caretaker.

campaign, the group was able to obtain its own community flat at James House, building on the model already laid down by the Settlement at Mosborough Crescent. A second project set up around the same time was the pilot Salvage Scheme which hired a local unemployed person on a part-time basis to collect large items of rubbish for disposal. Although the initiative folded when funding ran out, it laid the foundations for the appointment of a local person as an Area Caretaker to carry out home repairs in the St. George's area of Newtown. Funded by the Inner City Partnership and the Housing Department, the Caretaker dealt with issues such as broken locks, burst pipes or faulty tap washers. Such was the success of the scheme that the Settlement was able to withdraw its involvement in 1988-89, leaving the Local Authority to take on the Area Caretaker's post.

DARIUS and the Centre for Urban Ecology

Although the Settlement's prime concern was with contemporary housing and community issues, several of its projects at this time also had something of an environmental focus. This was certainly the case with regard to initiatives such as the Site Improvement or Salvage schemes, and was also true of two new ventures pioneered around the same time. In the late 1970s, the Settlement devised 'DARIUS' (Demonstration and Resources in Inner Urban Schemes). Inspired by the growth of hydrophonics in the United Sates, this initiative sought to use the Settlement's grounds to demonstrate ideas for alternative land use and technologies in the inner city. A key aim was to establish a 'hydroponicum' to grow food in Newtown in glass structures using nutrient-fed water, thereby helping local people to become more self-sufficient (Rimmer, 1980). With funding not forthcoming, the scheme was abandoned and attention turned temporarily to the Site Improvement project instead. However, the Settlement's concern with environmental issues was to re-emerge in 1984 with the creation of the Centre for Urban Ecology (CUE). Funded by the Inner City Partnership project, CUE was designed to improve wasteland areas and to provide education and advice on the urban environment:

> "The Birmingham Settlement Centre for Urban Ecology was set up to provide an advice service and demonstration centre on matters of urban landscape improvement. It helps promote and focus local initiatives on creating Nature areas, allotments, urban woodland and coppice, or indeed, any landscape solution which might be ecologically and socially beneficial. At the same time there is a strong educational function aiming to raise people's awareness of the processes underlying life in the city."
>
> (Dawe and Kunz, 1986, p.10)

To provide practical examples of what could be achieved, CUE planted an organic allotment at the Settlement, together with a series of gardens for insects, birds and butterflies. A roof garden was also created on top of the Settlement's buildings and a booklet produced to publicise the project's work (Dawe and Kunz, 1986).

In addition to this, CUE made improvements to local schools, to Birmingham parks and to a derelict area on Leonard Street in Lozells. A survey of wasteland and derelict areas was also conducted and presented to Birmingham City Council with recommendations for practical measures to improve the environment. As its reputation spread, the Centre for Urban Ecology began to develop into a promising commercial enterprise, selling plants and seeds, producing written material on the urban environment and preparing a national 'Communities in Action' pack for local environmental improvements. Funding from the European Commission also enabled the Centre to pilot environmental counselling projects in Newtown and Bournville, highlighting the links between everyday household activities and environmental quality with regard to issues such as recycling, energy conservation and gardening without chemicals. A series of 'Planaway Days' were also inaugurated in West Newtown, with a mobile exhibition bus travelling round the area to encourage resident involvement in planning decisions affecting their environment. Further publications, training material and environmental projects followed, with the Centre receiving visitors from as far afield as Denmark, France and the USA. Sadly, major cuts in funding restricted the Centre's growth and its losses proved unsustainable, culminating in its closure in 1992. By this time, however, the Settlement's environmental concerns had acquired increasingly mainstream support and many of the Centre's ideals have since been taken up as part of the 'green revolution' in the 1990s.

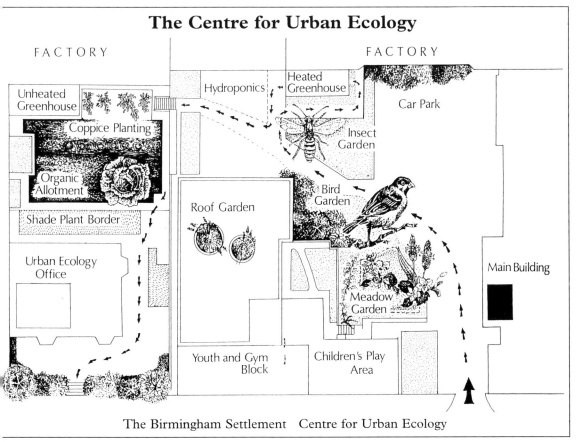

The Centre for Urban Ecology

FACTORY

FACTORY

Unheated Greenhouse

Hydroponics

Heated Greenhouse

Car Park

Coppice Planting

Insect Garden

Organic Allotment

Bird Garden

Roof Garden

Shade Plant Border

Urban Ecology Office

Main Building

Meadow Garden

Youth and Gym Block

Children's Play Area

The Birmingham Settlement   Centre for Urban Ecology

Dawe & Kunz, 1986, pp. 14-15

Crime and Community Safety

It was while the Centre for Urban Ecology was at its peak that the Settlement began to become increasingly involved in issues of community safety. This was a crucial concern at the time and its importance was later confirmed by a MORI poll carried out on behalf of Birmingham City Council:

A MORI (1992) survey of the people of Newtown found that:

- 71% were afraid of burglaries.

- 65% were frightened of muggings.

- 50% felt unsafe in the area.

- 45% said that they did not go out unless they had to.

- 40% did not feel safe in their own home.

- 34% did not like living in Newtown because of fear of crime or vandalism.

The Newtown Victim Support Scheme.

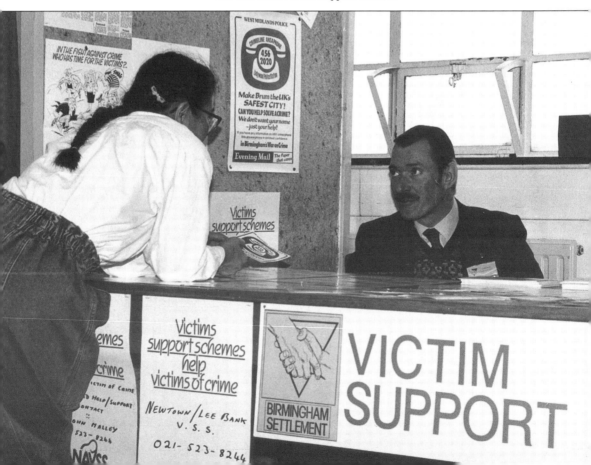

Crime then was an everyday fact of life in Newtown and local people simply did not go out if they could possibly avoid it. Often, it was possible to walk around Newtown for hours on end and hardly see a soul. In seeking to resolve some of these issues, the Birmingham Settlement was involved in developing the Newtown Victim Support Scheme to offer assistance and comfort to those who had experienced crime. Devised by the two Settlement community workers and three project leaders under the chairmanship of the rector of St. George's Church, the initiative became an independent organisation in 1987. By 1988, it was working with over 600 people in the Newtown and Lee Bank areas of the city and had developed a close working relationship with the British Transport Police, who referred every case in Britain via the Central Birmingham Victim Support Scheme (as it became known). With funding from the Home Office's Safer Cities Initiative, moreover, the Settlement was also able to launch a new Newtown Watch project in 1990. Focusing on the needs of women and the elderly, the scheme organised self-defence and safety awareness courses, developed Neighbourhood Watch Schemes and arranged for local police surgeries to make law enforcement services more accessible to local people. Although many problems remain, Newtown today is undoubtedly safer than it was ten years ago. Confidence is growing slowly and this is most clearly demonstrated by the greater visibility of local people on the streets. This is the result of many factors – not least the various regeneration initiatives which have been working in the area. However, the Settlement's role should not be forgotten in starting to grapple with the problem of crime and in making Newtown a slightly safer place to live.

Renewed Housing Problems

As the Settlement moved into the late 1980s and the early 1990s, the deterioration of the local housing stock and the fragmentation of the community were such that urgent action was required:

> "*One major problem that has come to the fore this year is the deterioration of the housing stock... Nearly all the twenty-seven Tower Blocks in South Aston need substantial renovation, not to mention the low rise housing... We estimate around thirteen million pounds is needed to put the housing in reasonable order, probably more to create a neighbourhood people will want to stay in and not move out of when they can. If you look around the neighbourhoods where Tower Blocks were built among new lower rise housing by the City in the 1963-73 period, you can see all the signs of decay. Decay resulting from too low a level of maintenance, lack of sufficient caretaking or litter control, inadequate community facilities and what we now see were poor building standards in the original construction. Rubbish collects uncleared for weeks in neglected corners, walls become graffiti boards, passageways smell of urine, people bar themselves in their home and especially the old, rarely venture out at night for fear of mugging or assault... It is time for an effort to prevent the deterioration of this valuable public housing stock into*

slums. It cannot be good economic or social policy to allow a capital asset like our public housing to deteriorate. We urge the City to see if the launch of some kind of a national initiative for a Community Housing Renovation and Improvement Programme is possible. We need to persuade Parliament to act to prevent the re-slumming of our cities and the waste of our national housing asset."

(Birmingham Settlement, 1986, p.5)

The Aston Commission and SRB

In addition to the national action it called for, the Settlement introduced its own projects to promote and support the regeneration of Newtown and the areas around it. One such initiative was the Aston Commission, set up in 1989 to investigate the problems of the neighbourhood and to make recommendations for action to improve the area and foster networks between residents, local businesses and the voluntary and public sectors. Based on the principle of partnership and the involvement of local people, the Commission undertook a resident-led survey of local issues and hazards, produced a directory of voluntary organisations working in the area and contributed to the development of the successful City Challenge bid. Such action was long overdue in Aston, an area which had many of the same problems as other areas of the inner city, but which had previously received less attention from policy makers. With funding from the Inner City Partnership, the Commission was able to establish Focus Groups to initiate action in areas such as youth, health, housing, the environment and business and training. Developments were reported back to local people via the *Aston Express* newsletter and an Aston Investment Backers Group was set up to attract money into the local economy. Although the Commission was terminated in 1993 when its funding expired, much of its work was taken over by the City Challenge programme. In addition to this, the Commission was also successful in laying the foundations for its successor, the Aston Reinvestment Trust, which was to work with financial rather than housing and community issues (see chapter 3).

Building on the work of the Aston Commission, the Settlement has since participated in *Breaking the Cycle*, a voluntary sector partnership funded by SRB money which is seeking to build a healthy, active, culturally diverse and sustainable neighbourhood in Aston for the twenty-first century. To achieve this aim, the partnership has devised a seven-year programme which will provide training opportunities, increase the skills of local community organisations, encourage sustained economic growth and promote the involvement of residents in the future of Aston. In the process, a number of initiatives will be targeted specifically at the Bangladeshi community, one of the most deprived ethnic groups in Birmingham (Birmingham City Council, 1996b). To ensure that this regeneration scheme succeeds where previous efforts have failed, the partnership will focus on developing skills and knowledge within the local community so that the benefits of the programme will continue long after its funding has ceased.

The Newtown Regeneration Initiative

A second project designed to build a better future for local people was the Newtown Regeneration Initiative (later the Newtown South Aston Regeneration Initiative or NSARI) launched in 1992. Working in partnership with Birmingham City Council, the Settlement developed a number of services to prevent further decay in Newtown and to create lasting change by supporting resident involvement in the community. This period saw a range of initiatives, some of which are described below:

- *Newtown Housing Work* dealt with queries relating to homelessness, repair problems, evictions, rent arrears, Housing Benefit problems and neighbour disputes. Advice sessions were held at one of the Community Flats and at emergency drop-in sessions at the Settlement itself. A key aim was to enable local people to have a greater say in what happened in Newtown by establishing new tenant groups and supporting existing organisations.

- The *Visiting Scheme* recruited local volunteers to befriend and support lonely and isolated people in the Newtown and Aston areas of the city. This project, now called *Homebased Care*, has since developed into a culturally sensitive home care service with funding from Birmingham Social Services. Seeking to enable

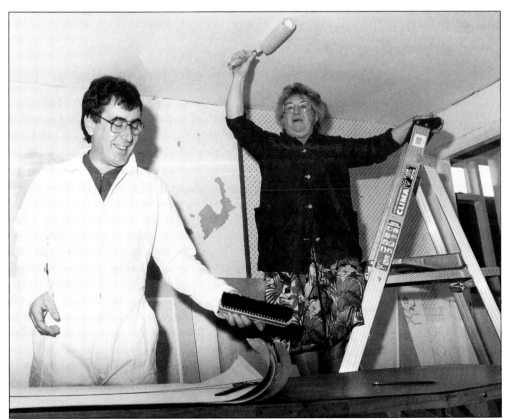

Brushstrokes, part of the Newtown Regeneration Initiative.

people to integrate themselves into mainstream society and to promote individuals' choice and independence, the scheme supports over 300 older people and those with physical disabilities or mental health problems in the community. It now runs in the evenings and at weekends, provides staff with NVQ training and works especially closely with the Afro-Caribbean community. In 1998, Homebased Care provided 450 hours of care per week, made 157 visits each week and employed 3 staff, 30 carers and 6 volunteers (Birmingham Settlement, 1998b).

• The *Secure-a-door* scheme installed door and window locks for people living in one of the 27 tower blocks or in the numerous maisonettes. It was designed to offer peace of mind to those who needed it most, such as older people, people with disabilities or lone parents. Working in conjunction with the West Midlands Fire Service, the project also began to distribute smoke alarms. Between April 1994 and July 1995, 233 Secure Door and Window Lock packages were fitted, together with 315 smoke alarms.

• *Brushstrokes* offered free painting and decorating courses and an equipment loan facility. Its aim was to help local people increase their DIY skills, improve the quality of their own internal environment and raise their self-confidence.

• The *Garden Project* helped older and disabled residents by tending their gardens. In 1995, some 35 gardens were restored to order and 34 were maintained on an ongoing basis.

Unfortunately for the Settlement, these projects were rapidly overtaken by the activities of the new City Challenge programme and a number of the City Council representatives initially involved in NSARI were redeployed to the latter scheme. While some of the NSARI projects were subsumed into City Challenge, the majority simply ceased to operate. The one major exception was Homebased Care, which continues to function and has since developed an excellent reputation for its culturally sensitive services.

Firment

At the same time as these projects were making contributions to improving the housing stock and community spirit of Newtown, a series of more fundamental and far-reaching initiatives was starting to take shape. In 1994, the Birmingham Settlement and Fircroft College established a new joint venture to build community capacity through outreach education and training. With funding from City Challenge, the Firment Project sought to empower local people to have a say in the regeneration of Newtown by building effective community organisations and by increasing the skills of individuals not otherwise involved in training. In general, the Settlement was responsible for making initial contact with individuals,

Prince Charles with members of the Firment Project.

groups and organisations to identify training needs, while Fircroft undertook the course delivery. The training provided covered topics such as equal opportunities, counselling, self-defence, group work skills and work with people. More recently, the project has arranged an educational exchange with Denmark and has sought to establish educational links between the Sylheti and Mirpuri communities in Bangladesh and Birmingham.

Capacity Building

As the Firment project progressed, the desire to improve community capacity on which the initiative was based was taken forward by the creation of a Capacity Building Team in November 1997. Building on the community development and community-based training which took place in the early 1990s, the Settlement sought to introduce a new initiative to increase the confidence, information and strategic capacity of people so that they could help themselves, their families and their community to take better advantage of the opportunities available to them. Based at the Aston Council House, the project targeted members of ethnic minorities, young people and local resident groups, developing specific programmes for Bangladeshi women, Asian young men and Asian deaf people. In 1999, the Capacity Building Team is operating according to a multi-functional approach, working in partnership with Fircroft and the Aston Ward Team to encourage participation in local social, economic and environmental regeneration.

RAIL and Cicero

Two further projects concerned with encouraging local people to take a more active part in the decisions which affect their lives and communities were set up in the last couple of years. The first of these, the Residents Association Information Link (RAIL), seeks to empower residents to be able to influence local policy effectively through existing mechanisms and to identify specific training needs not addressed by agencies locally. At a wider level, Community Initiatives in Citizen Education Regionally Organised (CICERO) was established to give people with very little access to power in their daily lives a voice in national and European politics. Birmingham was chosen as one of seven areas of Britain to pilot this project and, working with Fircroft College, the Settlement has supported local young people to learn about policy-making and to develop community organisations to inform this process. The ultimate aim is to encourage the European Union to fund developments in the disadvantaged communities around each of the pilot projects. As part of CICERO, a group visited Brussels to meet MEPs and links have been established with similar organisations in countries such as Spain and Ireland.

The Settlement's Own Buildings

Finally, no discussion of housing issues would be complete without reference to the Settlement's own property and buildings. While a detailed description of the Settlement's housing problems is beyond the scope of this publication, a brief overview of some of the main changes sheds light on some of the hardships and disruptions faced by Settlement workers in the course of their duties. When the Settlement first acquired ownership of 316 – 320 Summer Lane, for example, extensive repairs were required to put these houses into proper sanitary and structural condition. Piecemeal alterations were to follow as the Settlement's work increased and a new Settlement Hall was opened during the First World War by the Bishop of Birmingham. Electric lights were installed in 1923 and the Settlement's houses were totally repainted and renovated in 1927-28 following a concerted fundraising campaign. After this, the next major building project came in the 1930s when the Rotary Club paid for a new Hall at Summer Lane and when the Lord Mayor opened the new Kingstanding Settlement.

Thereafter, a Building Fund was established to rebuild the entire residence (which by this time was over 120 years old and very costly to maintain) and to construct a new Junior Block (which was duly completed and opened in 1940). An adjacent building was acquired in 1942 to expand the work of the Kingstanding Settlement and extensive repairs were carried out in Summer Lane in 1948. By this stage, the Summer Lane buildings were in a poor state of repair and the roof was leaking badly. Resolving this problem cost well over £5,000, but added an estimated 25 years to the predicted life expectancy of the buildings concerned and was ready in time for the Settlement to celebrate its jubilee in 1949. After this, housing issues came somewhat to the fore in the late 1950s when the

Sir Austen Chamberlain walking in procession to open the Rotary Hall at the Birmingham Settlement. Behind is Mr. Walter Higgs, President of the Rotary Club.

redevelopment of Newtown and the rapid deterioration of the residence forced the committee to consider relocation to different and less costly premises. Once the decision was taken to stay in Summer Lane, however, some form of rebuilding was inevitable, and the Settlement Hall was demolished in 1961 to make way for an extended youth block. Two years later the residence was demolished and replaced with a three-storey building next to the Rotary Hall with help from the Young Friends International Work Camps.

Work was also undertaken in Kingstanding, but the cost of maintaining the buildings there proved so prohibitive that the Settlement was forced to cut its losses, disposing of the premises to the Local Authority in 1974. Further alterations have been carried out more recently, but the examples above are sufficient to demonstrate the fact that the Settlement's buildings have been an almost constant source of worry and expense, making its work all the more demanding. That an organisation which has done so much to support local people with their housing problems should itself experience so many difficulties in this area is a testimony to the Settlement's commitment to overcoming its own obstacles in order to serve the needs of others.

The Boys' Club Room erected at the Birmingham Settlement by the Rotary Club.

Summary

Throughout the last hundred years, housing and community development have been one of the most crucial aspects of the Settlement's work. While housing has been a key issue across Birmingham as a whole, it has been particularly important in areas such as Newtown, where whole neighbourhoods have been destroyed and redeveloped to replace inadequate back-to-back housing with newer yet equally inadequate tower blocks. During this time, there has been a remarkable continuity in the Settlement's work, with an almost constant emphasis on accurate knowledge about local conditions, networks with other agencies, resident involvement, self-help and community capacity building. However, there has also been significant change, with the Settlement having to respond to the demolition of the community around it and the ongoing social problems that this created. In the process, the Settlement has been a major source of innovation, pioneering a number of new and successful projects and supporting several more initiatives to become independent agencies in their own right. That the

Settlement has been able to achieve so much in spite of its own housing difficulties is all the more to its credit. Overall, numerous problems remain in inner city areas such as Newtown and the millions of pounds invested under the various regeneration programmes seem only to have scratched the surface. However, there is light at the end of the tunnel, and agencies such as the Birmingham Settlement which work not only to improve physical conditions but also to empower local people, may well hold the key to future success.

Chapter 7:

'Idleness' – employment and recreation

Meaningful employment and meaningful recreation are central to wellbeing, yet are frequently denied to those in poverty. This chapter outlines the Settlement's work with regard to these issues, examining:

- Employment trends in Birmingham and Newtown.
- The effects of unemployment.
- Settlement projects concerned with unemployment. These include work with women and members of minority ethnic communities, as well as the provision of training and child care facilities.
- The lack of leisure opportunities in inner city areas such as Newtown.
- Recreational Settlement projects such as clubwork, play schemes, organised holidays and initiatives concerning the arts.

Beveridge's final *giant*, 'idleness', covers a multitude of sins and demands a range of responses. As a result, this chapter is divided into two sections, the first dealing with employment and the second with recreation. In particular, it is interesting to note how the Settlement's work in these areas has changed over the last hundred years, shifting from the recreational focus of the early and middle years of the century to one which, in the late 1990s, is very much concerned with overcoming the barriers to employment.

A. Employment

Although poverty has traditionally been seen as the result of individual failings, there is now an increasing recognition that it is not just a personal issue, but the product of social and economic factors frequently beyond the control of the individual (Becker and MacPherson, 1988). A classic example is unemployment, which remains a major cause of poverty today and has a massive impact on the lives of the people who experience it.

The effects of unemployment

- **Financial effects** – people without paid work have less money on which to survive.

- **Social effects** – people facing unemployment report a loss of identity and purpose. Reduced incomes also prevent participation in many leisure activities.

- **Psychological effects** – lack of employment can create feelings of disorientation, distress, anxiety and apathy.

- **Health effects** – many of the factors above can impact upon mental health, leading to depression and even suicide attempts. Money is also a major health resource denied to the unemployed.

(Haralambos and Holborn, 1990)

Of course, unemployment does not affect all sections of the population equally and there is significant evidence to suggest that some groups find themselves not only out of work, but also unable to regain employment due to discriminatory attitudes and practices within society. This is particularly true of young people, women, members of ethnic minorities and older people (Blackburn, 1991; Haralambos and Holborn, 1990). For all these reasons, unemployment is an issue to which agencies working with the effects of poverty must respond if their contribution is to be effective.

Local Trends

In the West Midlands, employment issues have come to the fore at various stages over the last hundred years. Birmingham has a long-established reputation as a city of a thousand trades and its industrial diversity has tended to protect it from the worst ravages of unemployment. In nineteenth century Summer Lane, for example, local people were involved in occupations such as carpentry, printing, badge making, bookselling, bricklaying, painting, plumbing, hairdressing, brewing and shoemaking (Simon, 1993). By the 1930s, it was estimated that there were at least 12,000 small firms across Birmingham employing less than 100 workers apiece (Bournville Village Trust, 1941), and this variety enabled people to find alternative work if one particular trade was doing badly:

"Trades come and go, small arms succeed cutlery, buttons succeed nails, cycles succeed watches... but the tradition of handicraft and the skilful manipulation of material goes on from generation to generation. The multitude of trades makes it more possible than in most places to dovetail into one another, so that the town rarely suffers from general unemployment."

(Muirhead, 1912)

Despite this, Birmingham's prosperity has nevertheless been heavily dependent on the manufacturing industry and its fortunes have suffered as a result of the long-term decline of this sector of the economy (Birmingham Settlement, 1986). In addition, employment trends in Britain have fluctuated considerably over the last century and no large urban area has been free from job scarcity, insecurity or loss during periods of economic downturn. In Birmingham, as elsewhere, unemployment has been highest during periods of international economic recession in the 1920s, 1930s, 1970s and 1980s. Of these, the latter two periods were particularly damaging, resulting in large-scale redundancy and a growth in long-term unemployment in certain areas of the city. By the mid-1980s, Birmingham's inner wards had male unemployment rates of between 45 and 55 per cent, with half of those out of work having been so for a year or more (Birmingham Settlement, 1985, 1986). Such a situation introduced many thousands of people to levels of poverty which they previously would have found difficult to imagine, causing untold financial, emotional and psychological damage. Unemployment then was a major social issue and one which agencies such as the Birmingham Settlement could not afford to overlook.

The Settlement's Response

In the early years of the twentieth century, the Settlement's response to unemployment was focused mainly on the distribution of financial aid to those in need (see chapter 3). While the Settlement's annual reports and its contributions to *Women Workers* occasionally contained appeals for paid positions to be found for those without work, this was rare and did not represent a large-scale or comprehensive solution to the issue of employment. In the main, the Settlement confined itself to working with the Charity Organisation Society and paying sums of money to 'special cases'. As has already been mentioned, this did not entail ongoing support, but one-off payments to help those facing temporary difficulties to re-establish their independence (see chapter 3). Often, this was related to helping someone gain employment, whether it be by purchasing the clothes needed for an individual to enter occupations such as domestic service or the navy, or by making an interim payment to tide a new employee over until they received their first wages. Useful though this must have been to the individuals concerned, however, it did no more than scratch the surface of what was a large and intractable problem.

After-care

After this initial period of relative inaction, the first major Settlement project to work with unemployment issues began to develop. From 1900 onwards, Settlement workers had started to supervise the welfare of a small number of young people who had recently left special schools (a type of work known as "after-care"). Visiting continued on a piecemeal basis until 1908 when a Registry and Information

Bureau (later called the Employment Committee and finally the After-Care Committee) was established to bridge the gap between school and employment. In its first nine months, the bureau received the names of 190 young women seeking work as they left school, but had only 30 employers with whom to match them. Trade at this time was slack and the majority of opportunities were in domestic service, for which the Settlement provided training and loaned money for clothes. As the project developed, it became more sophisticated, visiting girls from three local schools in their last term and working with their parents to discuss the various types of trade available and emphasise the importance of further training. A key aim was to encourage young people to enter skilled occupations rather than dead-end jobs and to ensure that school leavers had access to leisure activities in their spare time. To ensure that this aim was being met, those girls who were successfully placed in employment remained in touch with the Settlement and their progress was monitored.

In 1910, the Education (Choice of Employment) Act enabled local authorities to engage in after-care work, and in 1911 a Central Care Committee was established in Birmingham. In the same year, the Settlement's after-care project merged with this body, although the Settlement continued to be responsible for visiting in the Summer Lane area. A Juvenile Labour Exchange also met at the Settlement to provide advice to parents and children, although it was little used due to the high demand for juvenile workers at this time. By 1915, the Settlement had some 1,000 young women on its books and was visiting final year pupils in three local schools. Home visits, parents' meetings and leavers' parties were all used to develop friendly relations and the practical work of visiting was carried out by the Settlement's students under a committee of local headteachers, clergy and others chaired by the Settlement's warden. A fourth school was added in the 1920s, although the Settlement soon decided to focus the attention of its own students solely on Summer Lane School, leaving voluntary helpers to visit the other three schools. In this way it was hoped to spend more time and care with each individual person. Unfortunately, the committee's work was severely restricted by a lack of volunteers, and by the 1930s it was achieving little more than recruiting young people for the Settlement's clubs (Rimmer, 1980).

In addition to its ongoing after-care work, the Settlement became involved in two short-term and time-limited projects designed to respond to a temporary increase in unemployment in the immediate post-war period. In 1919, the Settlement granted use of its Hall to the Education Committee for an unemployment centre for young women discharged from the munition works. The centre was open from January to June and was run by a former Settlement student. Two years later, the Settlement lent the Hall and another room to the same committee, this time for an unemployment school for the young men of the area. A total of 30 boys attended the school, which ran for two months and taught English, hygiene and civics as well as devoting a good deal of time to organised games. The classes were organised by two teachers previously engaged in continuation schools, and the Settlement was pleased with the impact this initiative had on the local community. As levels of unemployment fell, however, such measures were no longer required and the Settlement turned its attention elsewhere.

Full Employment and Consensus Politics - 'You've never had it so good'

Following the gradual demise of the Settlement's after-care work, there is a large gap in the Settlement's history when there were no major employment-related projects at all. Settlement workers were briefly involved in interviewing married women for the Employment Exchange in 1942 and in an experimental co-operative workshop for older men in the early 1960s, but there was no concerted action against unemployment until the 1980s and 1990s. This middle period of the twentieth century was, after all, a time of consensus politics when full employment was the goal of both major political parties. People had "never had it so good" according to Harold Macmillan, and the problems of unemployment could not have been further from people's minds. It was not until the mid-1970s that this stability was eventually destroyed, with industrial and economic crises looming large on the horizon. Unemployment then was an ever-present reality and an issue that could no longer be ignored.

The Re-emergence of Unemployment

The first indication that the Settlement's lack of attention to employment issues might change came in 1979 with the introduction of a work experience programme for young unemployed people organised through the Manpower Services Commission. The scheme quickly disappears from the Settlement's records, although the first trainee to complete the programme was taken on by the Settlement as a receptionist shortly afterwards. However, the following year saw a radical reversal of previous policy and an acknowledgement that unemployment was a problem with which the Settlement must engage. From this time onwards, employment issues have been a central feature of the Birmingham Settlement's work:

> *"We are increasingly bombarded by the statistics of unemployment. Redundancies and lay-offs are announced weekly. The pundits tell us that we are now entering an unprecedented situation and that it will perhaps get worse with no prospect of ever getting better. There is obviously a real problem. There is another and more insidious problem that is often not seen. These unemployment statistics are about people and families, and they represent waste and suffering. The over-40's are particularly badly hit. Many of them are facing unemployment for the first time, and they find it a disturbing experience. A loss of confidence is followed by depression, and they talk of feeling ashamed and even dirty."*

(Birmingham Settlement, 1980, p.10)

Job Change

In response to this situation, the Settlement set up a new initiative in 1979. Working with Birmingham Polytechnic, the Job Change Project was a unit based at the Camp Hill Centre for unemployed men and women over the age of 40. Here, unemployed people could obtain information about re-training opportunities and welfare rights, receive individual counselling, explore the benefits of self-employment or voluntary work and increase their interview and self-presentation skills. Office equipment, telephones and daily newspapers were also provided and support was offered in drawing up career histories and completing application forms. The demand for this service was extremely high from the very beginning and the Settlement found itself receiving over 500 new applicants each year. 'Satellite' groups soon sprang up in other areas of the city, meeting independently and making use of the project's resources whenever appropriate. In this way it was possible to develop networks of similar employment schemes across Birmingham and throughout the country, with Job Change outposts in towns such as Coventry, Dudley and Wolverhampton. Close links were also established with the County Council's Economic Development Unit and funding from the Inner City Partnership guaranteed the project's existence up until 1989. In light of the national attention which has recently been focused on the problems of unemployment among middle-aged and older people (Age Concern, 1998; Department for Education and Employment, 1998), the Job Change Project should be seen as a major innovation many years ahead of its time.

SEAN

As the manufacturing industries continued to decline in the Midlands, the number of people facing long-term unemployment (and its consequent loss of income and self-esteem) increased dramatically. By 1987, the Job Change project was receiving 6,000 visits by unemployed people a year and began to extend its work into Sutton Coldfield through the SEAN (Sutton Employment Action Network) initiative. Working in partnership with the Sutton Citizens' Advice Bureau, SEAN provided a similar service to the Job Change Project, while at the same time recognising that unemployed people in such an affluent area were often more isolated than elsewhere. Unfortunately for the Settlement, both projects were hard hit by a combination of funding difficulties and a turnover of staff and were forced to close in the late 1980s. Despite this, the Settlement's expertise in this field was not wasted, with energy being channelled into a series of new employment projects.

Women's Job Change and Training

By 1982, concern at the Settlement was mounting that the Job Change Project was achieving more success with men than it was with women:

"Women tend to hold back from seeking support in their quest for work, feeling often that they should not be asking for work while there are so many men unemployed. It has always proved difficult to help them realise that, even in the absence of jobs, there is work to be done and jobs to be made."

(Birmingham Settlement, 1984, p.12)

To resolve this problem, the Settlement set up a Women's project with funding from the Equal Opportunities Commission. This was initially very similar to the Job Change Project, but soon began to develop its own priorities and ways of working. As the initiative progressed, it became apparent that the women who

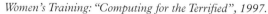

Women's Training: "Computing for the Terrified", 1997.

attended were interested in two distinct things. Firstly, there were those who sought to develop existing skills into money-making activities by working with other people in a similar situation to themselves. A good example of this was the 'C Team', a group which provided catering, clerical, cleaning and caring services on a commercial basis. By 1986, the C Team was preparing food for functions of 100 people, providing not only a much-needed part-time income to its members, but also a forum conducive to mutual support and skills development. Secondly, there were those who were more interested in expanding their social networks. These women enjoyed the informality and friendliness of the Women's project, using it as a place where they could go to discuss their problems in a supportive environment and to overcome the isolation which unemployment engendered. Both these groups of people were catered for at the Settlement and the steady increase in the number of referrals is testimony to the project's popularity.

In 1985, the Women's project and Birmingham Polytechnic organised a series of six consultation days on the issues facing women returning to work. The results of these consultations were not only disseminated through the Settlement's publications, but also fed back into the Women's Job Change in order to make the service more effective. Working once again with Birmingham Polytechnic, the Settlement began a Women and Information Technology course, combining computer skills with assertiveness training in a six-week programme. Well women sessions were also held and an 'under 5's' group was established to provide creche facilities for women with children. Funding from the City Council's Economic Development Unit enabled the project to survive the financial difficulties of the late 1980s, paving the way for a major expansion of the project's work in the 1990s.

As Women's Job Change has progressed, it has developed a separate Training Programme to increase the skill levels and qualifications of unemployed women and to create new employment and training opportunities. Whereas the Job Change project concentrates on intensive one-to-one support, Women's Training offers a supportive learning environment in which women can develop confidence and increase their skills through a range of vocational courses. After an initial assessment, the Settlement provides quality training to enable participants to progress into skilled jobs and to move from a basic to a more advanced level of study. Working closely together, the two projects now provide a combination of personal, career, group and employment support services as well as access to pre-vocational and vocational training courses. From 'black' women's assertiveness to basic computing and from women returners to business studies, the Women's Job Change and the Women's Training Programme offer assistance and training to a wide range of women. These include those who have left school with no qualifications, women who have been out of a learning environment for a long time, single parents with young children, members of ethnic minorities and women suffering from domestic violence or mental health problems. In 1998 alone, 150 women gained new skills and qualifications, with 75 per cent progressing into employment or further training (Birmingham Settlement, 1998b).

Women's Job Change and Training

"Janet Gunter, a mother of two, decided in 1991 to retrain for work after concentrating on her family for many years. She successfully completed a Return to the Office Course with Women's Job Change, gaining a clutch of qualifications in Business Administration and New Technology. Spurred on by this success Janet proceeded to do a Business Studies Access Course. Her numeracy skills became very apparent and, filled with extra confidence, Janet applied for a place at the University of Central England to do a BA Hons. Degree in Accountancy. Janet recently heard that she had won a place for the next course."

(Birmingham Settlement, 1993, p.14)

Associated Resources

A second initiative to arise out of the Job Change Project was Associated Resources. This was set up in 1981 when white collar members of the Job Change Project, many of them former managers and professionals, began to offer their knowledge and experience to the small business community. These people gave their time freely, with the nominal fee which they charged being reinvested in the project. Sponsored by the West Midlands County Council, Associated Resources became involved in around 36 businesses during the course of a year's work, undertaking a variety of projects. Often, these fell into three main categories:

● Small companies needing temporary specialist help to overcome a particular problem or carry out a one-off piece of work. Examples include the conversion of manual business control systems to new technology or the up-dating of salary scales through job evaluation.

● Feasibility studies and ongoing monitoring of proposed new co-operatives funded by the West Midlands County Council.

● Support to would-be entrepreneurs through specialist advice, practical help, market research and assistance with the development of business ideas. This section of the project found that particular groups of people faced more difficulties and prejudices than others. These included the young, women, older people and members of ethnic minorities.

In many ways, this was a new way of working, harnessing the talents of skilled but unemployed people to encourage others in a similar situation to themselves to transform their business ideas into reality.

CEBD Ltd.

In 1984, the Settlement facilitated the foundation of a new employment project with the opening of a 12,500 square foot Centre for Community Enterprise and Business Development (CEBD Ltd.) in Hockley Street. Supported by the County Council's Economic Development Unit, CEBD was an independent company designed to offer training opportunities in technical and business skills, together with workshop space and individual support in order to develop and market business ideas. As with previous initiatives, this is a classic example of the way in which projects founded by the Settlement can develop into separate organisations which leave their creator and begin to make their own way independent of the Settlement.

Always a separate company, CEBD later relocated to Southside on the Ladypool Road, Sparkhill, where it became known as the Community Enterprise Centre (CEC) and focused primarily on one-to-one counselling and business start-up. Despite this, the name CEBD was later revived as a commercial arm of CEC and, together with a second company, Southside Training, sought to supplement CEC's grant funding through training and consultancy work. These companies later disbanded due to funding problems, although several members of staff remained together and went on to form a new agency: Birmingham Enterprise Limited. City-wide in its remit, Birmingham Enterprise claims to see more clients than any similar agency in Birmingham and specialises in business start-up, ongoing support for new businesses and encouraging workers in the shadow economy to form legal businesses.

CEBD Ltd., Hockley.

Facilitating Employment

As the Settlement began to develop its expertise with regard to employment issues, it was also able to experiment with a number of new and much-needed initiatives. During the mid-1980s it was involved in a range of small-scale schemes, encouraging unemployed people to make use of their skills through voluntary work and setting up an exchange system whereby the unemployed could trade skills and services with each other on the basis of barter rather than money. Training schemes were also run in conjunction with the Manpower Services Commission and two six-day programmes in project management and development were piloted in Lancashire and West Yorkshire to introduce the Settlement's innovative approaches to staff in employment agencies in these areas. The Settlement also became increasingly involved in job creation, supporting unemployed people to establish new initiatives. Probably the biggest success was Evergreen Leisure Products, a business comprising six previously unemployed members of the Job Change Project which manufactured labour-saving garden tools for sale at home and abroad. Less extravagant and more typical examples included projects concerned with garden fencing and landscaping, steam-cleaning heavy goods vehicles, an executive courier service, print framing, export packing, garden summer-house construction and production rabbit-breeding.

BURN and National Development

Before long, the Settlement found itself at the forefront of a movement which was rapidly gaining momentum at a local and national level. In 1981, the Settlement had sponsored a workshop for representatives from over 50 employment initiatives. As a result of this, the need was identified for a national information network through which experience could be shared and new initiatives developed with relevant advice and information from those with expertise in that particular area. It was also recognised that unemployed people could achieve more collectively than individually and needed a credible voice with which to influence policy-making. The outcome of these discussions was the British Unemployment Resource Network (BURN), set up with funding from the Voluntary Services Unit of the Home Office. In particular, BURN provided three main services:

- A two-monthly newsletter to keep people in touch with the experience and ideas of other groups across the country.

- Regional workshops to stimulate the growth of strong local networks of groups.

- Practical information through the publication of a 'start-up kit', the BURN Directory on how to set up a self-help employment group and a listing of existing projects.

This work was greatly facilitated by the appointment in 1983 of a national development worker, whose job it was to travel round the country to assist the development of the various self-help groups in existence. Typical problems included the need for a meeting place, funding and access to the experience and good practice of similar organisations, although the development worker also found himself increasingly involved in semi-rural communities where there were no established support networks. Based at the Settlement, the development worker visited projects throughout Britain, introducing the pioneering methods of the Job Change Project to areas with less well developed employment support services. By 1989, work was being undertaken with over 120 groups across England and Wales, almost half of whom were primarily concerned with how to attract funding. Increasing interest from women's groups also led to the creation of special projects for women, and there was considerable demand for help in developing services such as tool libraries, bulk buy clubs and credit unions. However, this success was not to be sustained, and references to the Settlement's national development work disappear from its records in the late 1980s, presumably another victim of the funding difficulties experienced at the time (see chapter 3).

The Job Preparation Club

As the Settlement moved into the 1990s, unemployment continued to be an important issue in Birmingham in general and in Newtown in particular. In 1991, a weekly Job Preparation Club was set up at the Newtown Community Centre to provide practical help in seeking work. Services included support

The Job Preparation Club, 1997.

with curriculum vitaes and interview preparation as well as free access to newspapers, journals, vacancy notice boards, telephones, postage and envelopes. Working with the City Challenge Employment Team and Joblink, in-house training was organised with companies such as LDV Vans and Johnsons Controls, with members guaranteed an interview on successful completion. Other participants either set up their own businesses, gained access to further education, undertook further training through the Settlement or were even employed by the Settlement itself. The project soon moved to Reynolds House, but its membership continued to grow. By 1995, the Job Preparation Club was working with 171 people, 36 of whom gained employment in the course of the year. Just as important as actually getting a job, however, was the self-esteem and dignity which the Settlement was able to encourage:

The Job Preparation Club

"I've just got an interview... I wouldn't have got that far without the [Job Preparation] Club."

"You're not pushed into taking any old low paid job... or training which does not meet your needs or leaves you worse off."

"You're treated as an adult... a real person."

"You get treated like a person... not just a statistic."

(Birmingham Settlement, 1994, p.10)

Sustainable Strength

In 1995-96, the Settlement was able to develop new expertise in the field of women's self-employment through a new venture. Supported by the Aga Khan Foundation, the Barrow Cadbury Trust and the Esmee Fairbairn Charitable Trust, the Settlement established the Sustainable Strength project to provide training, advice and practical support to groups of women entering self-employment. The scheme was piloted in two areas, one in Newtown and the other in Ladywood, with the outcomes being evaluated by an independent researcher. While both positive and negative views emerged, the evaluation found that the project was important in providing practical support, helping participants to improve their confidence and self-image and encouraging the development of supportive social networks (Lowndes, 1997).

As the project progressed, it began to focus more on the Bangladeshi community in Aston, founding an Asian Women's Co-operative Development

Sustainable Strength, 1998.

Project. Building on research carried out by the Settlement into the employment opportunities available to Asian women, this initiative seeks to provide training for Asian women and to encourage their participation in co-operative groups. In 1998 alone, the project helped to develop some 26 personal training plans for women from ethnic minorities, incorporating issues ranging from English classes and driving lessons to management training for the self-employed. In the course of this work it was necessary to engage with members' families, taking time to ensure that they understood and supported their wives, daughters and daughter-in-laws in exploring employment opportunities. In the past year, Sustainable Strength has worked with 8 women involved in setting up a textile co-operative, 13 women attending child care training, 13 women undertaking teacher training and 20 women completing English courses for speakers of other languages (Birmingham Settlement, 1998b). It has also contributed to a report on the restrictions which benefit legislation imposes on women seeking economic independence, shared good practice with similar projects throughout Britain and established a Woman's Support Network to provide successful role models of women actively contributing to the regeneration of their communities.

Interworks

One of the Settlement's newest employment-related initiatives is the Interworks Project (also known as the Intermediate Labour Market programme or ILM). Based on the premise that it is easier to find a job if you are already in employment, this scheme was set up in 1998 to provide temporary jobs for local people unemployed for a long time. Working in partnership with small businesses, community groups and voluntary organisations, Interworks offers training, personal development plans and support in jobseeking. In its first six months, the project trained and secured permanent jobs for 14 people, with a 100 per cent success rate. Although the scheme is too new to evaluate in detail, its initial achievements are very impressive and it is clearly appreciated by participants:

> "I had been unemployed since 1991, I was depressed and felt trapped. Now I have a job I enjoy, friends at work and I can buy things for my son – now we have a future."
>
> (Sarah, quoted Birmingham Settlement, 1998b, p.5)

Following these initial successes, additional funding has been secured to ensure that the ILM project can continue until at least June 2000 and there is every indication that the initiative will continue to expand. To date, 62 people have participated in the programme, 35 per cent of whom are expected to gain employment within their placement organisations with the remainder seeking employment in the open labour market (Spencer, 1999).

New Deal

The most recent of the Settlement's employment projects concerns the Welfare to Work programme introduced by the New Labour government. Focusing initially on young unemployed people, this scheme offers training and work experience through state subsidies paid to employers and other providers, some of whom are voluntary sector organisations. As part of this 'New Deal' (as it has become known), the Birmingham Settlement provides work placements and training in the voluntary sector for younger longer term unemployed people. With the choice of over 100 placements in more than 20 voluntary sector organisations, participants work according to an individually tailored training plan and can also access job search support, employment guidance, money advice and training needs analysis. Between September 1998 and April 1999, the Settlement has recruited 52 people to its programme, and early indications are that it is outperforming other voluntary organisations (Spencer, 1999).

Child Care

Last but not least, the Settlement's work with women's unemployment has been greatly facilitated by the availability of a range of ancillary support services. For

The Out of School Club, 1997.

many women seeking to enter paid work, the greatest barrier is often not that of a lack of skills or even of discrimination in employment, but that of inadequate child care facilities. This was particularly the case in Newtown, where many of the women with whom the Settlement worked were single mothers and the only potential source of income for their families. For this reason, the Settlement's various child care projects have been an essential feature in enabling many women to undertake training and to gain employment. The first of these, the Out of School Club, was established in 1978 to look after the children of working mothers before and after school and during holidays. Commencing with some 15 children, the project had doubled in size by 1984 and began to build up a waiting list. Activities ranged from painting, sewing, cookery or craftwork to swimming, skating or day-trips.

Further children's clubs were added in the early 1990s and a creche, mobile creche and day nursery were introduced to cater for all age ranges. The latter, in particular, opened by the late John Smith M.P. on Valentine's Day 1994, was a direct link to the Settlement's past, creating direct parallels with the Kindergarten and Nursery which met at Summer Lane in the early part of the twentieth century (see chapter 5). By the mid-1990s, the Settlement had a major National Quality Standard Award under its belt, was running a holiday and several sports clubs and had supported local women to become involved in setting up a child care business. These projects are now a much-needed source of recreation for the children involved, but, more importantly, offer the safe and affordable child care required for local women to re-enter the job market. It would not be putting it too strongly to suggest that the Settlement's children's services are now the lynchpin of its work with women, undertaking and making possible a range of employment projects.

Child care at the Settlement.

B. Recreation

While gaining employment is a crucial stepping stone on the way to overcoming poverty, it is not in itself a complete solution to the *giant* of 'idleness.' Although those in paid work may expect to spend perhaps eight hours a day at their place of employment, this leaves a similar proportion of the waking day unaccounted for. This is the time that many people choose to fill with recreational activities, whether it be through social contact, sport, music, drama or a whole host of other pastimes. This may sometimes seem superfluous, but meaningful recreation is not a luxury. Often it is the simple things in life – a trip out or some other form of entertainment – that make life worth living and seem more bearable. Without recreation, the world would be a sadder, duller and less stimulating place. Yet, it is precisely this release from the monotony of daily living that is denied to people in poverty, and it is precisely such people that need it the most.

Local Trends

Recreational opportunities for people in inner city areas such as Newtown or on pre-war estates such as Kingstanding have traditionally been all but non-existent. That this was true in Summer Lane was demonstrated as early as the 1920s, when a recreational survey conducted by the Settlement found that local facilities were totally inadequate when compared with the density of population. This was particularly the case for children and young people, who had nowhere to go and nothing to do, doing their best to occupy themselves and make their own entertainment:

> *"The streets were the playgrounds; there was nowhere else to go... The street could be a cricket or football pitch, a poor man's tennis court, an athletic track, and provided space for hopscotch beds, a stage for dancers and acrobats and play actors. Games like marbles in the gutter, fag cards across the pavement, communal skipping, with the rope stretched across from one side of the horseroad to the other, only letting both ends go to allow the occasional traffic through."*

(Mannion and Mannion, 1985, p.40)

There were occasional trips to some of the larger parks or to the Lickey Hills, but the main problem with the inner city was the lack of open space. In 1938, there was less than three-quarters of an acre of open space per 1,000 inhabitants in the 14 innermost wards of the city, an area which contained two-fifths of the population of Birmingham. The figure recommended by the National Playing Field Association was at this time six acres of open space for playing fields alone, quite apart from parks and other areas of greenery required by those people who did not play sport (Briggs, 1952). For older youths and adults, the situation was

All dressed up but nowhere to go: a lack of recreational opportunities in the inner city, 1967.

little better. While the cinema, the theatre and the dance halls were popular with those who could afford them, the main social outlet in Summer Lane was through one of the many public houses, and the excessive consumption of alcohol was a major problem (see chapter 4). Over in Kingstanding, there was a major lack of social amenities, prompting the Settlement to open a branch there for previous members who had moved away and were unable to travel back to Summer Lane. The dearth of leisure facilities was recognised immediately, and became a major part of the Settlement's work on the estate:

> "It is not necessary in these days to stress the needs of the new housing areas. There is endless scope for Settlement work in Kingstanding and though much has been done in the last few years to improve conditions on the estate, there is still a great shortage of social amenities especially for children and young people. In view of what is being done by... other bodies, the Settlement has so far confined its work mainly to an attempt to provide for the leisure time of some of these thousands of boys and girls who so often have nothing to do and nowhere to go when they come home from school or work."

(Birmingham Settlement, 1934, p.47)

Even after the redevelopment of Newtown and the closure of the Kingstanding Settlement, a lack of recreational opportunities has remained synonymous with the inner city. In 1992, research commissioned by Birmingham City Council revealed twice as many residents (41%) dissatisfied with local leisure facilities as satisfied (22%). While specific features such as Aston Hall, the library and the Community Centre were popular, fear of crime prevented many people from accessing those services that did exist (MORI, 1992). In 1999, there have been some improvements, but the outlook remains bleak. A good example is one of the new playgrounds built as part of the City Challenge programme. While this was designed to give local families somewhere to play, it is usually too full of alienated young people or wandering alcoholics for the children to get anywhere near. Broken glass abounds and the children can do nothing more than gaze at the playground through the windows of the nearby tower block. After a century of 'progress', the need for leisure remains as acute as ever.

Recreation and the Settlement Movement

The importance of meaningful recreation for people in poverty was realised from the very beginning by people such as Samuel Barnett, the founder of the Settlement movement. In the speech at St John's, Oxford where he first proposed the idea of a Settlement, Barnett emphasised the need for recreation, both to enrich the lives of the poor and to foster a sense of community:

> *"Parties will be frequent, and whatever be the form of entertainment provided, be it books or pictures, lectures or reading, dancing or music, the guests will find that their pleasure lies in intercourse. Social pleasure is unknown to those who have no large rooms and no place for common meeting."*

(Barnett, quoted Pimlott, 1935, p.270)

Barnett was true to his word, and Toynbee Hall became renowned for its parties, guest nights, visits, games, exhibitions and concerts (Pimlott, 1935). It was this emphasis on recreation and leisure which was taken up by the Birmingham Settlement and which has characterised its work ever since.

Recreation and the Birmingham Settlement

Throughout a hundred years of work, the Birmingham Settlement has always been known for its clubs, its camps, its holidays and its activities. In 1939, for example, there were some 30 clubs at the Settlement, let alone all the other activities, events and initiatives which took place at the same time (Rimmer, 1980). Such was the Settlement's contribution to recreation, indeed, that it is impossible to describe every single project in detail. However, some of the more important schemes are outlined below to give a flavour of what life at the Settlement has been like over the last century.

Happy Evenings

In 1899, the Settlement began to organise Happy Evenings every Tuesday in the Summer Lane Board School for boys and girls alternatively. Working in conjunction with the Society for Providing Happy Evenings for Children in Board Schools, the Settlement distributed 100 tickets each week through teachers at the school. These tickets allowed children entry to a play hour, during which they were not only given access to games and toys, but were also taught how to play with them by the Settlement's helpers. This was an important project, since many of the children concerned had no toys of their own at home and were unaccustomed to spending a whole hour such as this in play. Such was its popularity that the Settlement found itself having to turn away children who had tried to gain entry without the required tickets.

From 1907, the children were also able to make use of the new play areas built by the Settlement on wasteland at the back of its buildings. With a garden, a swing and a sandpit, the Settlement was something of an oasis in the built-up and smoky environment of Summer Lane. This was truly an important resource and the Settlement made full use of it by opening it up to its own clubs, local schools, young people from the streets and nearby factory workers. Visitors found the garden and play area a "much valued privilege" (Birmingham Settlement, 1910, p.17), and the Settlement never ceased to marvel at how much pleasure such simple amenities could bring to the area. This was very much a learning experience, and the importance of play was something to which the Settlement was to return through play hours held for local children in the 1920s and the play projects of the 1970s.

Girls' Clubs

In addition to its Happy Evenings, the Settlement also set up a Girl's Club for older children soon to leave school. The project began on a small-scale basis in 1899, but expanded considerably after the acquisition in 1900 of 317 Summer Lane. Soon the club was meeting six evenings a week, offering activities such as Swedish Drill (a form of regimented gymnastics with exercises performed on the spot to numbers), cooking, writing, painting, singing and needlework. The club also entered several competitions in these activities and went on frequent trips to the Woodcock Street swimming baths or to the gardens of Committee members in Edgbaston. From 1901, the Club began to organise annual Whitsuntide holidays, with North Wales a popular destination. This was an entirely new experience for many club members, some of whom had never been further than the Lickey Hills before, and the girls eagerly saved their money throughout the year to raise the 15 shilling contribution required towards railway fares and board. As members of the club grew older, the project became known as the Senior Club and new initiatives were developed. These included Girl Guide and Brownie packs, as well as clubs for younger children (the Junior Club), those still at school and girls involved in street-trading.

Girls' clubs at the Settlement.

The Thursday Mothers

Shortly after the Settlement became involved in work with children, it also started to set up equivalent services for their parents. To begin with, the residents of the Settlement announced that they would be "At Home" on Thursday evenings to spend "an hour or more" in "conversation, reading, recitations, music etc." (Birmingham Settlement, 1901, p.5) with adults from the local area. As at Toynbee Hall, this group was designed both to provide local people with enjoyable leisure opportunities and to foster a sense of community between the Settlement and its neighbours. Both these objectives were achieved in full, and the At Homes were so popular that the Settlement had difficulty seating all the people who wanted to take part. By 1905, the average attendance was over 100 and the meetings soon became a thriving women's group known as the "Thursday Mothers." For some people, this was the only chance they had to spend time out of the house and the club was described by regular members as "the only bit of pleasure we get" (Birmingham Settlement, 1906, p.13). Competition for places was soon so strong that a temporary 'overflow' group was started on a Monday evening to meet the growing demand which the Settlement had initiated.

As the women's clubs progressed, they began to diversify their activities. Some members began to contribute to a hospital collection for disabled children, while others took the opportunity to participate in the numerous trips and entertainments which sprang up. Examples included day trips to places such as Bristol Zoo or Worcester Cathedral as well as parties of almost every type imaginable – tea parties, garden parties, summer parties and so on. The women were also especially interested in current affairs, receiving eminent guests to speak on issues of national importance. Such was their appetite both for entertainment and for knowledge that the warden in 1912 wrote that "the members seem to have no difficulty in going from folk-song to the Insurance Act and back again to games in the course of an hour" (Birmingham Settlement, 1912, p.19). This was particularly the case during the First World War, when attendance increased dramatically as more and more women sought diversion from the troubles of the outside world. With many husbands and brothers overseas, club-goers often took the opportunity to share news and to read letters from family members at the Front. Despite this worry and anxiety, however, they were still able to consider the feelings of others less fortunate than themselves, receiving a group of Belgian refugees with a great ovation and expressing their sympathy for German wives and mothers similarly parted from their loved ones.

Following a temporary decline in attendance in the latter stages of the war, the Thursday Mothers went from strength to strength. Attendance reached well over 300 and similar meetings were held for younger mothers and their babies on a Monday afternoon. The Settlement's warden also sought to introduce an educational element by asking students to speak for ten minutes each on current affairs. This had the advantage not only of keeping club members informed of recent events, but also of preparing students for public speaking. Further mothers' meetings were held in Kingstanding and later became affiliated to the Federation of Women's Clubs (Rimmer, 1980). In one form or another, mothers' clubs were to continue to meet at the Settlement until the 1960s, when the redevelopment of Summer Lane, the demolition of Settlement Hall and a general ageing among club members prompted a change in the Settlement's focus and a greater emphasis on work with older people (see chapter 4). By this time, financial restrictions had prompted the Settlement to reconsider some of its more traditional projects, and the various women's groups had become self-sufficient, managing their own finances and paying rent for the use of the Settlement's premises. Despite this, the central role of the At Homes and the Thursday Mothers has never been forgotten, with former members still able to recall their fond memories of these projects.

Boys' Clubs

Following the success of its girls' and mothers' groups, the Settlement started a Boys' Club in 1912 with male workers enlisted from an organisation known as the Street Children's Union. Progress was initially slow, and it was not until 1932 that the Settlement was able to appoint a resident male worker of its own with sole responsibility for work with boys and men. By this time, however, the various boys' clubs that had developed had become involved in a variety of activities ranging from boxing to meccano, from carpentry to football and from singing to play writing. There was even a jazz band, described by the warden as consisting of "seven combs, twelve trombones of cardboard, mouth organs, bones for castanets, two violins, a biscuit tin for a drum, a piano of sorts, plus several piercing human whistles!" She continued: "Rhythm we have but modulation of tone we seek for diligently" (Rimmer, 1980, p.60). This presumably had to

The Junior Gym Club waiting to get in, 1931.

be seen to be believed, and one can only imagine the result when the jazz band was asked to give a rendition of the Marseillaise to welcome two French girls visiting from a Parisian Settlement in 1922-23. Boys' clubs were also a key feature of the Kingstanding Settlement and a group of Scouts was established in both branches of the Settlement. Such was the reputation of the Kingstanding Settlement for its youth clubs, that it later became involved in the Kingstanding Youth Parliament, a co-ordinating body of local youth clubs which is mentioned in the official history of the city (Sutcliffe and Smith, 1974). Members of the Boys' Club were also involved in producing their own magazine, the Summer Lane *Settler*, during the 1940s.

The Junior Gym Club in the playground.

Men's Clubs

Arising naturally out of the boys' clubs was the introduction in 1924 of a weekly Men's Club. From the beginning, it had an educational focus, receiving speakers to talk about current affairs and to stimulate debate. An early lecturer was James Mallon, the warden of Toynbee Hall, and the topics covered included trade unionism, the dangers of tuberculosis, the work of the Discharged Prisoners Aid Society, racial problems in America and the national minimum wage. Regular club suppers and summer parties were held, and the club engaged in formal debates with the Fircroft Working Men's College in Selly Oak. During the 1930s, the club had a membership of well over 100 and was boosted by the

The Boys' Camp.

addition of a new Rotary Hall, the presence of male residents at the Settlement and the formation of a new young men's club. By this time, in any case, the Men's Club had begun to take control of its own affairs following the creation of a men and boys' advisory committee (mirrored by a women and girls' committee) to advise the Settlement with regard to its clubs. Work with men was now an increasingly important part of the Settlement, and it was in recognition of this that the word 'Women's' had been dropped from the Settlement's title in 1919. The Birmingham Women's Settlement was now well and truly a Birmingham Settlement, working with men and women alike.

Entertainment and Activities

Throughout all this change and development in the Settlement's club work, there was an almost constant stream of parties, trips, entertainments, holidays and sporting events. These are far too numerous to describe in full, but tended to revolve around five main themes:

● **Parties and events** – Samuel Barnett had emphasised that "parties will be frequent" (quoted Pimlott, 1935, p.270) and this was certainly true of the Birmingham Settlement. All the main clubs held their own parties, and there were particular special events such as the Club Display (1927), the reunion supper for demobilised soldiers (1946), the Festival of Britain (1951) or the Twelfth Night Party (1952) at which a founder member of the Thursday Mothers celebrated her golden wedding anniversary. Perhaps the most significant events, however, were those held to mark important stages in the Settlement's history, such as its fiftieth, eightieth and hundredth birthdays.

- **Holidays and camping** – Trips away were a key feature of the Settlement, whether it be the regular Girls' Club holidays in Wales or the one-off trip to a Parisian Settlement in 1923. Regular holidays, camping trips and rambles continued to be an important part of the Settlement's work, both before and after the war, with excursions and outings throughout the country and even overseas. This tradition continues today with a planned exchange between young people in Birmingham and Chicago due to take place as part of the Settlement's centenary celebrations.

- **Sport** – This was a crucial part of the Settlement's club work, with teams competing in football, netball, cricket, badminton and tennis. Such was the Settlement's reputation in this area that its cricketers played at the Warwickshire County Ground and its footballers took part in a competition in Spain. In Kingstanding, it was necessary to install a special cabinet to display and store the numerous trophies that the various teams had amassed.

- **Music** – This, too, was a key feature of Settlement life, whether through impromptu singing or through more formal projects such as the Boys' Club Jazz Band (1920s) or the Men's Light Orchestra (1940s). Summer Lane also had its own choir and Kingstanding set up a Music Group in 1952, with performances of works such as the 'Messiah' and the 'Quaker Girl.'

Whit. Monday 1930: Settlement club members.

- **Drama** – There have also been strong dramatic traditions at the Settlement, with the Kingstanding Drama Group in particular winning a number of competitions and awards. One of the undoubted highlights came in 1946 with a charity performance at the Aberdare Miners' Welfare Theatre in front of an audience of 800.

As some of the above examples suggest, the Settlement was a major centre of recreational activity from its foundation in 1899 onwards and for a significant proportion of its hundred-year history. The post-war period, too, saw further developments, with a new Citizens' Club for 18 to 30-year-olds, a play centre, a mother and baby group and a Scamps Club for young children in Kingstanding. Members of the Settlement were also involved in 1947 in a successful campaign to turn a piece of wasteland in Tower Street into a playground, petitioning the City Council and achieving a positive result (Rimmer, 1980).

A picnic in the country.

The Industrial Youth Project

Perhaps the most innovative scheme of all, however, was the Industrial Youth Project which was set up in 1964 with funding from the Department of Education and Science. Working with the National Association of Youth Clubs, the Settlement sought to provide a combination of recreational facilities and

A Midland Red Bus outing, June 1930.

training opportunities for young people employed in local firms. These included football tournaments, evening meetings and weekends away for recreation, teamwork building and initiative enhancement. Many firms were unco-operative, perhaps because they felt that the Settlement's work would encourage their young employees to leave and seek work with better promotion prospects. Despite this, the Industrial Youth Project continued to meet and in 1967 had an average attendance of 100 or so (Rimmer, 1980). The following year, the scheme was even able to set a world record for non-stop four-a-side football, with club members scoring over 1,700 goals and playing continuously for 33 hours! Sadly, the project ended in 1968 when its funding ran out and the scheme, although popular with the young people who used it, was never repeated. This was much to be regretted, for the club was an important venture while it lasted, enabling previously isolated young people to meet together and to engage in leisure activities.

Sport at the Settlement.

Changing Priorities: the End of an Era

Despite a long history of recreational work, the Settlement's emphasis was to shift to other matters in the latter part of the twentieth century and its contribution to leisure activities, while not insignificant, was never to be the same again. This was the result of a complex series of social, financial and organisational factors which combined to ensure that the Settlement had little choice but to focus its attention elsewhere:

● Youth work nationally was experiencing considerable difficulties in the post-war period. Training, pay and morale were poor, and many agencies experienced a constant turnover of staff. National concern was such that in 1958 the Minister of Education set up the Albemarle Committee to review the country's youth service. The Committee found that youth work had suffered from a shortage of money and proposed a development plan which sought to increase training opportunities for youth leaders. Despite this, problems remained.

- Similar difficulties were evident in both Summer Lane and Kingstanding throughout the 1950s and 1960s. There was a rapid turnover of club leaders, several projects were chronically understaffed and a number of clubs were discontinued altogether. In 1952, the Settlement felt it necessary to defend its youth work against the criticisms that had been voiced at a local and national level, devoting a considerable proportion of its annual report to this purpose. During the 1960s, the clubs also noted increasing incidents of violence among male adolescents and a greater tendency to challenge authority. One group at Summer Lane was closed temporarily in the mid-1960s following a particularly violent incident. This was a new generation in a new era and youth clubs simply were not fashionable or, ultimately, viable.

- At the same time, the redevelopment of Newtown resulted in the re-housing of some existing club members at some distance from Summer Lane. This was particularly true of the Thursday Mothers and the Nippers' Club (for boys 8-11), whose members lived locally one week and were miles away the next. To some extent, this is an issue with which the Settlement has never really come to terms. After many years of work at the heart of Newtown, it is now located on the edge of the community in a predominantly industrial area following the redevelopment of the neighbourhood, separate from the people it aims to serve.

- Extensive building work was also carried out at the Summer Lane Settlement with the demolition of the Settlement Hall and the extension of the Youth Block. While the latter ultimately benefited the youth clubs, the building work caused considerable disruption and traditional groups such as the Thursday Mothers were never fully reconciled to the loss of the Hall (Rimmer, 1980).

- To make matters worse, the 1960s were a difficult period for British Settlements as a whole, and a number closed altogether. Critics claimed that Settlements no longer had a role to play following the creation of the Welfare State and some lost the confidence to carry on. More generally, this was a period of low morale and disillusionment across the voluntary sector as a whole, with many agencies having to change the way they worked in order to survive (Matthews and Kimmis, n.d.; Rimmer, 1980).

- In Birmingham itself, the Settlement's own position was far from secure and, by 1964, it had accumulated debts of £11,650. The irony of this situation was not lost on the writer of the Settlement's annual reports who commented that "it would have been unfortunate if the Settlement found itself in the position of having new and improved premises... but unable to make full use of them owing to lack of adequate finances" (Birmingham Settlement, 1962, p.5). Financial restraints certainly restricted the Settlement's work with its adult groups, which by now were autonomous groups, managing their own budgets and renting rooms from the Settlement, but existing independently of it. People connected with the Settlement have suggested that the only thing that kept the organisation going was its links with the universities and the enthusiasm which its students brought. Without these, it is possible that the Settlement may have followed the example of so many of its counterparts elsewhere in Britain and ceased to function altogether.

- In addition, the Settlement's time was increasingly taken up with new initiatives, such as services for older people (see chapter 4). This trend was also re-inforced by the fact that members of more traditional projects were themselves growing older, prompting a reappraisal of the Settlement's role. At the same time, new centres in Newtown reduced the need for the Settlement's youth clubs (which closed in 1970) and the majority of the Kingstanding clubs were transferred to the Local Authority. As a result, there was very little funding for work in the local community and the Settlement had no choice but to turn its attention to other issues, shifting its focus from local to more city-wide and national projects such as money or legal advice (see chapter 3).

For all these reasons, the recreational work of the Settlement could not continue as it had done in the past. This, of course, may not have been a bad thing in the long run, since it was this period that saw such innovative projects in areas such as money advice, energy conservation, urban ecology and communal living with students and young people in care (see chapters 3, 5 and 6). For those people who had been coming to Summer Lane and Kingstanding for many years, however, the passage of the Settlement's clubs was the end of an era which many to this day remember with pleasure and happiness:

"I was in the Birmingham Settlement at Kingstanding. I am 71 years old and I was [involved] in the club[s] from 1935-1947... The club was open every evening but Sunday. We had a drama group, table tennis, needlework, ...cooking and a discussion group... It was a very nice building. There were two halls, one older than the other. The other, the newest one, had a stage. We had our own dance band who played for us on Saturday nights... I think we paid about 10 pence a night and 2 shillings on a Saturday. It was open from 7.30 to 10.30... I look back now at the enjoyable times we had... If any of the people that went to the club at the same time as I was there get in touch... I would very much like to meet up again."

Personal communication from Betty Roberts (nee Phillips), 11.02.99

"I was sad when I heard that the clubs had closed. I used to help out with the under 7's and at a fortnightly club for adolescents. I was the 'DJ', I suppose you'd call it, and I had to learn how to do the latest dances – 'The Twist' I think it was... I'd left by the time the clubs closed, but it was a shame – they were an important part of the Settlement."

Personal communication from Gillian Brown (nee Vinter), 28.06.99

CHIC

Following the gradual demise of the Settlement's recreational projects and the redevelopment of Newtown, new initiatives were required to meet the needs of local children. In response, the Settlement established a number of projects which drew heavily on work which it had undertaken in its early years at the turn of the century. The first of these was the Children's Holiday Information Centre (CHIC). Country holidays had been an important activity at the Settlement from the early 1900s onwards, yet by 1972 research carried out by the Settlement had revealed the inadequacy of existing holiday services for deprived young people. Out of 22,000 children in the city eligible for free school milk, only 4,000 were being offered an opportunity to go on holiday away from home. The Settlement also found that existing schemes were almost entirely unco-ordinated, duplicating each other's work and failing to pool their resources.

To rectify this situation, the Settlement called a conference for social workers, teachers and holiday organisers. The conference met in 1972 and subsequent discussions led to the formation of CHIC. Intended to help, advise and co-ordinate holiday projects for Birmingham children and to bring to the notice of the Local Authority the need for play facilities, CHIC was successful in securing additional funding for many of its members and in publishing an information booklet for relevant professionals. The Settlement was also responsible for setting up a Resources Centre which collected surplus materials such as paper, paint and rope from local firms and distributed them to local play initiatives as required. Film shows, theatre groups and a Punch and Judy show were also organised by CHIC to save play leaders the time and administrative difficulties of arranging such entertainments themselves. From 1975, CHIC became an independent organisation, continuing to campaign for increased holiday and play facilities for Birmingham children until its funding expired in 1979.

Colony Holidays

At the same time as it was working to co-ordinate Birmingham's holiday services, the Settlement was also developing its own initiatives in this area. At the holiday conference of 1972, the Settlement received a speaker from the Council for Colony Holidays for School Children (CCHS) and was clearly impressed with what it heard. From 1973, it began to operate as a local branch of CCHS, running Colony Holidays to locations such as Tenby, Malvern and Northampton. Two nine-day holidays were organised in 1973-4 for some 78 children and numbers increased steadily. By 1978, the Settlement was taking over 120 children from Newtown, Kingstanding, Lozells and West Heath on holiday, many of whom would not otherwise have had the chance to spend time away from home. In addition to this, the Settlement also worked with the Family Service Unit, the Lane Neighbourhood Centre, Forty Hall Road Action Centre and the Duddeston Friendship Camp to run holidays for 52 families at a caravan site at

Brean Sands. Many of these families had not had a holiday for several years and their social workers provided positive feedback on the scheme's impact on families otherwise unable to get a break from the stresses and strains of living in the inner city. These family holidays were later incorporated into CHIC, which by this time was an independent agency operating separately from the Settlement.

Play Projects

Also arising out of the CHIC experiment was the Settlement's summer play projects in both Summer Lane and Kingstanding. Once again, these drew on a long heritage of play work at the Settlement, harking back to the Happy Evenings introduced when the Settlement was first founded in 1899. The first modern play scheme was held for four weeks in 1971 at St. George's Junior School and received over 100 children. The scheme was subsequently repeated in a number of different locations in partnership with St. George's Church Centre, Newtown Community Centre and the Lawler Centre. By 1979, there were play schemes taking place during the Easter, Summer and October holidays, with a regular programme of games, outings, drama, art and craftwork. Before long, the project was being managed by a group of local residents called the Action Group on Play. Under their leadership a library service was added and there

Children at play.

were frequent trips to leisure centres, swimming pools and places of interest across Birmingham and beyond. The schemes continued to run throughout most of the 1980s, but disappear from the Settlement's annual reports in 1989, presumably as a result of funding problems. Despite this, recreational work with children still continues via the Settlement's nursery (see previous section).

Children at play.

The Arts

Two further recreational projects which draw on strong traditions within the Settlement's history were developed in the 1970s and early 1980s. The first of these, the Birmingham Arts Laboratory, was an independent charity which leased premises at the Settlement from 1970 to 1977 in order to experiment with new forms of dramatic art. During its time at Summer Lane, it provided a cinema club, drama and dance groups, musical performances, workshops, art exhibitions and printing and photography facilities. Best known for its cinema (the only one in Newtown), the Arts Laboratory relocated to Aston University in 1977 (Rimmer, 1980). After its departure, the Settlement's next tenant was the Second City Theatre Company. Dedicated to taking professional live theatre into the community, Second City developed a good relationship with its landlord, performing for the Settlement's day centre and play schemes before being disbanded in 1982. Despite the departure of the Arts Laboratory and Second City, however, the cultural heritage which the Settlement helped to develop and sustain in Newtown is continued to this very day by the Drum, a prestigious 'black' and Asian arts centre established in the area as part of the City Challenge programme.

SYMPh

Undeterred by these departures, the Settlement embarked upon a final recreational project in 1985 with the introduction of the SYMPh Youth Electronic Music Centre. Designed to encourage the musical skills of local young people, the centre provided training in electronic music, access to expensive musical instruments, an opportunity to meet and play with others and the chance to use the Settlement's fully professional 24-track recording studio. This was a major investment on the part of the Settlement and an invaluable service for the centre's members, many of whom were unemployed and unable to gain access to musical equipment in any other way. A second studio was opened in 1989 together with the Settlement's own record label, Switchback. As its reputation spread, the centre's facilities were used not only by local people to make demonstration tapes of their work, but also by well-known professional groups such as Magnum, the Glitter Band and Black Sabbath. Unfortunately for the Settlement, however, a grant of £35,000 which had been promised towards SYMPh failed to materialise, placing the project and the Settlement as a whole in a very difficult position. Although this particular storm was initially weathered, SYMPh was disbanded shortly afterwards at great financial cost to the Settlement.

Summary

Summing up attempts to combat the *giant* of 'idleness' is not easy, since the Settlement has probably done more in this area than in any other. With recreational projects in particular, the Settlement has been so active that this chapter has not been able to undertake a detailed description of each initiative, concentrating instead on providing a broad overview of events and trends. What is interesting is the way in which the Settlement's focus has shifted dramatically in response to the changing social, political and economic climate. When Birmingham's industries were thriving, there were very few employment-related projects at the Settlement and the majority of its work was taken up with recreational and leisure activities. This was to change almost entirely in the latter part of the twentieth century as a result of increasing difficulties in youth work, financial problems, post-war social reforms, a reappraisal of the Settlement's role and the gradual decline of Birmingham's manufacturing industries. By the 1980s, the Settlement was working with employment issues on a regular basis and spent

The SYMPh Project.

much less of its time on leisure projects. While recreation was still an important part of the Settlement, it was never as prominent a feature as it had been prior to the Second World War. This was very much a time of continuity and change: continuity in the ongoing attempts to resolve the problem of 'idleness', but radical change in terms of the Settlement's priorities and the particular issues which it sought to address.

Conclusion

This chapter summarises:

- The changes and continuities experienced by the Birmingham Settlement, 1899-1999.

- The factors contributing to the Settlement's ability to survive for one hundred years.

- The Settlement's position in the current policy context.

- The Settlement's future.

Continuity and Change

On the eve of its centenary, the Birmingham Settlement can look back over one hundred years both of continuity and of change. On the one hand, there have been radical shifts in the nature of poverty, of Newtown itself and of the Settlement's work, with policy developments in the areas described in this book creating new opportunities and avenues for the Settlement to pursue. That the Settlement has been able to respond to the changing circumstances in which it has found itself is testimony to its resilience, flexibility and innovation. At the same time, however, much remains the same, both in terms of the way in which the Settlement works and the scale and nature of the problems it is seeking to resolve. Although the Newtown of 1999 is very different to that of 1899 in many respects, it is also very similar – some would say depressingly similar – and remains just as impoverished relative to the area around it as it ever was. As a result, many of the Settlement's initiatives today, although operating in a different context and with a different emphasis, are working with the same issues first identified at the turn of the century by the Settlement's early projects. Perhaps the greatest continuity of all, however, lies in the principles on which the Settlement bases its activities. Key themes include self-help, education, shared learning, partnership, social innovation, research and campaigning, all of which derive directly from founding figures such as Denison, Toynbee and Barnett and continue to influence the Settlement movement as a whole to this very day.

Secrets of Success

A centenary celebration is an important yet rare occurrence in the life of a voluntary social agency. Few such organisations survive for anything like one hundred years and many fall by the wayside long before. This can be for a host of reasons: financial problems, the increasing trend towards time-limited, short-term funding, a changing policy context and internal difficulties, to name but a few. The Birmingham Settlement has experienced all these issues, yet continues to operate from its base on Summer Lane and to meet the needs of the people it serves. In as complex and unpredictable a world as the voluntary sector, the very act of survival is in itself a major achievement. This can be attributed to a number of factors:

1. Any successful organisation cannot afford to stand still for long and must adapt itself to the changing circumstances in which it finds itself. A key feature of the Settlement's history to date has been its ability to respond to change, developing new services to meet newly identified needs on the one hand, and reprioritising and refocusing its work in a changing policy context on the other.

2. Innovation is also crucial to survival, and this the Settlement has had in abundance. At different times in its history, many of its workers have been true visionaries, taking the lead nationally and even internationally in particular fields of work.

3. No agency can prosper in isolation and a degree of collaboration is required to ensure stability and coordination. Throughout its history, the Settlement has worked in partnership with local people, other voluntary organisations, academic institutions and the public and private sectors. This has been enhanced by the Settlement's role as an originator of new organisations, developing projects to fill gaps in existing service provision and supporting them to become independent agencies in their own right.

4. Funding is a constant concern for the voluntary sector and the Birmingham Settlement is no exception. However, the Settlement has been fortunate in the ongoing support it has received from a range of prominent local families and individuals. When funding crises loom, it is not unknown for the necessary resources to be donated, often at the eleventh hour and sometimes anonymously, from one of the Settlement's generous well-wishers. In many ways, this is a life-line that few voluntary agencies enjoy and has at times made the difference between survival and bankruptcy.

5. Successful voluntary agencies need committed personnel, and individuals involved with the Settlement have typically been extremely dedicated to their work. Over the last hundred years, the Settlement has overcome numerous

difficulties and hardships, and this is testimony to the commitment of its volunteers, staff and supporters alike.

6. A key theme throughout the Settlement's history has been its ability to combine continuity and change, remaining true to its founding ideals and sustaining core work, while at the same time retaining the flexibility to respond to new opportunities.

7. The Settlement movement was established to bring together people from different social and educational backgrounds to learn from each other and develop joint solutions to the problem of poverty. In Birmingham, this has created something of a 'human melting pot' with the rich and poor, the educated and uneducated, the employed and unemployed and people from different cultures bringing diverse skills and experiences and working together to achieve effective responses to oppressive social problems. In theory, the diverse and often contradictory nature of the Settlement's constituent parts means that its work should not be successful. In practice, however, these provide a creative tension, a dynamism and a pooling of abilities which make for exciting and effective ways of working.

Above all, however, voluntary social agencies can only survive in the long-term if there is an overriding demand for the services they offer and the expertise they bring. Poverty in Newtown is just as pervasive in 1999 as it was in 1899, and the Settlement's work is just as valuable today as it was then. There is therefore a continued need for an agency like the Settlement to work in Birmingham's inner city areas in order to alleviate the plight of those in poverty. Sadly, there will always continue to be such a need unless radical political, social and economic change can finally eradicate the conditions, exclusion, lack of choice and denial of life opportunities which poverty engenders.

The Current Policy Context

After a century of change and continuity, the Birmingham Settlement finds itself ideally placed to augment its already impressive achievements and with a strong future ahead. For the past twenty years, public welfare services in Britain have been restructured and reduced in favour of a more mixed economy of service provision. This has given greater impetus to the independent sector, with both private and voluntary providers increasingly working in areas of welfare provision traditionally monopolised by the public sector. Despite this, the independent sector has never actually replaced the role of the state, working instead alongside public service providers rather than as a substitute for them.

In the late 1990s, the New Labour government is promoting a 'third way' in which services will be developed and delivered through partnerships between public, private and voluntary sector agencies. This is intended to heal the traditional divisions in British welfare in which the state is either the sole provider (associated with the Left) or in which individuals must provide for themselves through the market (associated with the Right), uniting the best aspects of both approaches in a new way of working. The resultant 'third way' will be based on partnerships between providers from different sectors, with an explicit concern to ensure that 'best value' is achieved, irrespective of the status of the particular provider. This offers unprecedented scope for voluntary agencies such as the Birmingham Settlement to expand their work and influence considerably.

At the same time, the government is also promoting regional and local action to combat poverty and social exclusion. As a result, community-based activity, built on partnership between all local organisations with a commitment to capacity building, is now being encouraged and subsidised. Support for such work also comes from the European Union Commission. In such a situation, voluntary agencies with a strong community base will be well positioned to play a pivotal role in such regeneration activity, working in partnership with central and local government to develop policy and deliver services.

A key feature of the Settlement movement has always been its community base, its collaborative working and its ability to work alongside and supplement the activities of the state. As a result, the Settlements are well placed to take a leading role in the 'third way' for welfare delivery at the beginning of the 21st century. A key challenge for the Birmingham Settlement will be to respond to these opportunities, both in continuing its current role in local and national service provision and in developing new partnership initiatives with other providers to access new sources of support and to meet continuing social needs.

The Future

Although this publication has so far concentrated on the last hundred years, the Settlement's centenary celebrations are focusing not just on the past but also on the future. While the Settlement is justifiably proud of its work to date, it is equally aware of the need to prepare for the challenges, changes and problems which lie ahead. As a result, it has a number of proposals for expanding its services and building on its past successes.

In terms of individual projects, the Settlement has plans to enhance particular aspects of its existing initiatives. Examples include an expansion in culturally sensitive day care provision for Asian older people, the development of Business Debtline into a national service and an increase in the number of subsidised places within the Nursery. In addition, however, there are three main areas of activity in which the Settlement is committed to developing its work and focusing its attention in the future:

1. **Advice services** – this is a crucial aspect of the Settlement, empowering service users and providing them with the information they require to regain and retain control over their own lives.

2. **Employment and training opportunities** – these are important ways of equipping people with the skills and access to resources they need to combat their own poverty. A particular priority will be those members of minority groups who do not usually access mainstream services.

3. **Care services** – continuing to provide high quality services for groups such as children and older people.

As part of this process, the Settlement is committed to working in partnership with a broad range of organisations from the public, private and voluntary sectors, developing innovative ways of responding to previously unmet needs and supporting members of disadvantaged communities to access the opportunities available to them. Admirable though these aims may appear, however, an inevitable reality of the voluntary sector in the late 1990s is that the Settlement's aspirations will require substantial funding if they are to come to fruition. It is for this reason that the Settlement has launched a special appeal to raise £500,000 (above and beyond its normal annual fund-raising programme) as part of its centenary celebrations. This is intended to achieve three main objectives (Birmingham Settlement, 1999):

● To strengthen the Settlement's operating position, providing greater financial security.

● To resource the exploration of new initiatives in advance of established funding.

● To enable particular new ventures and extensions of present services.

If the appeal is successful and if these objectives are met, there seems no reason why the work of the Birmingham Settlement cannot continue for another hundred years and even further beyond that. As it stands on the verge of a new millennium, the Settlement occupies a unique vantage point, looking back to one hundred years of achievement and innovation, and looking forward to the challenge of a second century of poverty and opportunity.

Appendix A:

The Birmingham Settlement's Wardens*

Summer Lane

- Miss M. C. Stavely   1899-1905
- Miss Dawkins   1905-1906
- Miss M. C. Albright   1906-1910
- Miss M. C. Matheson   1908-1916
- Miss H. Madeley   1917-1919
- Miss M. Boyd-Mackay   1919-1921
- Miss K. C. Dewar   1921-1926
- Miss C. E. Muirhead   1926-1928
- Miss B. M. Botsford   1928-1933
- Miss M. V. Moffat   1928-1933
- Miss E. M. Batten   1933-1938
- Miss G. M. Truscott   1938-1941
- Miss B. Watson   1942-1947
- Miss N. Dawson   1947-1955
- Miss S. de C. Forster   1955-1968
- Mr. P. D. Houghton   1968-1989
- Mr. C. Kunz (acting)   1989-1990
- Ms J. Skinner   1990-1995
- Ms S. Spencer   1995-

Kingstanding

- Miss A. K. Lloyd   1931-1934
- Miss O. D. Clarke   1934-1937
- Miss N. E. Fear   1938-1953
- Miss A. J. Clark   1953-1955
- Mr. C. J. Blamire   1955-1970

*   Sometimes referred to as Directors or Chief Executives

Bibliography

A.A.B. (1916) The employment of school children, *Women Workers, the quarterly magazine of the Birmingham Ladies Union of Workers among Women and Children*, 26(2), 52-55.

Abel-Smith, B. (1964) *The hospitals 1800-1948.* London, Heineman.

Age Concern (1998) *Age discrimination: make it a thing of the past.* London, Age Concern.

Alcock, P. (1993) *Understanding poverty.* Basingstoke, Macmillan.

Aston Reinvestment Trust (1997) *Aston Reinvestment Trust: a social investment fund for Birmingham.* Unpublished information document, Aston Reinvestment Trust.

Aston Reinvestment Trust (1998) *Aston Reinvestment Trust: annual report 1998 – social investment for Birmingham.* Unpublished annual report, Aston Reinvestment Trust.

Aston Reinvestment Trust (1999) *Aston Reinvestment Trust.* Unpublished information sheet, Aston Reinvestment Trust.

Audit Commission (1986) *Making a reality of community care.* London, HMSO

Baggott, R. (1998) *Health and health care in Britain* (2nd ed.). Basingstoke, Macmillan.

Ball, S. (1986) *Sociology in focus: education.* London, Longman.

Ballard, P. (ed.) (1985) *A city at war: Birmingham 1939 – 1945.* Birmingham, Birmingham Museum and Art Gallery.

Barclay, I. and Perry, E. (1929) *Five hundred Birmingham houses.* Birmingham, COPEC.

Barnett, H. (1918a) *Canon Barnett: his life, work and friends – volume one.* London, John Murray.

Barnett, H. (1918b) *Canon Barnett: his life, work and friends – volume two.* London, John Murray.

Barnett, S. and Barnett, H. (1915) *Practicable socialism* (new series). London, Longmans, Green and Co.

Becker, S. (1997) *Responding to poverty: the politics of cash and care.* London, Longman.

Becker, S. and MacPherson, S. (1988) *Public issues, private pain: poverty, social work and social poverty.* London, Insight/Carematters Books.

Bedford, N. (1990) Sixty years at the Settlement, *Carrs Lane Journal*, November, 10-11.

Berg, J. (1994) *Positively Birmingham.* Solihull, Birmingham Picture Library.

Beveridge, W. (1942) *Social insurance and allied services.* London, HMSO.

Beveridge, W. (1953) *Power and influence.* London, Hodder and Stoughton.

Bird, V. (1970) *Portrait of Birmingham.* London, Robert Hale.

Birmingham City Council (1989) *Developing Birmingham 1889 to 1989: 100 years of city planning.* Birmingham, Birmingham City Council.

Birmingham City Council (1992a) *Success in the city: Newtown South Aston, Birmingham – Newtown housing strategy.* Birmingham, Birmingham City Council.

Birmingham City Council (1992b) *Success in the city: Newtown South Aston, Birmingham – Gunsmith's Quarter regeneration opportunities.* Birmingham, Birmingham City Council.

Birmingham City Council (1992c) *Success in the city: Newtown South Aston, Birmingham – programme details.* Birmingham, Birmingham City Council.

Birmingham City Council (1992d) *Success in the city: Newtown South Aston, Birmingham – executive summary.* Birmingham, Birmingham City Council.

Birmingham City Council (1992e) *Success in the city: Newtown South Aston, Birmingham – Newtown skills audit.* Birmingham, Birmingham City Council.

Birmingham City Council (1993) *Constituency and ward profiles* (1991 census topic reports). Birmingham, Birmingham City Council.

Birmingham City Council (1996a) *The Afro-Caribbean community in Birmingham: a community profile.* Birmingham, Birmingham City Council.

Birmingham City Council (1996b) *The Bangladeshis in Birmingham: a community profile.* Birmingham, Birmingham City Council.

Birmingham City Council (1996c) *The Chinese in Birmingham: a community profile.* Birmingham, Birmingham City Council.

Birmingham City Council (1996d) *The Irish in Birmingham: a community profile.* Birmingham, Birmingham City Council.

Birmingham City Council (1997) *The Pakistanis in Birmingham: a community profile.* Birmingham, Birmingham City Council.

Birmingham Council for Old People (1996) *50 golden years: 1946-1996.* Birmingham, Birmingham Council for Old People.

Birmingham Family Service Unit (1952) *First annual report, 1951-1952.* Unpublished annual report, Birmingham Family Service Unit.

Birmingham Health Authority (1997) *Public health information directory.* Birmingham, Birmingham Health Authority.

Birmingham Museum and Art Gallery (1985) *City children: Birmingham children at work and play, 1900 – 1930.* Birmingham, Birmingham Museum and Art Gallery.

Birmingham Public Libraries (1968) *Kingstanding past and present.* Birmingham, Birmingham Public Libraries.

Birmingham Settlement (1899) *Birmingham Women's Settlement: first annual report, 1889.* Unpublished annual report, Birmingham Settlement.

Birmingham Settlement (1901) *Birmingham Women's Settlement: annual report, 1900-1901.* Unpublished annual report, Birmingham Settlement.

Birmingham Settlement (1902) *Birmingham Women's Settlement: annual report, 1901-1902.* Unpublished annual report, Birmingham Settlement.

Birmingham Settlement (1903) *Birmingham Women's Settlement: annual report, 1902-1903.* Unpublished annual report, Birmingham Settlement.

Birmingham Settlement (1904) *Birmingham Women's Settlement: annual report, 1903-1904.* Unpublished annual report, Birmingham Settlement.

Birmingham Settlement (1905) *Birmingham Women's Settlement: annual report, 1904-1905.* Unpublished annual report, Birmingham Settlement.

Birmingham Settlement (1906) *Birmingham Women's Settlement: annual report, 1905-1906.* Unpublished annual report, Birmingham Settlement.

Birmingham Settlement (1907) *Birmingham Women's Settlement: annual report, 1906-1907.* Unpublished annual report, Birmingham Settlement.

Birmingham Settlement (1908) *Birmingham Women's Settlement: annual report, 1907-1908.* Unpublished annual report, Birmingham Settlement.

Birmingham Settlement (1909) *Birmingham Women's Settlement: annual report, 1908-1909.* Unpublished annual report, Birmingham Settlement.

Birmingham Settlement (1910) *Birmingham Women's Settlement: annual report, 1909-1910.* Unpublished annual report, Birmingham Settlement.

Birmingham Settlement (1911) *Birmingham Women's Settlement: annual report, 1910-1911.* Unpublished annual report, Birmingham Settlement.

Birmingham Settlement (1912) *Birmingham Women's Settlement: annual report, 1911-1912.* Unpublished annual report, Birmingham Settlement.

Birmingham Settlement (1913) *Birmingham Women's Settlement: annual report, 1912-1913.* Unpublished annual report, Birmingham Settlement.

Birmingham Settlement (1914) *Birmingham Women's Settlement: annual report, 1913-1914.* Unpublished annual report, Birmingham Settlement.

Birmingham Settlement (1915) *Birmingham Women's Settlement: annual report, 1914-1915.* Unpublished annual report, Birmingham Settlement.

Birmingham Settlement (1916) *Birmingham Women's Settlement: annual report, 1915-1916.* Unpublished annual report, Birmingham Settlement.

Birmingham Settlement (1917) *Birmingham Women's Settlement: annual report, 1916-1917.* Unpublished annual report, Birmingham Settlement.

Birmingham Settlement (1918) *Birmingham Women's Settlement: annual report, 1917-1918.* Unpublished annual report, Birmingham Settlement.

Birmingham Settlement (1919) *Birmingham Settlement: annual report, 1918-1919.* Unpublished annual report, Birmingham Settlement.

Birmingham Settlement (1920) *Birmingham Settlement: annual report, 1919-1920.* Unpublished annual report, Birmingham Settlement.

Birmingham Settlement (1921) *Birmingham Settlement: annual report, 1920-1921.* Unpublished annual report, Birmingham Settlement.

Birmingham Settlement (1922) *Birmingham Settlement: annual report, 1921-1922.* Unpublished annual report, Birmingham Settlement.

Birmingham Settlement (1923) *Birmingham Settlement: annual report, 1922-1923.* Unpublished annual report, Birmingham Settlement.

Birmingham Settlement (1924) *Birmingham Settlement: annual report, 1923-1924.* Unpublished annual report, Birmingham Settlement.

Birmingham Settlement (1925) *Birmingham Settlement: annual report, 1924-1925.* Unpublished annual report, Birmingham Settlement.

Birmingham Settlement (1926) *Birmingham Settlement: annual report, 1925-1926.* Unpublished annual report, Birmingham Settlement.

Birmingham Settlement (1927) *Birmingham Settlement: annual report, 1926-1927.* Unpublished annual report, Birmingham Settlement.

Birmingham Settlement (1928) *Birmingham Settlement: annual report, 1927-1928.* Unpublished annual report, Birmingham Settlement.

Birmingham Settlement (1929) *Birmingham Settlement: annual report, 1928-1929.* Unpublished annual report, Birmingham Settlement.

Birmingham Settlement (1930) *Birmingham Settlement: annual report, 1929-1930.* Unpublished annual report, Birmingham Settlement.

Birmingham Settlement (1931) *Birmingham Settlement: 32nd annual report, 1930-1931.* Unpublished annual report, Birmingham Settlement.

Birmingham Settlement (1932) *Birmingham Settlement: 33rd annual report, 1931-1932.* Unpublished annual report, Birmingham Settlement.

Birmingham Settlement (1933) *Birmingham Settlement: 34th annual report, 1932-1933.* Unpublished annual report, Birmingham Settlement.

Birmingham Settlement (1934) *Birmingham Settlement: 35th annual report, 1933-1934.* Unpublished annual report, Birmingham Settlement.

Birmingham Settlement (1935) *Birmingham Settlement: 36th annual report, 1934-1935.* Unpublished annual report, Birmingham Settlement.

Birmingham Settlement (1936) *Birmingham Settlement: 37th annual report, 1935-1936.* Unpublished annual report, Birmingham Settlement.

Birmingham Settlement (1937) *Birmingham Settlement: 38th annual report, 1936-1937.* Unpublished annual report, Birmingham Settlement.

Birmingham Settlement (1938) *Birmingham Settlement: 39th annual report, 1937-1938.* Unpublished annual report, Birmingham Settlement.

Birmingham Settlement (1939) *Birmingham Settlement: 40th annual report, 1938-1939.* Unpublished annual report, Birmingham Settlement.

Birmingham Settlement (1940) *Birmingham Settlement: 41st annual report, 1939-1940.* Unpublished annual report, Birmingham Settlement.

Birmingham Settlement (1941) *Birmingham Settlement: 42nd annual report, 1940-1941.* Unpublished annual report, Birmingham Settlement.

Birmingham Settlement (1942) *Birmingham Settlement: 43rd annual report, 1941-1942.* Unpublished annual report, Birmingham Settlement.

Birmingham Settlement (1943) *Birmingham Settlement: 44th annual report, 1942-1943.* Unpublished annual report, Birmingham Settlement.

Birmingham Settlement (1945) *Birmingham Settlement: 46th annual report, 1944-1945.* Unpublished annual report, Birmingham Settlement.

Birmingham Settlement (1946) *Birmingham Settlement: 47th annual report, 1945-1946.* Unpublished annual report, Birmingham Settlement.

Birmingham Settlement (1947) *Birmingham Settlement: 48th annual report, 1946-1947.* Unpublished annual report, Birmingham Settlement.

Birmingham Settlement (1948) *Birmingham Settlement: 49th annual report, 1947-1948.* Unpublished annual report, Birmingham Settlement.

Birmingham Settlement (1949) *Birmingham Settlement: 50th annual report, 1948-1949.* Unpublished annual report, Birmingham Settlement.

Birmingham Settlement (1950) *Birmingham Settlement: 51st annual report, 1949-1950.* Unpublished annual report, Birmingham Settlement.

Birmingham Settlement (1952) *Birmingham Settlement: 53rd annual report, 1951-1952.* Unpublished annual report, Birmingham Settlement.

Birmingham Settlement (1953) *Birmingham Settlement: 54th annual report, 1952-1953.* Unpublished annual report, Birmingham Settlement.

Birmingham Settlement (1954) *Birmingham Settlement: 55th annual report, 1953-1954.* Unpublished annual report, Birmingham Settlement.

Birmingham Settlement (1955) *Birmingham Settlement: 56th annual report, 1954-1955.* Unpublished annual report, Birmingham Settlement.

Birmingham Settlement (1956) *Birmingham Settlement: 57th annual report, 1955-1956.* Unpublished annual report, Birmingham Settlement.

Birmingham Settlement (1957) *Birmingham Settlement: 58th annual report, 1956-1957.* Unpublished annual report, Birmingham Settlement.

Birmingham Settlement (1958) *Birmingham Settlement: 59th annual report, 1957-1958.* Unpublished annual report, Birmingham Settlement.

Birmingham Settlement (1959) *Birmingham Settlement: 60th annual report, 1958-1959.* Unpublished annual report, Birmingham Settlement.

Birmingham Settlement (1960) *Birmingham Settlement: 61st annual report, 1959-1960.* Unpublished annual report, Birmingham Settlement.

Birmingham Settlement (1961) *Birmingham Settlement: 62nd annual report, 1960-1961.* Unpublished annual report, Birmingham Settlement.

Birmingham Settlement (1962) *Birmingham Settlement: 63rd annual report, 1961-1962.* Unpublished annual report, Birmingham Settlement.

Birmingham Settlement (1963) *Birmingham Settlement: 64th annual report, 1962-1963.* Unpublished annual report, Birmingham Settlement.

Birmingham Settlement (1964) *Birmingham Settlement: annual report, 1963-1964.* Unpublished annual report, Birmingham Settlement.

Birmingham Settlement (1965) *Birmingham Settlement: annual report, 1964-1965.* Unpublished annual report, Birmingham Settlement.

Birmingham Settlement (1966) *Birmingham Settlement opens its files, 1965-1966.* Unpublished annual report, Birmingham Settlement.

Birmingham Settlement (1967) *Birmingham Settlement: annual report, 1966-1967.* Unpublished annual report, Birmingham Settlement.

Birmingham Settlement (1968) *Birmingham Settlement: annual reports and statement of accounts, 1967-1968.* Unpublished annual report, Birmingham Settlement.

Birmingham Settlement (1969) *Birmingham Settlement: annual report, 1968-1969.* Unpublished annual report, Birmingham Settlement.

Birmingham Settlement (1970) *Birmingham Settlement: annual report, 1969-1970.* Unpublished annual report, Birmingham Settlement.

Birmingham Settlement (1971) *Birmingham Settlement: annual report, 1970-1971.* Unpublished annual report, Birmingham Settlement.

Birmingham Settlement (1972) *Birmingham Settlement: annual report, 1971-1972.* Unpublished annual report, Birmingham Settlement.

Birmingham Settlement (1973) *Birmingham Settlement: annual report, 1972-1973.* Unpublished annual report, Birmingham Settlement.

Birmingham Settlement (1974) *Birmingham Settlement: annual report, 1973-1974.* Unpublished annual report, Birmingham Settlement.

Birmingham Settlement (1975) *Birmingham Settlement: annual report, 1974-1975.* Unpublished annual report, Birmingham Settlement.

Birmingham Settlement (1976) *Birmingham Settlement: annual report, 1975-1976.* Unpublished annual report, Birmingham Settlement.

Birmingham Settlement (1977) *Birmingham Settlement: annual report, 1976-1977.* Unpublished annual report, Birmingham Settlement.

Birmingham Settlement (1978) *Birmingham Settlement: annual report, 1977-1978.* Unpublished annual report, Birmingham Settlement.

Birmingham Settlement (1979) *Birmingham Settlement: annual report (80 years, 1899 to 1979), 1978-1979.* Unpublished annual report, Birmingham Settlement.

Birmingham Settlement (1980) *Birmingham Settlement: annual report, 1979-1980.* Unpublished annual report, Birmingham Settlement.

Birmingham Settlement (1981) *Birmingham Settlement: annual report, 1980-1981.* Unpublished annual report, Birmingham Settlement.

Birmingham Settlement (1982) *Birmingham Settlement: annual report, 1981-1982.* Unpublished annual report, Birmingham Settlement.

Birmingham Settlement (1983) *Birmingham Settlement: annual report, 1982-1983.* Unpublished annual report, Birmingham Settlement.

Birmingham Settlement (1984) *Birmingham Settlement: annual report, 1983-1984.* Unpublished annual report, Birmingham Settlement.

Birmingham Settlement (1985) *Birmingham Settlement: annual report, 1984-1985.* Unpublished annual report, Birmingham Settlement.

Birmingham Settlement (1986) *Birmingham Settlement: annual report, 1985-1986.* Unpublished annual report, Birmingham Settlement.

Birmingham Settlement (1987) *Birmingham Settlement: annual report – nurturing new growth in the community, 1986-1987.* Unpublished annual report, Birmingham Settlement.

Birmingham Settlement (1988) *Birmingham Settlement: annual report and accounts – nurturing new growth in the community, 1987-1988.* Unpublished annual report, Birmingham Settlement.

Birmingham Settlement (1989) *Birmingham Settlement: annual report and accounts, 1988-1989.* Unpublished annual report, Birmingham Settlement.

Birmingham Settlement (1990) *Birmingham Settlement: annual report and accounts, 1989-1990.* Unpublished annual report, Birmingham Settlement.

Birmingham Settlement (1991) *Birmingham Settlement: annual report and summary accounts, 1990-1991.* Unpublished annual report, Birmingham Settlement.

Birmingham Settlement (1992) *Birmingham Settlement: annual report and summary accounts, 1991-1992.* Unpublished annual report, Birmingham Settlement.

Birmingham Settlement (1993) *Birmingham Settlement: annual report and summary accounts, 1992-1993.* Unpublished annual report, Birmingham Settlement.

Birmingham Settlement (1994) *Birmingham Settlement: annual report and summary accounts, 1993-1994.* Unpublished annual report, Birmingham Settlement.

Birmingham Settlement (1995) *Birmingham Settlement: annual report and summary accounts, 1994-1995.* Unpublished annual report, Birmingham Settlement.

Birmingham Settlement (1996) *Birmingham Settlement: annual report and summary accounts, 1995-1996.* Unpublished annual report, Birmingham Settlement.

Birmingham Settlement (1997a) *Birmingham Settlement: annual report, 1996-1997.* Unpublished annual report, Birmingham Settlement.

Birmingham Settlement (1997b) *Birmingham Settlement: annual review, 1996-1997.* Unpublished annual review, Birmingham Settlement.

Birmingham Settlement (1998a) *Birmingham Settlement: annual report, 1997-1998.* Unpublished annual report, Birmingham Settlement.

Birmingham Settlement (1998b) *Birmingham Settlement: annual review, 1997-1998.* Unpublished annual review, Birmingham Settlement.

Birmingham Settlement (1999) *Community and opportunity: the centenary appeal of the Birmingham Settlement.* Unpublished fundraising appeal, Birmingham Settlement.

Blackburn, C. (1991) *Poverty and health: working with families.* Milton Keynes, Open University Press.

Bournville Village Trust (1941) *When we build again: a study based on research into conditions of living and working in Birmingham.* London, George Allen & Unwin.

Boyd, N. (1982) *Josephine Butler, Octavia Hill and Florence Nightingale: three Victorian women who changed their world.* Basingstoke, Macmillan.

Brasnett, M. (1964) *The story of the Citizens' Advice Bureau.* London, The National Council of Social Services.

Bridges, L., Sufrin, B., Whetton, J. and White, R. (1975) *Legal services in Birmingham.* Birmingham, University of Birmingham Institute of Judicial Administration.

Briggs, A. (1952) *History of Birmingham volume II: borough and city, 1865 – 1938.* London, Oxford University Press.

Briggs, A. and Macartney, A. (1984) *Toynbee Hall: the first hundred years.* London, Routledge and Kegan Paul.

Brown, S. and Gloyne, E. (1966) *The field training of social workers.* London, George Allen and Unwin.

Brown, M. and Payne, S. (1994) *Introduction to social administration in Britain* (7th ed.). London, Routledge.

Byrne, T. and Padfield, C. (1990) *Social services* (4th ed.). Oxford, Made Simple Books.

Carson, M. (1990) *Settlement folk: social thought and the American settlement movement 1885 – 1930.* Chicago, University of Chicago Press.

Chadwick, E. (1842) *Report on the sanitary conditions of the labouring population of Great Britain.* London, HMSO (Reprinted 1965, Edinburgh University Press).

Chinn, C. (1991) *Homes for people: 100 years of council housing in Birmingham.* Birmingham, Birmingham Books.

Chinn, C. (1993) *Keeping the city alive: twenty-one years of Urban Renewal in Birmingham, 1972 – 1993.* Birmingham, Birmingham City Council.

Chinn, C. (1994) *Birmingham: the great working city.* Birmingham, Birmingham City Council.

Chinn, C. (1995) *Poverty amidst prosperity: the urban poor in England 1834 – 1914.* Manchester, Manchester University Press.

Chinn, C. (1996) *Brum undaunted: Birmingham during the Blitz.* Birmingham, Birmingham Library Services.

Chinn, C. (1997a) On the royal road to fame: Kingstanding, in C. Chinn, *Our Brum.* Birmingham, Birmingham Post and Mail.

Chinn, C. (1997b) Sunshine and smiles in Summer Lane, in C. Chinn, *Our Brum.* Birmingham, Birmingham Post and Mail.

Citron, J. (1989) *The Citizens' Advice Bureaux: for the community by the community.* London, Pluto Press.

Coley, A. (1911) The council schools, in J. Muirhead (ed.) *Birmingham Institutions.* Birmingham, Cornish Brothers.

Cummins, J. (1901a) Scenes in Slumland number one, *Birmingham Daily Gazette,* 4 March 1901, p. 4, vol. LXXVII, number 10116.

Cummins, J. (1901b) Scenes in Slumland number two, *Birmingham Daily Gazette,* 5 March 1901, p. 4, vol. LXXVIII, number 10117.

Davis, A. (1984) *Spearheads for reform: the social settlements and the progressive movement 1890 – 1914.* New Brunswick, Rutgers University Press.

Dawe, G. and Kunz, C. (1986) *Practising ecology in the city: the Birmingham Settlement Centre for Urban Ecology.* London, BASSAC.

Dayus, K. (1982) *Her people.* London, Virago Press.

Dayus, K. (1985) *Where's the life.* London, Virago Press.

Dayus, K. (1988) *All my days.* London, Virago Press.

Dayus, K. (1991) *The best of times.* London, Virago Press.

Dayus, K. (1994) *Omnibus.* London, Virago Press.

Department for Education and Employment (1998) *Action on age: report of the consultation on age discrimination in employment.* Sudbury, Department for Education and Employment.

Dobraszczyc, U. (1989) *Sociology in focus: sickness, health and medicine.* London, Longman.

Douglas, J. (1979) *From Summer Lane.* Birmingham, Second City Publishers.

Douglas, J. (1983) *A walk down Summer Lane.* London, Remploy.

Edwards, F. and Lewis, B. (eds) (1992) *Talk about Newtown.* Birmingham, Birmingham Library Service in association with Yorkshire Art Circus.

Fenter, M. (1960) *COPEC adventure: the story of the Birmingham COPEC House Improvement Society.* Birmingham, COPEC.

Focus Housing Group (1998) *Focus Housing Group: a social investment agency – catching the wave, annual report 1998.* Unpublished annual report, Focus Housing Group.

Gaine, C. and George, R. (1999) *Gender, 'race' and class in schooling: a new introduction.* London, Falmer Press.

Gardiner, J. and Wenborn, N. (eds) (1995) *The History Today companion to British history.* London, Collins and Brown.

Gorst, J. (1895) Settlements in England and America, in J. Knapp (ed.) *The universities and the social problem.* London, Garland Publishing.

Ham, C. (1992) *Health policy in Britain: the politics and organisation of the National Health Service* (3rd ed.). Basingstoke, Macmillan.

Haralambos, M. and Holborn, M. (1990) *Sociology: themes and perspectives* (3rd ed.). London, Unwin Hyman.

Harrow, J. (1998) *The English University Settlements, 1884 – 1939: a social movement becalmed?* Unpublished paper presented to the Voluntary Action History Society, London, 12 May, 1998.

Hastings, A. (1991) *A history of English Christianity* (3rd ed.). London, SCM Press.

Heward, C. and Whipp, R. (1983) Juvenile labour in Birmingham: a notorious yet neglected case, 1850 – 1914, in A. Wright and R. Shackleton (eds) *Worlds of labour: essays in Birmingham labour history.* Birmingham, University of Birmingham.

Hill, M. (1997) *Understanding social policy* (5th ed.). Oxford, Blackwell.

Howard Association (1892) *Edward Denison, M.P., Arnold Toynbee, and social problems.* London, Howard Association.

iSSUE (1994) *Fighting for life: annual review and summary accounts.* Unpublished annual report, iSSUE.

iSSUE (1996) *Annual review and summary accounts.* Unpublished annual report, iSSUE.

iSSUE (1998) *Infertility is a lonely path: annual report and accounts, 1996-98.* Unpublished annual report, iSSUE.

iSSUE (n.d.) *We want to have a baby...why can't we? A guide to prospective parents.* Unpublished promotional leaflet, iSSUE.

Johnson, C. (1995) *Strength in community: an introduction to the history and impact of the International Settlement movement.* Derby, International Federation of Settlements and Neighbourhood Services.

Jones, J. (n.d.) *A history of the hospitals and other charities of Birmingham.* Birmingham, Midland Educational Company.

Jones, K. (1984) *Eileen Younghusband: a biography.* London, Bedford Square Press/ NVCO.

Jones, K. (1994) *The making of social policy in Britain, 1830-1990* (2nd ed.). London, The Athlone Press.

Knapp, J. (ed.) (1895) *The universities and the social problem.* London, Garland Publishing.

Lay-Flurrie, J. (1982) *Old roots Newtown: the development of the Summer Lane area of Newtown.* Birmingham, Lay-Flurrie.

Lethbridge, J. (1993) *Birmingham in the First World War.* Birmingham, Newgate Press.

Lowndes, V. (1997) Sustainable Strength pilot programme: an evaluation, *Social Services Research*, 2, 37-51.

Lloyd, J. (1911) The hospitals, in J. Muirhead (ed.) *Birmingham Institutions.* Birmingham, Cornish Brothers.

Mannion, P. and Mannion, B. (1985) *The Summer Lane and Newtown of the years between the wars, 1918 – 1938.* Birmingham, Mannion and Mannion.

Mannion, P. and Mannion, B. (1987) *Pub memories of Summer Lane and Newtown between the wars.* Birmingham, Mannion and Mannion.

Mantle, J. (1891) Distress in North Birmingham, *Birmingham Daily Post*, 8 January.

Matheson, C. (1912) Birmingham Women's Settlement, *Women Workers, the quarterly magazine of the Birmingham Ladies Union of Workers among Women and Children*, 22(1), 23-24.

Matheson, C. (1916) Social study diplomas, *Women Workers, the quarterly magazine of the Birmingham Ladies Union of Workers among Women and Children*, 26(3), 75-80.

Matthews, J. and Kimmis, J. (n.d.) *A history of the English Settlement movement.* Unpublished article, London, BASSAC.

McGregor, S., Upton, C. and Coxon, N. (1995) *Architecture and austerity: Birmingham 1940 – 1950.* Birmingham, Birmingham City Council.

Meacham, S. (1987) *Toynbee Hall and social reform, 1880 – 1914: the search for community.* London, Yale University Press.

Means, R. and Smith, R. (1998) *Community care: policy and practice* (2nd ed.). Basingstoke, Macmillan.

M.E.L. (1992) *Success in the city: Newtown South Aston, Birmingham – Newtown shopping survey.* Birmingham, M.E.L. Social and Consumer Research Unit.

MORI (1992) *Success in the city: Newtown South Aston, Birmingham – survey of Newtown residents.* Birmingham, Birmingham City Council.

Morris-Jones, J. (1985a) Redevelopment and renewal in Birmingham, in J. Morris-Jones, *Essays in local history.* Birmingham, Morris-Jones.

Morris-Jones, J. (1985b) Birmingham under the Chamberlains, in J. Morris-Jones, *Essays in local history.* Birmingham, Morris-Jones.

Muirhead, J. (1912) *Social conditions in provincial towns: VIII Birmingham.* Unpublished manuscript, Birmingham City Central Library (Local History section).

Newtown South Aston City Challenge (1998) *Birmingham City Challenge in Newtown South Aston 1993-1998: new life in the community.* Birmingham, Birmingham City Council.

Novak, T. (1996) Empowerment and the politics of poverty, in B. Humphries (ed.) *Critical perspectives on empowerment.* Birmingham, Venture Press.

Picht, W. (1914) *Toynbee Hall and English Settlements.* London, G. Bell and Sons.

Pimlott, J. (1935) *Toynbee Hall: fifty years of social progress 1884 – 1934.* London, J. M. Dent and Sons.

Priestley, J. (1977) *English journey.* Harmondsworth, Penguin (First published by William Heinemann Ltd in 1934).

Rimmer, J. (1980) *Troubles shared: the story of a Settlement, 1899 – 1979.* Birmingham, Phlogiston Publishing.

Ring, F. (1911) Birmingham white ribbon bands, *Women Workers, the quarterly magazine of the Birmingham Ladies Union of Workers among Women and Children,* 21(2), 46-49.

Ring, F. (1914) Wage-earning school children, *Women Workers, the quarterly magazine of the Birmingham Ladies Union of Workers among Women and Children,* 23(4), 94-96.

Rogers, F. (1973) *Labour, life and literature: some memories of sixty years.* Brighton, Harvester Press.

Sachs, A. and Wilson, J. (1978) *Sexism and the law: a study of male beliefs and legal bias in Britain and the United States.* Oxford, Martin Robertson.

Sherard, R. (1905) *The child-slaves of Britain.* London, Hurst and Blackett.

Showell, R. (1885) *Dictionary of Birmingham.* Oldbury, Walter Showell and Sons (This edition published 1969, Wakefield, S. R. Publishers Ltd).

Simon, C. (1993) *La vie dans les taudis de Summer Lane, 1881-1891.* Unpublished mémoire de maîtrise, Université de Franche-Compté.

Spencer, S. (1999) *Update on the Interworks and New Deal Programmes.* Unpublished report to the Board of Trustees, Birmingham Settlement, 15th April 1999.

Stocks, M. (1956) *Fifty years in every street: the story of the Manchester University Settlement* (2nd ed. with an additional chapter on the years 1945-1955 by B. Rodgers). Manchester, Manchester University Press.

Sutcliffe, A. and Smith, R. (1974) *Birmingham 1939 – 1970.* London, Oxford University Press.

Tillyard, F. (1906) Poverty in Birmingham, *Women Workers, the quarterly magazine of the Birmingham Ladies Union of Workers among Women and Children,* 15(4), 74-79.

Townsend, P., Whitehead, M. and Davidson, N. (1992) *Inequalities in health.* London, Penguin.

Trolander, J. (1987) *Professionalism and social change: from the Settlement House movement to neighbourhood centres, 1886 to the present.* New York, Columbia University Press.

University of Aston Public Sector Management Research Unit (1985) *Five year review of the Birmingham Inner City Partnership.* London, HMSO.

Vince, C. (1902) *History of the Corporation of Birmingham volume III, 1885 – 1899.* Birmingham, Cornish Brothers.

Vince, C. (1923) *History of the Corporation of Birmingham volume IV, 1900 – 1915.* Birmingham, Cornish Brothers.

Wadsworth, R. (1971) *The story of the Citizens' Advice Bureau in Birmingham, 1939-1969.* Birmingham, Birmingham Citizens' Advice Bureau.

Webb, C. and Phillips, J. (1983) *An investigation into the provision of Dial-a-Ride as a form of public transport for those who cannot use conventional public transport.* Unpublished undergraduate dissertation, University of Aston, Birmingham.

Women Workers (1905) Day nurseries, *Women Workers, the quarterly magazine of the Birmingham Ladies Union of Workers among Women and Children,* 15(2), 42-44.

Women Workers (1908) The Birmingham branch of the National Union of Women Workers, *Women Workers, the quarterly magazine of the Birmingham Ladies Union of Workers among Women and Children,* 18(1), 1-5.

Woods, R. and Kennedy, A. (1922) *The Settlement horizon: a national estimate.* New York, Russell Sage Foundation.

Young, A. and Ashton, E. (1956) *British social work in the nineteenth century.* London, Routledge and Kegan Paul.

Younghusband, E. (1947) *Report on the employment and training of social workers.* Dunfermaline, Carnegie United Kingdom Trust.

Younghusband, E. (1951) *Social work in Britain.* Dunfermaline, Carnegie United Kingdom Trust.

Younghusband, E. (1978) *Social work in Britain, 1950-1975: a follow-up study – volume 2.* London, George Allen & Unwin.

Younghusband Report (1959) *Report of the working party on social workers in the local authority health and welfare services.* London, HMSO.

Jon Glasby is a researcher and qualified social worker. Having studied at the University of Birmingham for the past five years, he has both a degree in history and a masters/diploma in social work. As a freelance researcher, he has undertaken a range of research projects, studying topics such as the emergency hospital admission of older people, the role of health visiting services and user involvement in service provision. Particular interests include community care, working with older people, social history, local government finance and the interface between health and social services.

Subject Index